THE STORY-TAKERS

M000266571

Public Pedagogy, Transitional Justice, and Italy's Non-violent Protest against the Mafia

The Story-Takers charts new territory in public pedagogy through an exploration of the multiple forms of communal protests against the mafia in Sicily. Writing at the rich juncture of cultural, feminist, and psychoanalytic theories, Paula M. Salvio draws on visual and textual representations including shrines to those murdered by the mafia, photographs, and literary and cinematic narratives to explore how trauma and mourning inspire solidarity and a quest for justice among educators, activists, artists, and journalists living and working in Italy.

Salvio reveals how the antimafia movement is being brought out from behind the curtains, with educators leading the charge. She critically analyses six cases of communal acts of antimafia solidarity and argues that transitional justice requires radical approaches to pedagogy that are best informed by journalists, educators, and activists working to remember not only victims of trauma, but those who resist trauma and violence.

(Toronto Italian Studies)

PAULA M. SALVIO is a professor in the Department of Education at the University of New Hampshire.

The Story-Takers

Public Pedagogy, Transitional Justice, and Italy's Non-violent Protest against the Mafia

PAULA M. SALVIO

UNIVERSITY OF TORONTO PRESS
Toronto Buffalo London

© University of Toronto Press 2017
Toronto Buffalo London
www.utorontopress.com
Printed in the U.S.A.

ISBN 978-1-4426-5031-2 (cloth)   ISBN 978-1-4875-2177-6 (paper)

∞ Printed on acid-free, 100% post-consumer recycled paper with
vegetable-based inks.

Toronto Italian Studies

Library and Archives Canada Cataloguing in Publication

Salvio, Paula M., author
The story-takers : public pedagogy, transitional justice, and Italy's non-violent protest
against the mafia / Paula M. Salvio.

(Toronto Italian studies)
Includes bibliographical references and index.
ISBN 978-1-4426-5031-2 (cloth).   ISBN 978-1-4875-2177-6 (paper)

1. Mafia – Italy – Sicily – Case studies.   2. Organized crime – Social aspects –
Italy – Sicily – Case studies. 3. Social movements – Italy – Sicily – Case studies.
4. Nonviolence – Italy – Sicily – Case studies.   I. Title.   II. Series: Toronto Italian studies

HV6452.5.S25 2017   364.10609458   C2017-903474-X

University of Toronto Press acknowledges the financial assistance to its publishing
program of the Canada Council for the Arts and the Ontario Arts Council, an agency
of the Government of Ontario.

**Canada Council
for the Arts**

**Conseil des Arts
du Canada**

ONTARIO ARTS COUNCIL
CONSEIL DES ARTS DE L'ONTARIO

an Ontario government agency
un organisme du gouvernement de l'Ontario

Funded by the   Financé par le
Government   gouvernement
of Canada   du Canada

Canadä

For Alexandra, Lily, Zoe, and Una

Contents

Acknowledgments

The stories told in this book have been made possible by many extraordinary people. This book has benefited from the enthusiasm and challenging exchanges among my colleagues in the Department of Education at the University of New Hampshire, particularly Suzanne Graham, Joe Onosko, and our exceptional doctoral students: Clio Stearns, Shay Cassily, and Sara Clarke-Vivier. I also want to extend my gratitude to the Department of Education, the College of Liberal Arts, and the University of New Hampshire Center for the Humanities for their generous research funds, including a sabbatical leave for 2013, a 2012 Center for the Humanities Senior Scholar Fellowship, and support for the publication of this book. This scholarship also benefited from generative conversations and lively seminar discussions among my colleagues at the Boston Psychoanalytic Society and Institute during my residence as a Julius Silberger Fellow between 2011 and 2012, specifically with Bonnie Smolen and Dawn Skorczewski.

The *Story-Takers* is intended to honour the history of non-violent protest against mafia infiltration into the Italian state and the larger global field. I owe a great deal to the teachers, scholars, activists, and photojournalists who took time out of their demanding schedules to meet with me during my research visits to Italy. In Sicily, I am indebted to Edoardo Zaffuto and the co-founders of Addiopizzo and Addiopizzo Travel. Edoardo introduced me to the contemporary campaigns against extortion and graced this project with his insights, generous critiques, and sensitivity. Corleone Dialogos members Cosimo Lo Sciuto and Giuseppe Crapisi and photojournalists Letizia Battaglia and Shobha Battaglia gave their time in interviews, through email exchanges, and in invaluable discussions about antimafia non-violent protest. Franco Zecchin offered many hours of valued discussions and intellectual insights into the ethics of using photography to document mafia violence. I benefited from correspondence with and challenging feedback from Deborah Puccio-Den and Umberto

Santino. I am also grateful to Antonella Lombardi and Vito Lo Monaco for extended discussions about antimafia legislation and educational initiatives. Maria De Carlo offered comfort and warmth during my research visits and made her home in Palermo feel like my own.

Many of the ideas in these chapters began as conference presentations. I thank all those who invited me to present my scholarship on transitional justice pedagogy and antimafia protests, including Lisa Farley, Sara Mathews, and R.M. Kennedy, who organized the conference Art in Times of Conflict: Curricular Explorations at Wilfrid Laurier University; Aparna Tarc and Mario Di Paolantonio, who invited me to speak at York University's Summer Institute's Pedagogies and the Arts of Memory; and Dennis Sumara and Mary Bryson, who invited me to speak at the University of British Columbia. William Pinar offered critical support from the very early stages of this project. This book has also benefited from the thoughtful comments and counsel of colleagues whom I have met and worked with at conferences and corresponded with over the years. My perspectives on transitional justice, public pedagogy, and antimafia education have been strengthened by the scholarship of Dana Renga, R.M. Kennedy, Derek Duncan, Bronwen Leebaw, Mario Di Paolantonio, Deborah Britzman, and the late Roger Simon. This project also benefited in profound ways from Warren Crichlow's astute reading and analysis. Robin Pickering-Iazzi and Piero Garofalo offered keen observations, unending support, and intellectual companionship. I extend my deepest gratitude to Amy Boylan, whose dynamic intellectual range in Italian cultural studies inspired this project.

It has been an absolute pleasure to work with Douglas Hildebrand, my editor at the University of Toronto Press, as well as with the anonymous reviewers who provided thoughtful and constructive feedback. My sincere thanks go to Alexandra Shaker, Kristen Scott, Dawn Hunter, and Mary Newberry for their sharp editorial skills and collaborative spirits. Peter Taubman fills each day for me with inspiration and intellectual and emotional riches. I am grateful for his patience during the long process of writing and revision – and for never failing to make me laugh.

Some sections of this book were first published in different forms. Chapter 2 first appeared as an essay in *Italian Studies* 67, no. 3 (2012): 397–410. Chapter 5 appeared as "Reconstructing Memory through the Archives: Public Pedagogy, Citizenship and Letizia Battaglia's Photographic Record of Mafia Violence," in *Journal of Pedagogy, Culture and Society* 22, no. 1 (2014): 97–116. Parts of Chapter 4 appeared under the title "'A Taste of Justice': Digital Media and Libera Terra's Antimafia Public Pedagogy of Agrarian Dissent" in *The Italian Antimafia, New Media, and the Culture of Legality*, edited by Robin Pickering-Iazzi (University of Toronto Press, 2017).

THE STORY-TAKERS

Public Pedagogy, Transitional Justice, and Italy's
Non-violent Protest against the Mafia

Introduction: Story-Taking, Public Pedagogy, and the Challenges of Transitional Justice

> No philosophy, no analysis, no aphorism, be it ever so profound, can compare in intensity and richness of meaning with a properly narrated story.
>
> – Hannah Arendt, *Men in Dark Times*

In fall 2011, with support from the Scholars at Risk Network and the New York City Police Department, Italian[1] journalist Roberto Saviano taught a graduate seminar on the mafia at New York University under an assumed name. His students were sworn to secrecy by the university, and no Twitter or Facebook postings were permitted. Why the clandestineness? Saviano's non-fiction book *Gomorrah* (2006), which has sold more than 10 million copies worldwide and been translated into 54 languages, and in 2008 was made into an award-winning film, delivered an intimate account of the Neapolitan mafia, the Camorra. Given the extensive reach of organized crime into toxic waste disposal, drug and human trafficking, extortion, and counterfeit goods, Saviano's riveting investigations resonated globally and brought him some unwelcome recognition.

In 2006, soon after *Gomorrah* had sold 10 thousand copies, Saviano was forced into hiding, becoming a kind of Italian Salman Rushdie. In an interview with E. Nina Rothe in 2012, Saviano recalled what he describes as the phone call that changed his life.[2] He was 26 years old, riding a train from Pordenone to Naples. An Italian police officer called him to say "there had been a series of disclosures by repented criminals, as well as intercepted phone calls that ... made it clear I was to be eliminated." Designated by the mafia as an "inconvenient citizen" (and accused by then prime minister Silvio Berlusconi of having defamed Italy with his book), Saviano continues to live under police protection. His team of armed escorts usher him to speaking engagements, seminar rooms, and apartments through alleyways, hotel kitchens, and vacant parking lots. "This," he reports, "is my life sentence."[3]

What kind of danger could a 26-year-old journalist possibly pose to the Camorra – a group of over 100 crime clans, also known as the "system," that has killed more people than any other criminal organization in Europe and has extended its interests and tentacles well beyond its regional and national borders? Why does Saviano elicit so much rage, not only among Naples' mafia (the Camorra and its allies have filed lawsuits against Saviano) but also among the youth of Casal di Principe, the hometown Saviano shares with several Camorra clans? When asked these questions, Saviano is clear: "They're not afraid of me, they're afraid of my readers."[4]

Infuriated at Saviano's depiction of criminal activity, the youth of Casal di Principe have flooded YouTube with videos indicting Saviano, calling him "a sewer, an assassin, a junkie, a liar who has destroyed our town."[5] Saviano believes the critical, at times furious, reaction to *Gomorrah* has everything to do with what I describe in this book as *story-taking*, that is, using narrative and visual representations to portray events we may be inclined to turn away from or to disavow. I take the term *story-taking* from social historian Carolyn Steedman and feminist philosopher Adriana Cavarero. The story-taker is a necessary collaborator in the act of telling, attuned to the challenges that trauma poses to language and to narrative. The story-taker listens and shapes a narrative by assuming that there is a story to be told that might too easily be forgotten or remain hidden. The story-taker takes the story not as appropriation but as part of an ethical deal so that the outcome – an entity, a story – might compel listeners to ethical, non-violent action.

Saviano describes his style of story-taking as a mash-up of "non-fiction, police reports, judicial documents, and personal experiences written like a novel, but with real facts."[6] Admired by many antimafia investigators, Saviano is praised for creating a new crime genre that has widened his audience to include ordinary people. "Saviano broke open a new front," observes Antonio Laudati, a top Justice Ministry official. "He informed the man on the street. He turned our prosecution files into literature."[7] In fact, he opened the world's eyes to the global reach of organized crime and challenged the stereotype of Sicily as the singular home of mafia activity and, in the words of Italian political thinker Leopoldo Franchetti, "a threat to the political and moral integrity of the nation."[8]

Cultural theorists describe Saviano's writing as an UNO – an unidentified narrative object – that combines novelistic devices, news reportage, trial transcriptions, social theory, and personal commentary to expose the Camorra's involvement in billion-dollar global rackets. This style, and not simply the revelation of naked facts, has expanded his audience to include both specialists and ordinary people. Saviano believes that simply presenting information is not enough to provoke readers to take ethical action. Why? Because today, he notes, in part because of social networking systems, "everything is said, everything comes and goes, it's very difficult for anything to remain secret anymore; but the real challenge lies in passing along this information to the public; making it become a subject that people want to talk about, discuss, repeat and want to understand better."[9]

Saviano underscores the pedagogical imperative and narrative challenges facing educators living and teaching in a time that is on the verge of massive social and political change. How do we tell stories about the struggle for ethical economies, the health risks that accompany acute poverty, and the abuse of resources and environmental devastation so that the public and our students will want to better understand and address the local and global challenges facing a participatory democracy? How do educators, journalists, and activists tell stories in ways that present difficult knowledge that we might ordinarily turn away from or disavow? As Saviano points out, to simply dispense information is not enough. The intergenerational call throughout the world for racial and gender justice, access to education and health care, economic opportunity, and dignity in response to repressive political conditions is evidence of a global trend in social movements that is best described as a process of transitional justice. I argue that the process of transitional justice calls for radical approaches to narrative and to teaching that are best informed by journalists, educators, and activists working in societies in transition.

The case of Saviano is one example of the mafia's current threat to freedom of the press and the dangers inherent in taking individual action against the mafia. As of January 2016, Saviano is one of 22,722 investigative journalists who have suffered threats and abuse because of their reportage on the mafia and one of 20 journalists living under police protection. Reporters Without Borders has documented the increasingly dangerous conditions facing journalists throughout Italy today, including intimidation, arson attacks on homes and cars, and the mafia's abuse of libel action and claims for damages in civil courts. Despite attempts to alter the law that makes libel a crime for investigative journalists exposing mafia crime, Italian journalists continue to be sentenced to prison for libel offences against members of criminal organizations. These acts of intimidation not only undermine the work of journalists, bloggers, and activists and place them in danger but also censor information and weaken the public's access to antimafia entries in the news media.

The case of Saviano also speaks to the dangers facing journalists who work in isolation. When Saviano wrote *Gomorrah*, he wrote outside the protection of organizations such as Reporters Without Borders and the Italian Federation of Journalists. And while *Gomorrah* has reached millions of readers (and Saviano has nearly 1.5 million Twitter followers), he continues to be exiled from colleagues and sentenced to a solitary, fugitive existence, all while the mafia tightens its grip on the Italian economy and poses, as stated earlier, serious threats to media freedom. Citing the power of solidarity among journalists, Roberto Natale, president of the Italian Federation of Journalists, argues that public radio and television should report more frequently on mafia news and that an inclusive solidarity, "in association with more visibility and public attention for media freedom provides the best protection for threatened journalists."[10] This includes showing solidarity with threatened colleagues and being committed to the ideal that no journalist should have to act alone against mafia criminality.[11] The concept of inclusive solidarity implied in Natale's call refers to a quality of association that holds a group of people together because of shared values, goals, or interests. Members are willing to act on one another's behalf or on behalf of the group when necessary. In story-taking and storytelling practices among communities in transition, solidarity among activists, citizen journalists, and educators is instituted to reject tyranny and oppression and to ameliorate the conditions that cause suffering, whether one directly suffers or not.

In contrast to Saviano's isolating himself, the storytellers portrayed throughout this book act in solidarity with others. Directing their attention to the legacy of human rights abuses committed by Italy's criminal associations, storytellers participating with antimafia activist groups, such as Addiopizzo and Corleone Dialogos, use social media and social entrepreneurial practices, photojournalism, and collective spontaneous expressions of grief and mourning to directly address the challenges to collective action, and they work to build and sustain social bonds of solidarity. They seek to recover collective memories of non-violent dissent against a mafia that would prefer an absolute erasure of this history. In what follows, I take Saviano's commitment to listen and to tell difficult stories as a point of departure for exploring the narrative forms structuring the non-violent art of public dissent against another mafia in Italy: Sicily's Cosa Nostra. I argue that a productive ground for theorizing the narratives that give expression to transitional justice among communities traumatized by violence can be found in the public pedagogy of antimafia activists currently working together in Sicily.

Transitional Justice and Education

The field of transitional justice traces its roots to the Nuremberg trials after World War II. Although the Nuremberg trials have been criticized on many levels for being flawed, they provided a foundation for codifying international human rights law and set a precedent for holding accountable those responsible for crimes against humanity, war crimes, and genocide.[12] The International Center for Transitional Justice describes transitional justice as "a set of judicial and non-judicial measures that have been implemented by different countries in order to redress the legacies of massive human rights abuses. These measures include criminal prosecutions, truth commissions, reparations programs, and various kinds of institutional reforms."[13]

Human rights activist Pablo de Greiff observes that "the number of transitional societies increases if one extends the domain of application of 'transitional justice' from its original context – namely, societies emerging from authoritarianism – to societies emerging from conflict."[14] He explains that societies emerging from conflict are often faced with acute poverty, poor governance, fractured infrastructures, and serious inequalities. Moreover, post-conflict countries typically face massive human rights abuses, as well as serious health care issues, the loss of educational resources, and the high costs of implementing justice initiatives.[15]

On a conceptual level, transitional justice emphasizes inclusive and non-adversarial frameworks that seek to keep a violent past from being repeated. The emphasis is placed on dialogue between victims and their perpetrators rather than solely allocating blame.[16] Given that transitional justice is foremost about challenging denial and forming a basis for learning from the past, it has, at its heart, a pedagogical impulse. The pedagogical dimension of transitional justice is grounded in a set of ethical questions: What memories are worthy of attention? What legacies are restored and sustained after social breakdown? How should past violence be judged?

Political scientist Bronwyn Leebaw points out several complicated issues that emerge within transitional justice institutions. She argues that the use of legalistic and restorative frameworks too often foster new forms of forgetting and mythmaking by relying on criminal justice models that depoliticize the terms of investigation and make disingenuous claims to impartiality.[17] "Depoliticization has been a strategy," explains Leebaw, "for promoting reconciliation and a common sense of justice" in an effort to alleviate the suffering of victims.[18] What inadvertently follows, she says, is a masking of the specific political and social values that frame the investigation and its judgments.[19] Drawing on critics of the human rights movement, Leebaw's analysis raises questions about the ways in which depoliticization works to foreclose debate, not only about the terms of global justice but about the ways in which international justice norms are gendered. Depoliticization also works to present the values and traditions associated with Western liberalism as universal and to remove problems from their historical and political context.[20] Also abandoned within the legalistic and restorative frameworks are stories of dissent. Too often, transitional justice limits official remembrance of past suffering to victims or passive bystanders and fails to recognize the role of those who took action, who engaged in dissent, and who resisted state-sanctioned violence.

The act of depoliticization – within both legalistic and restorative frameworks – neutralizes the political landscape in ways that undermine the pedagogical commitments inherent in transitional justice frameworks. One cannot learn well from the past or challenge denial by effacing political dynamics. The story-takers depicted throughout this book compose narratives that capture the complexities of suffering and agency. They use writing, photography, and imaginative acts of protest to tell stories of resistance and solidarity. These actions offer lessons in the complexities of working towards justice, particularly given that the mafia continues to thrive in Italy.

During a series of interviews in July 2013 with antimafia activists and educators in Palermo, I asked if they believed that Italy was indeed a society in transition as they work towards recovering from the economic, emotional, and environmental devastation created by the mafia. Vito Lo Monaco, former director of the Italian Communist Party and current president of the Pio La Torre Center (*Centro Pio La Torre*), reported that "the Republic continues to be in crisis and the lives of people in Italy continue to be impacted by organized crime, but Italy is not isolated in this struggle. Organized crime is an international enterprise, rooted in exploitation." In the context of the antimafia movement in Italy, transitional justice refers to projects taken up – legislative, economic, educational, aesthetic, and cultural – to redress victims, recognize the rights of victims, promote civic trust, and strengthen the rule of law. Given the mafia's infiltration into the state, eradicating the mafia from Italy requires similar transformations to those that occurred in countries such as South Africa and Argentina. The intention of this book, however, is not to compare the human rights abuses in Italy and other countries in transition but to place in relief the human rights abuses in Italy that might easily be overlooked if one fails to recognize the impact that large-scale corruption has on human rights. As Chris Cuneen has argued in his discussions of reparation, state crime is not restricted to genocide, mass murder, or torture. State crime can include petty corruption and large-scale corruption of political elites.[21] In partnerships with the state and manufacturers in Italy and beyond the Italian borders, the mafia has executed and continues to execute massive human rights abuses and environmental violations.[22] These collaborations have produced, to offer just one example, illegal waste dumping sites in Italy near Naples and the surrounding region of Campania that have resulted in clusters of nearby residents with liver, kidney, pancreatic, and other cancers. This is just one example of the extent to which the law has played a constitutive role in crimes against humanity. The law, in partnership with the mafia, too often legitimates unchecked environmental devastation and unchecked extortion, and facilitates the takeover of land for exploitation, as was made evident in the building of the Falcone-Borsellino Airport in Cinisi, Sicily. Add to this the fact that the mafia has not only established itself as an international organization but has also established "clean" methods for penetrating legal and illegal enterprises.

Lo Monaco maintains that making tangible reparation for mafia-related crimes cannot happen in the courtroom alone. Reparations must happen on the legislative, educative, social, and cultural levels as well. He offers Italy's Rognoni-La Torre Law as one example of a legislative process created to address the fiscal and emotional losses caused by Italy's neglect of the violence imposed on ordinary citizens by organized crime. Recognized by Italy in 1980 as the antimafia law, this legislation made mafia conspiracy a crime and allowed the courts to seize the assets taken by the mafia and return them to public use for the public good. At the same time, Lo Monaco emphasizes the importance of organizations that work with victims of mafia violence and create partnerships with educational institutions to design curricula that focus on what activists and educators describe as an ethical economy and *legalità*. The term *legalità* is used to distinguish between illegal actions sanctioned by the state and morally engaged civic action inspired by ideals of justice, freedom, and dignity. Part of this work includes processes of reclaiming half-spoken histories of dissent against mafia crime. In this sense Italian antimafia educators and activists make a significant contribution to transitional justice institutions and debates by telling and taking stories about the commitment to protest against mafia crimes, rather than focusing solely on victims of mafia violence. The theme of resistance, which is almost entirely neglected in discussions about transitional justice, offers important lessons about the experience of resistance and nonviolent dissent, and fulfils a moral obligation to recognize those who suffered as the result of protest or principled action.[23]

Implicit in acts of reparation made in the name of transitional justice is the intention to create new democratic governments that both separate from the past and sustain social peace.[24] Although formal institutional structures and acts of legislation are crucial to cultivating transitional justice, transitional law always includes, as implied by Lo Monaco and underscored by legal scholar Ruti Teitel, "a cultural logic ... transitional law is, above all, symbolic – a secular ritual of political passage."[25] Michael Rothberg argues that as a secular ritual, transitional justice possesses a strong narrative dimension that includes fiction/non-fiction, as we see with Saviano's work, courtroom testimony, truth commission reports, educational curricula, and cinematic, aesthetic, and musical scores. "Regardless of the medium," writes Rothberg, "such narratives give form to political transformation by helping shape the transitional era's time consciousness, both its space of experience and its horizon of expectations."[26]

What are the distinguishing features of transitional narratives and what implications do these features have for public pedagogical projects that are committed to educating citizens and residents to take part in a participatory democracy? Teitel identifies a set of key features:

1. Transitional narratives are not meta-narratives but mini-narratives that are nested in prior national stories.
2. Transitional narratives do not speak of new beginnings or origins but build on "pre-existing political legacies" by recategorizing central events from a nation's past.[27] They exist in relation to past narratives of trauma and violation.
3. They recategorize or recast central events from a nation's past in the context of new political dispensation that might, for example, translate "anti-terrorist measures" into "crimes against humanity."
4. They emplot a prior national history of injustice into a future narrative of hope and redemption.

Rothberg raises concerns about Teitel's fourth narrative feature because, he argues, narratives that follow a redemptive path tend to slip into the very form of disavowal Leebaw discusses in her analysis of depoliticization. Narratives that move from tragedy to comic resolution – stories of affliction that end happily, with gained insights into history – too often become master plots that inspire a "forgetful will to reconciliation" by "letting go of the past" in the name of hope for the future.[28] What is refuted, notes Rothberg, is the hold the past has on the present and "the ongoing inextricability of individuals from collective, social contexts."[29] In other words, narratives vulnerable to disavowal promote versions of democratic progress, in part, by denying continuities between the past and the present and by failing to recognize the global and local ethical obligations we have.[30]

Our ethical obligations are not contingent, I argue, on a shared language or a common life grounded in familiar landscapes or recognizable faces. The activists and educators introduced in this book solicit ethical encounters from local and global constituencies, and in so doing each project compels us to negotiate a set of ethical questions that resonate with those outlined by Judith Butler in her study of our moral obligation to respond to state violence and war: Is what is happening so far from me that I have no responsibility for it? Is what is happening so close to me that I cannot bear to take responsibility for it? If I am not responsible for this suffering, should I still take responsibility for it?[31] And what if I respond ethically and put my own life in danger?

I approach the question of education's ethical obligations to others with caution. I do so for several reasons. Given the strains of self-sacrifice and martyrdom in antimafia discourses, I am concerned with any ethic that invokes the call to preserve the life of another person if that ethic does not also call for self-preservation. The pedagogical ethic of remembrance this book pursues is one that persists in marshalling the life drive, to persist, following Butler, "in one's own being ... even if, as a super-egoic state, ethics threaten to become a pure culture of the death drive."[32] Arendt's concept of natality guides my discussions of a pedagogical ethic that values the political act of founding or making a new beginning without sliding into narratives of disavowal, naive hope, or denial. For Arendt, natality marks the moment when one is born into the political sphere and comes to understand how acting together can create the truly unexpected. The public pedagogy of, for example, anti-extortion organizations, such as Addiopizzo, and citizen journalists writing from Corleone present cases of social renewal that open spaces of possibility in relation to a traumatic past that informs rather than determines the future. Within what Arendt would call the "gap between past and future," antimafia activists, students, and teachers orient themselves towards a future that is neither in denial of nor fated by the past nor silenced by violence.[33]

Transitional justice marks a particularly complicated moment in a nation's development. Communities of and in transition do not necessarily occupy a post-traumatic state; consequently, composing narratives that make the work of mourning possible is especially challenging. Within the context of antimafia protest is the persistent infiltration of mafia crime and its attendant suffering. In her analysis of the mafia and Italian cinema, Dana Renga argues that "Italy does not inhabit a post-traumatic state during which time traumatic injury is understood and articulated as cultural trauma."[34] The mafia continues to thrive and to adapt to new market and social conditions; consequently, the period of latency so necessary for a trauma to be spoken about and worked through is not possible. Moreover, as Renga argues, the nature and anguish of victims, while apparently clear-cut, is not so, particularly when considering the pain of perpetrators and thousands, notes Renga, "who hold a liminal status within the organization, including many women and children. These individuals are bound to their clan through the code of honour, family loyalty, and frequently, fear. Yet, as they have never committed any illegal act, the line between victim and victimizer is nebulous ... essentially, the suffering of those who fit this category is denied."[35] This unrecognized suffering can be described as an experience of what Jill Stauffer terms "ethical loneliness."[36] Stauffer locates the causes of ethical loneliness in political and social institutions that fail to listen well to victims, perpetrators, and resistors who make claims for justice and reparation. Like Renga, Stauffer recognizes the porousness that exists between victims and perpetrators, particularly in cases of protracted conflict. In what ways are possibilities for mourning compromised when persons experience the anguish of being abandoned by communities and state institutions? To what extent can the work of mourning be taken up in a society that continues to experience traumatic injury? And how are competing interests and contradictory memories negotiated within communities in transition, particularly as these interests play out along socio-economic gendered lines?

This book explores the claim that societies must exist in a post-traumatic state in order to mourn. The case studies are designed to consider the conditions that make collective mourning possible in the midst of trauma and how competing interests can undermine a community's capacity to make sense of loss, particularly when groups occupy very different personal, political, and cultural positions. In her study of the debates in New York about establishing a memorial site at Ground Zero after the 9/11 attacks, E. Ann Kaplan makes clear how difficult it is for communities to establish consensus about how to work through trauma on several levels – personal, political, intellectual, emotional – so that they can marshall the life drive Arendt so highly values, turn to their city, and continue life as citizens of the world.[37] Kaplan uses Ulrich Baer's 2002 edited collection *110 Stories: New York Writes after September 11* to illustrate the need for narrative in the wake of disaster and the role that artists, poets, novelists, short-story writers, playwrights, and photographers can play in posing, in Baer's words, "uncomfortable questions and unflinching reflection."[38] Baer's approach to storytelling is akin to Arendt's belief in the power of narrative to restore memories that have been abandoned by history. Baer turns not to triumphant narratives drenched in sentimentality and consolation but rather to narratives that register complex meanings and call out for deliberation, reinterpretations, and revisionary practices that can establish communities of mourning and generate social and cultural transformation. Artists such as Baer and the antimafia activists and educators featured in this book's case studies are members of what cultural sociologist Jeffrey C. Alexander, following Max Weber, described in his sociology of religions as "carrier groups."[39] Members of carrier groups work as collective agents to represent loss and make claims for justice. They have, explains Alexander, "both ideal and material interests, they are situated in particular places in the social structure, and they have particular discursive talents for articulating their claims – for what might be called 'meaning making' – in the public sphere."[40] Working across generations, gender, sexual identities, and socio-economic interests, carrier groups can represent institutions, private and national interests, or political affiliations. Operating within the context of antimafia activism are complex struggles to mourn within the interstices of persistent traumatic injuries and competing interests among groups who carry ambivalent and conflicting commitments and ideals about civility and justice.

This book understands cultural trauma as a distinctly catastrophic event or series of events that irrevocably impact members of a community in ways that alter their sense of well-being, group consciousness, and sense of the future.[41] Drawing in part on the definition of cultural trauma posited by Alexander, each case study considers the ways in which members of communities use discourses and aesthetic practices to socially mediate trauma's impact. The underlying assumption made by Alexander holds that trauma is socially mediated – events in themselves are not inherently traumatic.[42] Alexander places a high value on the role of imagination in representing trauma, both real and imagined. The representation of social pain and the threat this pain poses to persons' well-being and sense of the future is understood to activate the "trauma process." In other words, the trauma process is constituted by the act of symbolization itself, the moment when a traumatic injury is articulated and claims for justice are made.[43]

Traumatic experience, irrecoverable loss, and persistent violence coexist within the dynamics of political transition.[44] I argue that within the dynamics of political transition, the work of mourning is possible when story-taking and storytelling provide alternatives to the neo- liberal story of transition and resist consoling narratives that depoliticize transitional justice. Furthermore, I argue that the pedagogical impulse of transitional justice is most efficacious when stories of resistance and refusal are part of the public memorial landscape. The difficult and interminable work of mourning requires not only a public pedagogy that refuses narratives of naive hope and consolation but also a public pedagogy that inspires ethically informed political judgment.

Drawing on the early work of Henry Giroux and building on the scholarship of Jennifer Sandlin and Glenn C. Savage, I use the concept of public pedagogy to analyse learning and educational experiences that take place outside formal school settings. Giroux's early scholarship contributes significantly to our understanding of how public pedagogy, such as advertising, cinema, and social media, perpetuates dominant, neo-liberal values. In this book public pedagogy is understood as a fluid concept that at times imposes a hegemonic force vis-à-vis "corporate pedagogies" while at other times is used to enact cultural and political resistance, counter-hegemonic possibilities, and cultural renewal. I also pay specific attention to the ways in which public pedagogy has the potential to generate critical engagements with knowledge that is difficult to recognize or to come to terms with.[45]

I use the term *difficult knowledge* to refer to the representations of social trauma and individuals' encounters with them in formal and informal educational settings. My focus here is on practices of remembrance that are associated with conflict, violence, loss, and death. But there is more. I am also interested in what it means, from a pedagogical point of view, to introduce knowledge that challenges participants' expectations and interpretive capacities, and provokes anger, confusion, or anxiety.[46] What can be learned when a shrine or monument provokes grief, shame, or rage? The stories embedded in many of the pedagogical projects represented in this book speak to complicities of countries, families, and cultures in the systemic violence of mafia crime. These projects hold difficult knowledge because they do indeed evoke anxiety and call for participants to bear witness to victims of violence, perpetrators of violence, and those identified as having passively stood by in the presence of mafia brutality.

What is difficult about the knowledge presented, however, is not intrinsic to the photographs, shrines, artefacts, or discourses themselves. Rather, following educational theorists Deborah Britzman, Alice Pitt, and Roger Simon, I argue that what makes knowledge difficult is located in its affective force. This force lies within the affective experience of the encounter and the extent to which the provocation challenges limits of thought.[47] In other words, the affective force of difficult knowledge has the potential to challenge our frameworks for acting ethically in the world. It cannot be specified in advance or assumed to be unitary, singular, or shared.[48] Public pedagogy bears the responsibility for cultivating an ethically informed judgment of how to shape the relation between affect and thought, recognizing the indeterminacy of response.[49] Exactly what constitutes an ethically informed judgment is explored throughout this book.

In an era saturated with media images of suffering, it is not enough, as Saviano reminds us, to simply tell stories of injustice. Public pedagogy calls for innovative narratives and methods of memory curation. The radical public teachings of antimafia educators, artists, and activists currently working in Sicily inspire innovations in exhibition, public and cultural interventions, and the creation of memorial sites. *The Story-Takers* maps the landscape of memory and non-violent protest, identifying their core pedagogical, narrative, and artistic features and investigating their impact via six case studies, each of which invite participation in repertoires of the making and remaking of cultural memory. *The Story-Takers* charts new intellectual, pedagogical, and political pathways in what has been, until now, an unprecedented exploration of public pedagogy's non-violent protest against the global reach of mafia violence.

Reclaiming Memories of Resistance

It is late in Naples as I board the night boat for Palermo. Naples, Messina, Capaci, Trapani all belong to the southern part of Italy, observes travel writer Peter Robb, where Europe is no longer entirely Europe but also Africa, Asia, America. Sicily is the farthest part of Italy from Europe and nearest to the rest of the world.[50] Separating North Africa from Europe, about 310 kilometres from Naples, Palermo emerges as a quintessential *noir* cityscape. Once steeped in vice and terrorism, contemporary Palermo no longer falls silent in the presence of the Cosa Nostra, the Sicilian mafia that held the city in its grip for generations. Within walls of citrus orchards long ago confiscated by the mafia resides another Palermo, a city committed to an ethical economy, security, and dignity. Today, activists, educators, social entrepreneurs, artists, and ordinary residents of the city publicly speak against mafia control by refusing to pay extortion fees or to be seduced by distorted codes of honour and perverse notions of family loyalty. Palermo's cityscape is an expression of the formation of a new identity as city and citizen work to challenge the law of *omertà*, a code of silence and practice of intimidation that threatened generations with death or the disappearance of loved ones if they spoke of mafia violence.

In March 2011 Edo Zaffuto, an antimafia activist and one of the founding members of Addiopizzo, a grassroots anti-extortion group based in Palermo, invited me to join him and a group of high school students from Turin and their teachers on what they describe as an "ethical tour of Palermo." Our plan was to meet early in the morning to explore sites that are symbolic in the fight against the mafia and to visit businesses that have said no to the mafia's demands for protection money. We boarded a bus early in the morning. Our first stop, about 20 minutes from the city centre, was by the side of the expressway leading to the Falcone-Borsellino Airport. The bus pulled up near a tall red obelisk that marks the stretch of highway where antimafia prosecutor Giovanni Falcone; his wife, Judge Francesca Morvillo; and three police bodyguards, were killed in an explosion while driving. We filed out of the bus and Zaffuto escorted us around the obelisk engraved with the victims' names, while he described the events that led up to the assassination. On 23 May 1992 Giovanni Brusca blew up a section of this expressway, following orders from then mafia head Salvatore (Totò) Riina to kill Falcone. We circled the monument and climbed a nearby hill to a small concrete outbuilding painted with the words "No More Mafia!" in big, blue block letters, a message from the people to the mafia that they will no longer be silent.

A period of intense conflict over building contracts, real estate, and drugs between a group of mafiosi from the interior town of Corleone and Palermo's mafiosi or families led to a series of brutal assassinations in spring 1992.[51] Following a decade of intensification of mafia brutalities between 1970 and 1983, Corleonesi "boss" Totò Riina masterminded a series of savage murders and, together with Giovanni Brusca, arranged to assassinate Falcone after placing him on their death list in the early 1980s. Falcone made their list by tracing the criminal organization's financial ties to politicians and making transparent, in the words of journalist Alexander Stille, "the Pirandellian world of Sicilian politics where appearance and reality are easily confused and where the face of the mafia may hide behind the respectable mask of lawyer, judge, businessman, priest or politician."[52] Italians can recite the details of the day Falcone died the way Americans recount the assassination of John F. Kennedy. Two months later, on 19 July 1992, Falcone's fellow prosecutor and close friend Paolo Borsellino and his five bodyguards were blown up in a massive car bomb explosion in downtown Palermo.

In the wake of the devastating loss of Falcone, Borsellino, and the long list of public servants who fell victim to the mafia, the past pressed up against the present as pre-existing legacies of public dissent took form. Inspired by the half-spoken Sicilian history of antimafia agrarian protests, the residents of the city openly expressed their outrage in the streets. Hanging from balconies throughout the city were white bed sheets printed with what has now come to be an iconic photograph of Falcone and Borsellino leaning in to each other, smiling. The sheets, spray-painted with slogans such as "Falcone Lives," "Palermo Wants Justice," "Get the mafia out of government," "Stop killing this city," and "Their ideas have not died, they walk on our legs" appeared throughout a city that, while having fallen on its knees in grief, refused to succumb. The women who formed the "committee of the sheets" (*Comitato dei lenzuoli*) were just one group who collectively responded to the devastating loss of virtually all Italian civil servants who dedicated themselves to dismantling mafia terror and devastation. Together, they inspired other grassroots organizations to take action. Spontaneous shrines, such as the Falcone Tree – the people's monument – sprang up overnight in front of Falcone and Morvillo's apartment in the heart of Palermo on Via Notarbartolo, where the tree still stands. The tree continues to serve as a civil shrine and is covered with letters and memorabilia commemorating Falcone, Borsellino, and other "martyrs of justice" who were systematically executed. Out of a deep desire to transform the image of Corleone and to resist the mafia presence in their town, youth activists turned citizen writers created a digital news centre, Corleone Dialogos. This project is dedicated, as explained in the mission statement on the website, to changing "the culture of our land, leaving a state of isolation to create the basis for new social and economic development."[53] This wave of activism and hope in

Palermo has extended to the larger Italian peninsula and has marked a new political era in Sicily that involves a process of transitional justice that seeks to transform civil society, culture, and the economy.

Throughout this book, I argue that the moving, emotional force behind the antimafia activism in Sicily is a desire for what Cavarero describes as "the narratable self" that longs for "receives and offers, here and now, an unrepeatable story in the form of a tale."[54] Cavarero brings to our attention the importance of continually and ritualistically transforming narratives about the difficult legacies people have inherited and the traumatic experiences they have lived through. I draw on the work of Cavarero to argue that communities negotiating societal trauma, especially during times of transitional justice, long for difficult legacies to be narrated in ways that are meaningful, but these narratives must be continually reordered, refined, and enlivened. As well, they must have the capacity to sustain the traces of the trauma's impact. This approach to composing transitional narratives stands apart from acts of remembering that compulsively recite the same national tales or slip into liberal narratives of redemption.

The narrative practices taken up by the antimafia activists introduced in this book offer educators a radical approach to understanding how communities negotiate societal violence outside the classroom through collective memory work that establishes storytelling as a relational politic that involves ethical action. Writing in 1943 in *War and Children*, Anna Freud (with Dorothy T. Burlingham) noted that educational systems are "always conservative insofar as they represent a society's attempts to transmit its values to the next generation."[55] The educational projects taken up outside formal schooling present possibilities that are open to challenging national and institutional forms of commemoration that rely too narrowly on the idealization of what has been lost, as well as what Simon describes as "pedagogically redemptive forms of representation."[56] This approach to commemoration, argues Simon, fails to cultivate "an interpretive concern with the past that is beyond cognitive expectation."[57] What too often accompanies this failure, Simon suggests, is an indifference or a lack of sensitivity to the ways in which the past presses up against the present.

What does it mean to exercise an interpretive concern that exceeds what is cognitively imaginable? Why would such a project be worthy of our attention? For Simon, the practice of an ethical pedagogy of remembrance is contingent on a "re-formation of historical memory, consciousness and imagination." Simon argues that educators practise this ethic by working with students to reinterpret "dominant narratives, reviv[ing] marginal ones, or bring[ing] to light those formerly suppressed, unheard, or unarticulated."[58] Social practices of remembrance, Simon goes on to say, imply relationships that collect around reading texts, speaking with and listening to others, and engaging in various forms

of cinema and art, all of which make it possible for people who have not literally lived through historical events to feel their force in their intellectual and
imaginative lives. Simon locates generative educational thought in the moment
when educators work "to affirm or transform established practices of historical memory through person-to-person encounters or the staging of engagements with text or image."[59] Furthermore, he makes a crucial normative point
with respect to curriculum design: implicit in pedagogies of remembrance are
a set of evaluations and assessments that determine what we believe should
be remembered, placed in relief, reframed, or infused with meaning. In other
words, curriculum design is never neutral. In the case of reworking narratives
of progress that deny or neglect the ongoing production of trauma and inequality in the present, we might start with taking an account of the tension between
continuity and discontinuity – how does the past live with us in the day-to-day
present?[60] Who is remembered and who is forgotten within an antimafia public
culture that relies on heroic discourses of self-sacrifice to educate communities
about mafia activism?

To develop the concept of a critical interpretive concern with the past that
reinvests transitional narratives with meaning, I use specific biographical figures who are active in the antimafia movement and the antimafia imaginary.
Throughout this book, I use the term *antimafia imaginary* to refer to how the
anti-criminal, civil, and social elements are imagined among antimafia activists, students, and teachers. At times in conversation, at other times through
digital archival research, fiction, and film, I explore the discourses of memory
and forgetting that pervaded the public spaces of Palermo immediately after
the murders of Falcone and Borsellino. The concepts of the story-taker and the
storyteller elaborated by Cavarero and Steedman guide my explorations of the
range of narrative and visual strategies activists use to tell stories of the many
Palermos and, in turn, to tell a story about themselves as citizens, residents,
teachers, artists, and social entrepreneurs who work to sustain a culture of what
they describe as dignity and *legalità*. Drawing on the scholarship of Steedman,
Cavarero describes the work of the story-taker as one who collects oral testimonies and elaborates on them in writing and in photographs. Cavarero draws
a link between the biographer and the psychoanalyst who gives "back to the
patient, the story of his or her life."[61]

Much of modern knowledge is provided by the *story-taker* – the one who
solicits and listens to life stories told by others, and then transcribes them into
the scientific canons of his or her discipline. As Carolyn Steedman rightly emphasizes, this figure finds its most famous and influential variants in psychoanalysis. The psychoanalyst might indeed be interpreted as a *story-taker* whose
purpose is "to give back to the patient the story of his or her life, welded into a

chronological sequence and narrative coherence, so that at the end of it all, the coming to psychic health might be seen as the re-appropriation of one's own life story."[62]

The story-takers in this book have developed relationships with victims of mafia violence; they have become conversant with half-spoken histories and have come to know and to work with courageous people who refused to be intimidated by mafia threats. As well, they incorporate the theme of resistance into the theory and practice of transitional justice. Taken collectively, contemporary antimafia activism also expresses a desire to offer Sicily a story that renews cultural attention on the citizens and residents denied protection by the state. And while death has a literal presence in much of the activism we explore in this book, death is also constitutively excluded and replaced, I argue, with a desire for new beginnings - what Arendt describes as *natality*.

The activists that I have worked with over the last seven years understand that although they have contributed to the reduction of mafia-related crime in Sicily, they face, in the Cosa Nostra, what John Dickie has described as a shadow state, literally a political body that sometimes opposes, sometimes subverts, and too often dwells within the body of the legal government.[63] In 2009 it came as no surprise to Palermitani that former Italian prime minister Silvio Berlusconi had a long alleged history of mafia involvement dating back to Berlusconi's creation of the Italian party, *Forza Italia*. Nor was it surprising to learn from testimony taken by mafia bosses turned state informants, such as Tommaso Buscetta, that the state failed to protect Falcone and Borsellino. Among the most devastating aspect of mafia violence, argues sociologist Umberto Santino, was

the connection between politics and crime. This mixture between illegal and legal, criminal and institutional, is at the heart of the mafia's historical model, but it has grown and spread independently of the presence of Sicilian mafiosos or Sicilian-Americans. It is not that the mafia has invaded the world, it is that the world has produced more and more groups of the mafia-type.[64]

Santino's analysis is as relevant today as it was in post–World War II Italy when the United States, in an effort to undermine Italy's Communist Party, covertly funded the Christian Democrats (who worked with the Cosa Nostra) and threatened to withhold Marshall Plan funds if the Communists were permitted to win national elections.[65] Today, the global community continues to turn its back on deeply rooted problems of poverty and unemployment, both of which make mafia support possible.[66] Anthropologists Peter Schneider and Jane Schneider have observed that the mafia's economic impact, specifically on the construction industry in major cities, makes the antimafia movement vulnerable because global economics has not adequately addressed issues of poverty and unemployment. This is perhaps why, they note, the graffito *"Viva la mafia!"* is inscribed on city walls and crumbling buildings in poor neighbourhoods.

Although it would be naive to claim that the antimafia movement has eradicated organized crime, the antimafia struggle sustains its efforts. Since the deaths of Falcone and Borsellino, the antimafia movement has continually been successful at destabilizing mafia-related crime, advocating for participatory democracy and transparency, and denouncing violence and corruption, in part by demanding investigations into mafia activities and their sources of funding, and directly challenging the state's complicity in mafia-related activities.[67] The solidarity and reform efforts sustained in Sicily contradict the stigma and stereotypes made by scholars such as Robert Putnam in his 1993 book *Making Democracy Work: Civic Traditions in Modern Italy.* Depicting southern Italians as lacking any capacity for the "spirit of association," or a capacity for civil consensus, his work undermined the strength and dignity of Sicilians. Schneider and Schneider remind us of the irony of Putnam's analysis given that his book was published "during the very years that the anti-Mafia movement flourished."[68] In fact, every antimafia activist I speak with – whether teacher, artist, journalist, or student – emphasizes that no one can accomplish anything significant alone. It is only through sustained, collective action that public spaces can be reclaimed. What continues to be of serious concern, however, is that while they remain steadfast in their resistance, the antimafia activists represented in this book simply do not receive sustained support and protection from the Italian state. Such support would offer the necessary foundation for cultivating a civil education and a civil society that are their best protection.[69]

Plan of the Book

The first and second chapters of the book examine the stories taken and told about antimafia prosecutors Giovanni Falcone and Francesca Morvillo. Specifically, these chapters examine the implications of institutionalizing subversive mourning practices that represent unspeakable losses in public life, as well as the narrative challenges involved when representing women who played a crucial role in the antimafia movement.

Chapter 1 examines the Falcone Tree, a spontaneous shrine created immediately after the 1992 murder of Giovanni Falcone. The analysis builds on Judith Butler's studies of precarity and examines what it might mean for public pedagogy to, in the words of Judith Butler, "tarry with grief" in the aftermath of atrocity. The chapter incorporates a study of Freud's 1917–29 works on grief and what he describes as "endless mourning," the spirit of what we find in Butler's call "to tarry with grief." Freud serves as a guide for considering the extent to which the discourses surrounding Falcone's memory resonate with the consoling, redemptive narratives Freud raised concerns about in his later writings on grief in response to World War I. The chapter argues that the institutionalization of Falcone's memory ironically promotes conformity to an antimafia discourse that idealizes martyrdom and encrypts the very memories of personal trauma and historical events that it intended to keep vibrant and alive. Rather than presenting as a clear case of collective mourning within the context of a society in transition, the Falcone Tree represents a clear case of the ways in which mourning can be taken up and refused, expressed, deferred, and silenced in the midst of social breakdown.

Chapter 2 presents a critical analysis of the memorial landscapes composed on Facebook to commemorate female martyrs of justice in the Sicilian antimafia movement. The chapter turns to the Facebook page of attorney and antimafia activist Francesca Morvillo and argues that while Morvillo's Facebook site functions as an archive of feelings, it eventually overshadows her memory in much the same way she is overshadowed in more mainstream antimafia public cultures. Thus, I suggest that Morvillo's Facebook page can be read as a site of struggle that displaces her memory with iconic images of antimafia history that commemorate masculine histories and relegate her to a figure who lacks political significance worthy of remembering. How, I ask, does Morvillo's Facebook page – this archive of feelings – articulate particular affective investments that resonate with the common, everyday understanding of invisible, forgotten figures and the ways in which discourses of memory and the memorable are taught? What implications do the stories taken and told on this site have for public pedagogy and the work of memory composed in transitional societies? The displacements of her memory pose specific challenges to sustaining Morvillo's legacy and raise important questions in the post-feminist moment about what, in 1990, Teresa de Lauretis described as the paradox of the "non-being of a woman."[70] This paradox serves as my point of departure for considering the absence of Morvillo's memory in the public imaginary specifically and the implications this absence has for imagining a feminist antimafia consciousness attached to ideals of self-sacrifice and martyrdom more generally.

Together, the first two chapters demonstrate how the logic of depoliticization undermines the capacity to generate narratives that come closer to the symbolic work of mourning in transitional societies. They demonstrate that the logic of depoliticization creates conditions for what Eric Santner describes as a "narrative fetishism," a narrative form that expunges the traces of the loss and trauma that called the narrative into being in the first place.[71] Both chapters also establish the limits of transitional narratives that, while emerging in an effort to retain memories of dissent among societies in transition, foreclose on mourning and perpetuate naive hope and denial.

Chapter 3 examines the Sicilian grassroots organization Addiopizzo, with a specific focus on Addiopizzo's public pedagogical commitment to educate residents and citizens in Italy for what they describe as an ethical economy. Founded in 2004 by five university graduates, Addiopizzo, analogous to fair trade, works towards eliminating the illegal taxes imposed on Sicilian businesses, most specifically, the payment of the coerced protection fee (the *pizzo*) paid to mafia leaders. I consider the extent to which a relatively small group of concerned citizens and residents are able to successfully protect business owners who refuse to participate in extortion activities. How effective has Addiopizzo been in creating a social protective shield that allows for the possibility for cultivating critical consumers? What is the promise and what are the limits of such an organization given the force of mafia infiltration into government, politics, and the global economy?

Building on extensive interviews, fieldwork, and archival research, the chapter opens with an introduction to the founding members of Addiopizzo and their use of story-taking and storytelling to curate courageous, non-violent campaigns against extortion. The chapter examines Addiopizzo's curriculum, designed in collaboration with teachers and antimafia cultural organizations such as *Libera* and the La Torre Institute, to educate youth and residents about the importance of addressing extortion, to quote La Torre president Vito Lo Monaco one more time, "as the most primitive, primary method of accumulating wealth and destroying democratic life."[72] I argue that the strategic narrative practices of storytelling and story-taking used by Addiopizzo come closer to a form of remembering that fulfils the work of mourning while at the same time retaining traces of the impact of the trauma of extortion. Hannah Arendt's writings on natality and belatedness provide a way to understand the public pedagogical value of Addiopizzo's curriculum. Addiopizzo offers a clear case of what teaching for natality looks like within a society in transition. The chapter demonstrates how the group's distinct public pedagogical approaches are grounded not only in remembering a history of dissent against mafia violence but also in teachings that direct the public's attention not to mortality alone but to articulating new beginnings and, in Arendt's words, "renewing a common world" in the context of a living history.[73]

In Chapter 4 we turn to Corleone, the home of Corleone Dialogos, an antimafia digitally networked project created by youth in Corleone that posts on Facebook, publishes a monthly newspaper, and is dedicated, as stated in its mission statement, to changing "the culture of our land" and to creating "the basis for new social and economic development." This chapter explores the concept of the citizen writer in Sicily who presents half-spoken histories of non-violent dissent against the mafia by using screen culture to create a counter-public sphere. Building on an analysis of its digital archive and on interviews with the founders of Corleone Dialogos and active members of the organization, I explore how the narrative strategies work to extend the memories of an agrarian history of antimafia protest into contemporary antimafia activism. The chapter argues that the citizen journalists at Corleone Dialogos use writing to insert themselves into the historical record and the current news production process as story-takers and curators of collective memory formation. Here I draw on a concept of the commons elaborated on by Michael Hardt and Antonio Negri to more fully understand the public pedagogy of Corleone Dialogos. I argue that Corleone Dialogos presents a compelling challenge to claims made by sceptics of social media that new media practices, such as blogging, posting, texting, and posting on Facebook, neglect organization and revolt. I argue that the public pedagogy of Corleone Dialogos offers a strong case of what anthropologist Baris Cayli describes as "public engagement and participatory reformist culture that works to reconstruct the public sphere in the name of an ideal: creating a new public culture as a moral force by spreading radical information."[74] I conclude with a call for educators to assess citizen writing as a form of radical public pedagogy that strives to cultivate political judgment and what Hannah Arendt describes as "enlarged mentality."[75]

Chapter 5 considers the extent to which photographs of politically motivated violence can call on us to affirm human rights and to respond ethically to suffering both in our midst and at a distance. I explore the public pedagogical projects of photojournalist and antimafia activist Letizia Battaglia. Bound up with traditions of social documentary and biography, Battaglia's archive of over six thousand photographs of the mafia's internal war in Sicily works as a moving, portable archive that challenges the world to understand mafia crime as far more than Italy's problem. Drawing on the work of D.W. Winnicott, Masud Khan, Elisabeth Young-Bruehl, and Ariella Azoulay, I argue that Battaglia uses her photographic archive to create shared political spaces of action for narrating the lives of persons who have been rendered non-existent by history. Battaglia's photography, read as a historical document of lives in and of transition, makes lives legible and present and insists on restoring civil relationships and forms of being together that imagine a future apart from violence and corruption. Most importantly, Battaglia's photographic archive opens spaces for introspection and the recovery of difficult knowledge that has been disavowed or denied. Battaglia uses this knowledge, unavailable within national commemorative narratives, to expand the arc of remembering and to persistently challenge the state repression of memory.

Chapter 6 charts the history of Franco Zecchin's work as a leading antimafia photographer. Zecchin uses photography to stage and invite participation in social, historical, and cultural memories that are shocking, empowering, mobilizing, and traumatic. The photographs Zecchin has taken of mafia victims and perpetrators offer Palermo a story from an angle quite distinct from his one-time collaborator and lover Letizia Battaglia. While Battaglia uses only a wide-angle lens and enters into the images she takes, Zecchin brings irony and distance to images of mafia horror and suffering. Working as a photojournalist for *L'Ora* during the height of mafia violence, Zecchin claimed public attention by setting up provocative pop-up galleries in schools and on street corners, depicting murder after murder in Palermo and Corleone. Curated apart from state control and without profit, Zecchin asked ordinary citizens and residents of the city to participate in active, social forms of recognition and remembering, by bringing them face to face with images of previously denied violations of human rights.

Drawing on interviews with Zecchin and studies of his archival documents, I explore the extent to which Zecchin's photographic exhibits offer educators lessons in how the photograph can challenge limits of thought about violence, and in turn, establish ethical relations with others whom we imagine we have nothing in common. To what extent does Zecchin's photography present not solely an objective truth but the truth that is not optically present but profoundly felt? To what extent did the photographic exhibits of Zecchin exert an affective force that challenged the limits of thinking and feeling among residents who disavowed the mafia's presence? Building on the argument in Chapter 5, I suggest that Zecchin's photography recovers difficult knowledge and narratives of protest within the context of transitional justice and, as a form of public pedagogy, cultivates collective resistance in response to atrocity.[76] Moreover, his approach to photography offers a clear case of Arendt's idea that political judgment requires active participation and deliberation in politics, as well as a critical distance, apart from violence, from which the storyteller or historian can imagine multiple points of view.

The epilogue synthesizes the analysis and discusses its implications for a public pedagogy that contributes to the challenges of transitional justice by integrating themes of resistance into the curriculum, along with narrative practices – biographical and autobiographical – that articulate the specificity of lives: desires, failures, longings, and losses. This form of narration has been elaborated on by scholars in curriculum theory, such as William Pinar, Madeleine Grumet, Mary Doll, Janet Miller, Peter M. Taubman, and me over the years. More recently, the work of narration, inspired by Arendt and Cavarero, has been explored by scholars such as Mario Di Paolantonio, Warren Crichlow, R.M. Kennedy,

Dina Georgis, Chloe Brushwood Rose, and Bronwen Low. Collectively, this body of work holds the assumption that life narratives offer an alternative to philosophical universalism and disembodied categories that efface bodily existence and sexual, socio-economic, and racial differences. Biographical and autobiographical narration, observes Kennedy, "highlights the relationality of experience: that we affect the other and come only to know ourselves through the web of relations with others."[77] The chapters that follow are inspired by this collective body of scholarship and are intended to extend understanding of the ways in which life narratives play a vital pedagogical-commemorative role in transitional societies and both give shape and are shaped by competing and dynamic terrains of public memory.

Chapter One

"To Tarry with Grief": Spontaneous Shrines, Public Pedagogy, and the Work of Mourning

Is there something to be gained from grieving, from tarrying with grief, from remaining exposed to its unbearability and not endeavoring to seek a resolution for grief through violence?

    – Judith Butler, *Precarious Life: The Powers of Mourning and Violence*

You are killed generally because you are alone or else because you have got into a game that is too big. You are often killed because you don't have the necessary alliances, because you are without support. In Sicily, the Mafia strikes the servants of the state that the state has not succeeded in protecting.

    – Giovanni Falcone, with Marcelle Padovani, *Cose di Cosa Nostra*

Introduction

What might it mean for public pedagogy to "tarry with grief" in the aftermath of unspeakable violence? What stories are taken and told by communities to bear their sorrow? In an effort to address these questions, this chapter offers an analysis of the Falcone Tree, a spontaneous shrine built from a magnolia tree immediately after the 1992 massacre of beloved antimafia prosecutor Giovanni Falcone (18 May 1939–23 May 1992). The creation of this shrine, which still stands outside Falcone's apartment in Palermo on Via Notarbartolo, broke the imposed oath of silence kept by so many of Palermo's residents who had lived for generations in the presence of mafia threats that exacted profound emotional and economic suffering. The acts of participation performed at the Falcone Tree have been made not only to bring about social transformation but also to provoke questions about the implications of institutionalizing subversive mourning practices over unspeakable losses in public life. Over time the

Falcone Tree has become spontaneously sponsored, if you will, by the Giovanni and Francesca Falcone Foundation, and the tree has become a spontaneous part of the civic curriculum called *legalità*. Given the institutionalization of this shrine, to what extent does it continue to express the emotional life of the people? I use Freud's 1917–29 work on grief and what he described as "endless mourning," the spirit of what we find in Judith Butler's call "to tarry with grief," as a guide for considering the extent to which the discourses surrounding Falcone's memory resonate with the anti-consoling practices Freud wrote about in response to World War I. I do so in order to bring us closer to what I describe as *registers of ethical action* when thinking about the work of public pedagogy as a collective act of mourning.

Remembering Giovanni Falcone

On 23 May 1992, hours after antimafia prosecutor Giovanni Falcone; his wife, Judge Francesca Morvillo; and their three police escorts were murdered by the Cosa Nostra in an explosion near Palermo, the citizens of Palermo transformed a magnolia tree outside the Falcone home into a spontaneous shrine. The death of Falcone and the creation of this shrine marked the start of a painful era for Sicilians, ending what Christian Democrat Palermo mayor Leoluca Orlando had named the "Palermo Spring." Inaugurated by Orlando in the mid-1980s, the Spring was a time of cultural, ethical, and societal renewal. This political era in Sicily embraced an ideology and a global project of transforming civil society, reforming Sicily's economy, and restructuring its political system. The Palermo Spring generated a new optimism and confidence among the people of Sicily as Palermo took civil action against the mafia in the maxi-trial of 1986–7, led by Falcone and his colleague Paolo Borsellino. Using what came to be known as "the Falcone method" of investigating the mafia, Falcone and Borsellino hunted down obscure financial records, which resulted in the conviction of major players in heroin trafficking in the early 1980s. Later, Falcone and Borsellino used wiretapping and surveillance to convince many high-ranking mafiosi to break the oath of silence, or *omertà*, and to work in partnership with the government to fracture the Cosa Nostra. The trial's most crucial evidence, based on testimony from Tommaso Buscetta, a former boss turned informant, led to 474 mafiosi going on trial for a multitude of crimes related to mafia activities, including trafficking in heroin, extortion, and murder. Buscetta was the first important *Pentito*, or collaborator with the state, who testified against the mafia and informed Falcone, Borsellino, and their colleagues about the methods used by the mafia to transfer illicit capital through a series of filters and stages that disguised its criminal origin and permitted its use in the legal economy.[1]

Later *pentiti* contributed information that allowed antimafia prosecutors to develop legislation directed at asset investigation and confiscation, leading to the state re-appropriating seized mafia property and then distributing it to people and communities in need.

Working in a heavily protected underground bunker the size of a football field, Falcone and Borsellino exposed links between the mafia and government officials. Three hundred sixty Cosa Nostra figures were convicted of serious crimes, including 119 in absentia, for a total of 2665 years, the worst legal defeat the Cosa Nostra had ever suffered.[2] "The trial succeeded," notes mafia scholar John Dickie, "in proving that the mafia was an actual organization, not a mentality or the actions of individuals." Falcone, recognized as one of the most distinguished antimafia crusaders, also came to be one of the most wanted men by the mafia, and it was no secret that he was targeted for death as part of a mass campaign of extermination that included the murder of over one thousand people – men of honour, their relatives and friends, police and government officials, children, and innocent bystanders. Falcone's brutal death was devastating to antimafia activists, citizens, and residents throughout Italy. The Palermo Spring ended in bloodshed, as antimafia judges, police officers, politicians, priests, and escorts were ruthlessly murdered, one after another.[3]

These assassinations proved, argues criminal law expert Cyrille Fijnaut, "that the Cosa Nostra was not only capable of controlling legitimate and illegitimate markets – and hence all of society – but it is also prepared to use intimidation and brute force against any government that attempts to break its grip."[4] In response to the assassinations of Falcone and Borsellino, the European Union (EU) launched programs to combat organized crime that included establishing a Working Group on International Organized Crime, set up in September 1992. Five years later, on 15 August 1997, a coherent policy plan entitled *Action Plan to Combat Organized Crime* was released.[5] Criminologists believe that the action plan took five years to finalize because the EU member states disagreed about how serious a threat the mafia posed to them as a group. It was not until the Gilligan drug gang in Dublin murdered Veronica Guerin in November 1996 that the EU recognized mafia violence was not simply Italy's problem.[6]

The Falcone Tree (*un albero di Falcone*) is among the best-recognized spontaneous shrines that emerged during this period of unprecedented murders in Palermo and the surrounding areas, and it was one of the first instances of public statements made by the Italian people protesting mafia control. Each day visitors from all over Europe come to pay homage to Falcone and leave letters, prayers, garlands, photographs, jewels, and pledges made directly to Falcone to commemorate and sustain his dedication to civil rights, active citizenship among youth, and an ethical economy. Wrapped around the large trunk of the tree is the red and yellow flag of Sicily with its distinctive image of the winged head of Medusa with her three wheat ears. A large photograph of Vito Schifani, one of the escorts killed in the car bomb explosion with Falcone, is posted on the trunk, along with the iconic photograph of Falcone and Borsellino, leaning into each other as if sharing a joke. The photograph, taken by Tony Gentile shortly before the men were murdered, is one of the most widely distributed images of public memory of the two prosecutors. Typical letters posted to the tree address Falcone as if he were still a living force:

> Dear Falcone, Your death is not in vain because your spirit lives permanently in this place where your purpose and mission is not yet complete ... peace and justice must reign on this land of Sicily.[7]

Folklorist Jack Santino, who coined the term "spontaneous shrines" to describe memorials created for victims of political assassination in Northern Ireland, points to the ways in which spontaneous shrines are "truly of the people."[8] They bring people together in what he describes as a "collective mourning in protest" that often references the social conditions that brought about the deaths of the people commemorated. "Improvised memorials," argue anthropologists Peter Jan Margry and Cristina Sanchez-Carretero, "should be read as more than an expression of grief. They are performative events in public spaces that often trigger new actions in the social or political sphere."[9] This is evident in the expressions of grief and rage appended to the Falcone Tree. Many of the postings on the tree reference the desire to be free from mafia control: "Liberate Sicily from the mafia. Thank you, Giovanni Falcone, for liberating our land." They also protest a government complicit with mafia violence: "*libertà* = *legalità*." Santino explains:

> [Spontaneous shrines] are not institutionalized memorials. They are shrines that mark the communication between the dead and the living and not only commemorate and memorialize rituals characteristic of private funerals and memorials, but they are sites of pilgrimage and invite participation even from strangers – open as they are to the public.[10]

Unlike institutionalized or government-sponsored monuments, spontaneous shrines engage the public in marking and decorating the shrine, inscribing on it notes and other forms of commemoration that express intense levels of identification. Such feelings are apparent in the numerous letters, drawings, and poems that promise to fulfil the dreams of Falcone: "Justice, State, duty to the point of sacrifice."[11] "We shall fulfill your dreams!" "You didn't want any children. I would like you to be my dad," Luisa from Naples writes in pencil.[12] "I will never have peace," writes Giuseppe, "until the work that you have started / and which it is our duty to continue / is accomplished." His signature is preceded by the words "WITH DUTY."[13] Letters left by law students from cities throughout Italy and Sicily after Falcone's state funeral testify to their identification with his professional excellence: "I'm studying law in Florence with the intention of carrying out my future profession as judge or lawyer as you did," writes L.[14]

Making these inscriptions is part of the experience of visiting the shrine and, as Santino observes, "demonstrate to an audience one does not know that one participated, that one contributed to this monument, that one was here, albeit anonymously."[15] Visitors to spontaneous shrines have been described as "rhetorical pilgrims," who use ordinary objects, such as necklaces and scarves and notes to the deceased as rhetorical strategies to express collective grief and to take part in national and international healing processes.[16] The unofficial, undirected nature of spontaneous shrines is not sanctioned by institutions, and shrines are most often created to commemorate sudden death – terrorist attacks, car accidents, murders, fires.[17]

This chapter directs its attention to mourning as a mode of political resistance. It explores the conditions under which a public process of mourning can contest and revise the meaning and significance of unspeakable violence and trauma, specifically among communities working through processes of transitional justice while simultaneously living in the midst of violence.[18] I argue that in the face of societal trauma, communities seek meaning that stands apart from nationalist agendas. This search involves revising the frames around which grief is organized, and re-signifying or refiguring the social and cultural norms around which grief is expressed. The cultural work of representing the losses of individuals and communities that are marginalized in public life presupposes that all lives are grievable and that we live in a world in which we are physically, emotionally, and politically dependent on one another.[19]

Indeed, the creation of a spontaneous shrine, such as the Falcone Tree, marks immediate, spontaneous expressions of grief, outrage, loss, and hope for the future, a call, if you will, "to tarry with grief," a phrase I take from Judith Butler's *Precarious Life*. The move to create a shrine suggests a capacity to remain exposed to the unbearability of grief and to refrain from seeking solace from grief through violence. Moreover, the capacity to create a spontaneous shrine immediately after Falcone's murder suggests a particular strength among the people of Palermo at the time – a strength that kept them from feeling passive and powerless, and instead, in the words of Butler, made them more sensitive to "human vulnerability, to our collective responsibility for the physical lives of one another." It is in grief, in being beside ourselves, unbounded and undone, that we might find, following Butler, who follows Freud, "the unconscious imprint of our primary sociality."[20] Butler's "ethics of grief" understands mourning as "an identification with suffering itself" that might emerge precisely from the "struggle to keep fear and anxiety from turning into murderous action."[21] The ethics of grief Butler renders in her study of violence, mourning, and politics asks us to consider mourning as synonymous with "agreeing to undergo a transformation, the full result of which one cannot know in advance."[22] Implicit in this agreement is the willingness to submit to a position of unknowingness.

When we grieve, we lose our bearings – we ask ourselves, "What has become of me? What is left of me? What is it that I have lost in the loss of my beloved?" These questions, observes Butler, point to the "I" in the mode of unknowingness and create a possible clearing for a new ethical position if the narcissistic preoccupation of melancholia can be replaced with an understanding of the vulnerability of others.[23] Butler proposes to make grief itself a resource for political life that might make possible a less violent politics. I will return to her proposal later as we consider what it might mean for public pedagogy "to tarry with grief."[24]

As noted in the Introduction, the acts of participation performed at the Falcone Tree are more than a collective act of grieving; they are intended to bring about social transformation. The acts of commemoration associated with the Falcone Tree raise questions about the implications of institutionalizing subversive mourning practices after indescribable public losses. The Falcone Tree has been spontaneously sponsored by the Giovanni and Francesca Falcone Foundation and has become a spontaneous part of the civic curriculum called *legalità*.[25] By virtue of the Tree being institutionalized, does the curriculum built around this shrine, designed in the name of "educating for legality," assume, as astutely pointed out by anthropologists Jane Schneider and Peter Schneider, that criminality can be suppressed through an education that colonizes consciousness through institutionalized rituals, even when the targeted people have no alternative livelihoods and continue to live in poverty and feel abandoned by the state?[26]

With these ideas in mind, and before turning to a closer analysis of the Falcone Tree, I will address a series of important themes in Freud's later writings on grief and what he described as "endless mourning," the spirit of which we find in Butler's call to "tarry with grief." Freud's work offers a guide for considering the extent to which the discourses surrounding Falcone's memory resonate with the anti-consolatory grieving process Freud wrote about in response to World War I, which, in my estimation, might bring us closer to what I describe as *registers of ethical action* when thinking about the work of public pedagogy, curriculum, and the limits of institutionalizing memory.

Freud, Mourning, and the Elegiac Formation

The medicalization of illness and dying in the closing decades of the nineteenth century not only rendered death an increasingly taboo subject but also contributed to the disappearance of Victorian mourning customs and demonized social displays of bereavement.[27] Writing about loss and melancholia during the closing decade of the nineteenth century, Freud challenged this cultural repression of loss by insisting on the necessary emotional labour of mourning, theorizing the psyche as an internal space for the work of grieving, and ushering a discussion of bereavement into the public realm.[28] In Freud's 1917 essay "Mourning and Melancholia," which provides a rich archive for thinking about societal grieving, mourning is associated with a call for the bereaved to triumph over the sadness of loss by finding a valid compensation for loss in the world of the living. In the early stages of his studies of mourning, Freud understood it less as a lament for the passing or loss of a beloved and more as a process directed at restoring a certain economy of the subject. During that time, Freud believed that mourning was a process through which the survivor sought a magical recovery of the lost love object for self-serving reasons, that is, to reclaim a part of the self she or he had projected onto the loved one, a part of the self that was necessary for the survivor to feel complete. "Losing a loved one," writes Tammy Clewell in her study of Freud's later understandings of loss, "threatens to shatter the mourner's imaginary psychic integrity, imaginary since this self-image depends on a relation external to the self."[29] At this stage of Freud's understanding of loss, he equated object-love – that is, love for the other – with a form of self-love.[30] Moreover, and this is an important point for understanding the protests in mourning performed at the Falcone Tree, in Freud's early writing on loss, he believed that a person can ease the pain of loss by accepting a consolation in the form of a substitution – a new lover, a new country, a new interest or social commitment.

In "Mourning and Melancholia," Freud focused most directly on how survivors use human substitutes and cultural fictions to stand in and offer consolation for the lost love object. Among the most vital means through which one seeks consolation is language. The distance achieved through symbolic systems puts the lost love at a greater distance so the bereaved can come to terms with the absence. We see the use of language to grieve put to work immediately after Falcone's death. The letters and commemorative documents appended to the tree can be understood as replacing the loss of Falcone, his literal body, with language, images, symbols, and consoling narratives. These remind us how language, as well as cultural and aesthetic objects, can substitute for absence by representing and giving figurative shape to the lost presence we yearn for. At the same time, we know that no collection of artefacts can substitute for the enormity of the absent referent that is Falcone's body.[31]

The idea that the anguish of loss subsides through practices of consolation and substitution has been challenged by many of the most respected cultural sites of contemporary mourning, including Maya Lin's Vietnam Veterans War Memorial, Claude Lanzmann's *Shoah*, Toni Morrison's fiction, and the poetry of Anne Sexton and Sylvia Plath, to name only a few. This "new practice of mourning" is evident in the modern elegiac traditions wherein the bereaved resist consolation, refuse recovery and transcendence, and criticize not only the dead but themselves as well.[32] Through the representation of lost others, these artists seek redress for personal, cultural, and political grievances. This mode of grieving, of refusing consolation, works to both criticize tradition and to rebel against cultural and familial structures of power, and the gender, racial, and sexual biases these structures imply.

In 1920 after Freud's 27-year-old daughter Sophie died in the Spanish flu epidemic, he began to write about grief a bit differently. He returns to the subject of mourning in several texts formulated in response to the shattering experiences of World War I. He does so in "On Transience," and in two papers he published together in "Thoughts for the Times on War and Death," where he advances an anti-consoling and anti-idealist approach towards mourning. This approach is most clearly evident in his 1923 work *The Ego and the Id*, in which he offers a theory of grief that recognizes the interminable qualities of normal grieving and registers an understanding of the character of the ego as an elegiac formation.[33] This understanding emerges out of Freud's recognized confusion about why mourners, in fact, do not easily turn to consoling objects to substitute for their loss. "But why is it," he writes in his essay "On Transience," "that this detachment of libido from its objects should be such a painful process is a mystery to us and we have not ... been able to frame any hypothesis to account for it. We only see that libido clings to its objects and will not renounce those that are lost even when a substitute lies ready at hand. Such then is mourning."[34] In "On Transience" we learn of Freud's diminished optimism for post-war recovery from loss and trauma.

Over time, Freud began to understand grieving as an interminable process and that the work of mourning becomes synonymous with taking the lost other into the structure of one's own identity.[35] On 11 April 1929 Freud wrote a letter to his close friend Ludwig Binswanger, who had also suffered the loss of a child, in which Freud confirmed the persistence of mourning, offering his experience of being inconsolable nine years after his daughter's death:

Although we know that after such loss the acute state of mourning will subside, we also know we shall remain inconsolable and will never find a substitute no matter what may fill the gap, even if it be filled completely, it nevertheless remains something else. And actually, this is how it should be. It is the only way of perpetuating that love which we do not want to relinquish.[36]

Freud eventually presented his understanding of mourning as an interminable process that resists consolation. In fact, Freud found that the ego itself is formed as a kind of archive filled with lost love objects; consequently, loss itself organizes the psyche.[37] This is why in 1990, Madelon Sprengnether described the ego as an "elegiac formation" whose very structure internalizes absence.[38]

Framing the Expression of Falcone's Memory

In her study of what she describes as the "literacy events" surrounding the making of the Falcone Tree, Deborah Puccio-Den frames the social memories of Palermo's war against the mafia that are inscribed in and circulate around the shrine as a form of political hagiography that raises Falcone to the status of a saint, a "martyr of justice." Puccio-Den argues that this political hagiography resonates with the political rhetoric Orlando put to work in his creation of the Palermo Spring and culminates in what she describes as the new "antimafia religion." The Falcone Tree continues to stand on Via Notarbartolo. The thick, heavy branches of the magnolia tree impose on the entrance of the apartment building where Francesca Morvillo's mother still lives. The Falcone Tree both leans into the building and sprawls into the street, standing like a trope, as Puccio-Den observes, for the Palermo Spring – a tree of hope. The tree has been entrusted with the work of continuing the dreams of Falcone and Morvillo – "Justice, State, duty to the point of sacrifice."[39] "You can crush a flower but you can't prevent spring," writes Simon, a young student, in 1992.[40] Puccio-Den goes on to observe that it is as if the fruits of the tree are the demonstrations, meetings, associations, curriculum, foundations, and new forms of protesting that have emerged since the judge's murder. Inspired by Falcone's "sacrifices," a term continually present in the antimafia vocabulary, devotees write of the betrayals Falcone suffered at the hands of colleagues, betrayals that echo those suffered by Christ.[41] Puccio-Den emphasizes that, since 1992, the writings and poster art that combine photography, drawing, and newspaper clippings have been used by visitors to express anger, bitterness, hopes, and sorrow, and to inscribe intimate feelings into the public arena, thereby forcing emotional life into the "registers of action" taken up in the name of social and cultural renewal.[42]

The observations and analyses made by Puccio-Den resonate with my observations of this shrine since 2008. After several visits to the Falcone Tree and interviews with the director of the Giovanni and Francesca Falcone foundation and with visitors, including activists, students and teachers, I noticed that the narratives and devotional practices performed to honour Falcone express modes of remembrance that indeed draw on conventional Catholic mourning practices that seek consolation. These practices tend to idealize Falcone as a martyr of justice, at times a Christ figure, who lived a life according to heroic codes of conduct. The Catholic resonances of the annunciation and rebirth surface in a message left by Anna in 1992: "With you, now, we speak more than before / and there will not be a night when / through you, a prayer does not rise up / to God, so we can bring the longed-for Spring to our land."[43] Since 1992 visitors to this shrine have engaged in a kind of "hyper-remembering" that Freud ascribed to the work of mourning. He described this process as an act of obsessive recollection or compulsive repetition of themes that seeks to replace the actual loss of the beloved with an imaginary presence. Freud understood acts of hyper-remembering as an effort to restore a certain economy or equilibrium after enduring a loss of a beloved that one had so profoundly endowed with love and ideals.[44] At the same time, this spontaneous shrine inscribes a body into the city that was ignored, according to many Italians, by the state, a body that was made vulnerable and left unprotected.

The obsessive labour associated with the writings, photographs, and poster art appended to the tree parallels the harrowing interminability not only of grief itself but also of attempts to master or understand – though never completely – a particular traumatic experience. Although the repetition of these consoling narratives "tarry with grief" in that they are inherently non-violent, they also raise questions about a potential rigidity that may have crept into the mass memory production and consumption of Falcone's memory.

In my visits to this tree since 2008, I have found little difference between the writings and art appended to the tree in 1992 and archived in the Falcone Foundation, and what was appended to the tree over 20 years later. In Palermo in July 2014, the tree was decorated with drawings, photographs, flowers, and notes from students attending schools throughout Italy, including messages such as the following:

Youth bring today this message, we are able to believe in your life, your testimony and a future of serenity in the presence of legality.

The mafia is a cancer that's still to be cured. This gang must be destroyed. Goodbye, Giovanni.

No to the Mafia! Liberate Sicily from the Mafia. Thank you Giovanni Falcone for liberating our land.

Peppino, Giovanni, Paolo ... their ideas are not dead. You did not kill them, their ideas are not dead, they walk on our legs.

Recently added notes include themes of gratitude, vows to continue to liberate Sicily from the grip of the mafia, as well as assurances to Falcone that his work lives on – "your ideas are not gone – they are carried on our legs." Not only does Falcone live on, but like Christ, he has achieved a new life in death.

Although national memorials to Falcone, with their stone engravings and steadfast promises to remember, are fixed around predetermined and encoded narratives of patriotism, the Falcone Tree demonstrates the potential that spontaneous shrines have to refuse such fixed narratives and thereby engage actively with grief and loss, as well as to provide meaning in the midst of societal trauma. The political commitment expressed in writing by visitors to the Falcone Tree commits them, observes Puccio-Den, to a "regime of action, through a written and signed contract, and brings writing out of the intimate sphere."[45] "Falcone: / Today, nearly one month since the / Capaci massacre, I find myself in / Palermo, you know, I felt the need to write these few lines / and to pin them to the tree below / your home, to testify that / your memory, and that of your wife / and bodyguards, is still alive in me," writes Giuseppe.[46] In his communication with the dead, Giuseppe's letter reads almost like a prayer that renews the vow to remember.[47]

Yet does the repetition of the same messages, tropes, slogans, and images since 1992 risk emphasizing the "memorialization of the past" over "its contemplation and study?"[48] Do the repetitive greetings to Falcone as saint, hero, and martyr suggest a compulsion to repeat and hence to reify his memory in ways that might foreclose on conflicted feelings about his death and conflicted, half-spoken meanings about its historical and social significance? How does the Falcone Tree negotiate the memorialization of the life of Falcone, Morvillo, and their antimafia comrades at the same time that it engages in sustained contemplation of mafia violence without monumentalizing what took place on 23 May 1992? What is culturally implied when a spontaneous shrine, created to establish meaning and express grief, encrypts the very memories of personal trauma and historical events that it intends to keep alive? Giovanni Falcone's death, spontaneously and publicly memorialized, appears to be ironically contained and controlled by the political hagiography of the Palermo Spring, as well as by the curriculum designed in the name of social transformation by the Giovanni and Francesca Falcone Foundation. If I am right about the repetition of memory themes inscribed in this shrine, where, then, does the possibility lie for what I earlier referenced as "registers of ethical action" that refuse to comply or to be consoled by a psychic compliance with nationalist agendas? If a public curriculum tarries with grief, it must simultaneously sustain a fidelity to what has been lost and be open to a valuable mode of unknowingness and to new possibilities and silences about what the memories of what and whom we have lost contain. The project of revitalizing memory and recollection, and the role that monuments, shrines, and other representations of loss play in our lives must remain spontaneously animate and open to questions that are often only half-spoken by society and culture. To more fully address the vicissitudes of this work, I turn now to the curriculum scholarship of Roger Simon,[49] Mario Di Paolantonio,[50] and my earlier work on anti-consoling practices and the curriculum.

Registers of Ethical Action and the Curriculum

In *The Touch of the Past: Remembrance, Learning and Ethics*,[51] Simon makes an astute observation about commemorative projects that rely too narrowly on graphic realism and reach for "pedagogically redemptive forms of representation."[52] He argues that any attempt to remember a traumatic past and confront a violent history one hopes never to repeat by memorizing facts privileges mastery, domination, and control. This epistemic attitude undermines the capacity to come to terms with the incalculability of trauma, as well as working towards what Simon describes as an "interpretive concern with the past that is beyond cognitive expectation."[53] Di Paolantonio draws on Simon's work in his analysis of the *Escuela de Mechanica de la Armada* (ESMA), one of the six hundred clandestine detention centres operative during the Argentine military's "dirty war." Di Paolantonio explores the extent to which this centre's public curriculum works to provoke what he describes as "difficult questions" that extend beyond information gathering and idealization. Both Di Paolantonio and Simon implicitly reference Butler's call to "tarry with grief" and challenge education to consider the role that vulnerability and the loss of mastery might play in creating an *ethics of grief* that would serve as a *register of action* against psychic and physical violence. Both Simon and Di Paolantonio also join Butler in exploring what it might mean to approach the work of remembrance in ways that could open us up and "put into question ... what is presently left unsaid or socially and psychically repressed."[54]

The work of attending to what is half-spoken in society has conventionally been the work of artists. This is one of the many lessons I learned from studying the teaching life of Anne Sexton – the work of the poet is to listen for the half-spoken image and to give it form, to give it a shape, to give it a life. Cultivating the capacity to attend to what is half-spoken requires a particular kind of listening that does not rely on literal understanding alone – it is, as Di Paolantonio suggests, grounded in a more "uncertain state of awareness." I want to emphasize the play on words here – an "uncertain state of awareness," that one is fully aware – and open to uncertainty. This is precisely what Butler has in mind when she speaks of an awareness grounded in disorientation, vulnerability, dislocation, and loss. Following Freud, Butler suggests that by making grief a resource for politics, we might recognize that in our very sociality as bodily beings, we are implicated in lives not our own, over which we have little control. And as Freud came to understand, in loss, we do not always know what we have lost in another person, place, or idea, or what we have lost within ourselves. Butler proposes that it is in this sphere of loss that we might begin to develop an identification with suffering and a patience with states of unknowability.

The offerings left at the Falcone Tree are grounded as much in suffering as in certainty. The ephemera posted to the tree in memory of Falcone and Borsellino emerge as a continuous stream of slogans, drawings, and prayers that mobilize sentiments and feelings tied to the mission of the Falcone Foundation, as well as to the antimafia civic curriculum, *legalità*. In this sense the ephemera can be read as a collective call for predictable and rational, rather than spontaneous, action – a call for justice, an ethical economy, and a life free from the violence of extortion. The ephemera and offerings left in memory of Falcone and Borsellino, persistently remembered as martyrs of justice, fail to pose difficult questions around the ruptures of identification with and idealization of both men. Nor do they consider the limits of the consoling narratives that circulate around the men's memories. Is it inevitable that institutionalizing memory more generally, and the consumption of Falcone's memory more specifically, cultivates a monumental rather than anti-monumental sensibility? And is it inevitable that by doing so, this spontaneous shrine is recast as a memorial where consoling narratives circulate and eventually foreclose on the forms of memory work that might express interpretive concerns that exceed our cognitive understanding? The Falcone Tree provokes education to consider what we might find ourselves open to if we were to refuse the comforts of consolation and pursue what it might mean for public pedagogy to "tarry with grief."

We might begin by asking how a study of the past events of societal trauma and massive mafia violence affects the present, how, that is, this "sad past" continues to have currency.[55] Following Simon, I explore the forms of curatorial selection and judgment that might inform ethical public pedagogical action. This work involves composing ethical and political discourses that serve as resources for bridging the past and the present without, in the words of John Willis, "reducing one to the other."[56] A public pedagogy that has the capacity to "tarry with grief" is built on several presuppositions. Each presupposition challenges education to understand spontaneous shrines, such as the Falcone Tree, as sites of mourning that stand apart from institutionalized memory and open up and sustain public conversation, debate, and feelings about the impact that history has on contemporary social life.[57] While many of the letters, slogans, and phrases appended to the tree speak of never forgetting (*per non dimenticare*) and of carrying Falcone's work into the present day, few expressive traces, as I noted earlier, suggest the visitors to the shrine have experienced a renewed connection with Falcone that provokes them to assess their relationship to the history of mafia violence in this contemporary time.[58] Eric L. Santner might read the narratives as forms of "narrative fetishism" that work to expunge the traces of the loss and trauma that called the narrative into being.[59] Santner develops the concept of narrative fetishism by directly contrasting it with the symbolic work of mourning. While the entirety of Santner's discussion of narrative fetishism is worth reading, I quote a short passage here:

> Both narrative fetishism and mourning are responses to loss, to a past that refuses to go away due to its traumatic impact. The work of mourning is a process of elaborating and integrating the reality of loss or traumatic shock by remembering and repeating it in symbolically and dialogically mediated doses; it is a process of translating, troping, and figuring loss and ... may encompass "a relation between language and silence that is in some sense ritualized." Narrative fetishism, by contrast, is the way an inability or refusal to mourn emplots traumatic events; it is a strategy of undoing, in fantasy, the need for mourning by simulating a condition of intactness, typically by situating the site and origin of loss elsewhere. Narrative fetishism releases one from the burden of having to reconstitute one's self-identity under "posttraumatic" conditions; in narrative fetishism, the "post" is indefinitely postponed.[60]

The commemorative practices performed at the Falcone Tree suggest the complex ways in which mourning can be taken up and refused, expressed, deferred, and silenced in the midst of social breakdown. The spontaneous shrine created by the people of Palermo in 1992 provided a public, collective vernacular expression of loss in the very midst of societal trauma. Although the intimacy with Falcone expressed at the shrine soon after his murder was an illusion to many visitors to the shrine, the grief was real. Moreover, Falcone was undoubtedly traumatized by the mafia, much as Italy was and continues to be. The antimafia discourse of martyrdom, as well as the institutionalization of Falcone's memory, obscures this fact by establishing Falcone as a saint who courageously sacrificed his life for the love of justice. Furthermore, the institutionalization of his memory ironically promotes conformity to an antimafia discourse that idealizes martyrdom and believes that sacrifice in the name of justice can cure the trauma of mafia brutality. By displacing the traumatic memories of mafia violence and Falcone's brutal death with consoling, normative narratives that memorialize him as a martyr of justice who will "always live on," the traumatic memories associated with Falcone are relegated to a past that lies elsewhere, as well as to a level of consciousness that is neither repressed nor fully expressed. By refusing to emplot the traumatic events, the stories taken and told about Falcone that are appended to the tree come closer to narrative fetishism than to acts of mourning. Perhaps this is because the traumatic memories continue to be too dangerous, for political and social reasons, to recall, just as, argues E. Ann Kaplan in her study of trauma and cinema, the "forgotten" contents in individual consciousness are too dangerous to remember.[61]

Conclusion

A public pedagogy that tarries with grief cannot be assigned learning outcomes in advance. It should, however, be informed, as noted earlier, by public debate, feelings, and conversations that stand apart from state control and institutionalized memories. As well, a public pedagogy that takes up the collective act of mourning as a mode of political resistance continually and imaginatively refigures the symbolic and affective norms around which grief is expressed. This work is taken up in the name of intentional educational work that challenges privatization and values the public sphere. The Falcone Tree offers a clear case of how institutionalized memories can become vulnerable to the logic of private interests. This is perhaps made most evident in the Falcone Foundation's investments in sustaining a heroic, monumental image of Giovanni Falcone at the expense of opening up spaces for deliberation about Falcone's memory today. In this sense one might conclude that over time, the "rhetorical pilgrims"[62] who visited the Falcone Tree have taken on the character of individual consumers of memory who are excluded from collective deliberations about how Falcone is remembered in the context of protracted mafia violence. A public pedagogy that intends to use the work of mourning to pursue public memory requires a different kind of social interaction than is experienced in privatized settings or private relationships of love and friendship.

The kind of action I have in mind for a public pedagogy of remembrance involves Hannah Arendt's concept of action – that is, to bring something new into the world in the company of others. The defining quality of action, argues Arendt, is freedom – not, however a freedom that is private or individual but, rather, a sense of freedom that is public and hence political. Humans are free only to the extent to which they act and to the extent to which others respond to their initiatives. The response of others to our actions is often what can frustrate or undermine the initiatives we value. Arendt reminds us that if no one takes up our beginnings, nothing comes of our actions. In other words, we must act in solidarity with others despite how difficult this work is because, according to Arendt, "to be isolated is to be deprived of the capacity to act."[63] The principle of plurality – a condition that values difference rather than eradicates it – is, for Arendt, the condition of human action and freedom, and emerges in the public rather than the private realm. Thus, the action that characterizes a public pedagogy of remembrance understands freedom within the context of a public sphere that values plurality and the rights of everyone to act, to be free to participate in deliberations. These conditions are so necessary for a public pedagogy of remembrance precisely because they have a vital interest in what is strange, unfamiliar, and distant, rather than a naive attachment to establishing and sustaining common ground. For Arendt, plurality is another name for the human condition of multiplicity, interconnectedness, and differences in perspectives, values, and commitments. Thus, the idea of the public in the term *public pedagogy of remembrance* is best framed as educational work that cultivates human togetherness and political existence to make action possible amid the tensions and challenges that plurality brings. A public pedagogy of remembrance is not intent on instruction or learning. It is, however, intent on challenging the press of the market, private interests, and the state on memory formation. The Falcone Foundation and the memories circulating around the Falcone Tree offer a clear case of how public pedagogy can unwittingly depoliticize memory when pedagogy is understood as a curriculum that must be directly taught, memorized, and learned, as well as when it is privately sponsored or supported by state resources. Not only do the narratives appended to the Falcone Tree reduce Falcone's humanity by failing to include the specificity of his life, but the discourses of martyrdom also make evident an absence of plurality within the structures of memory that commemorate him.

Although the discourses of martyrdom surrounding the memory of Falcone commemorate masculine histories that establish antimafia martyrs of justice as saintly and courageous, they play out very differently for imagining a feminist antimafia identity. In Chapter 2 we turn to a critical analysis of the memorial landscapes composed on Facebook to commemorate female martyrs of justice in the Sicilian antimafia movement. The chapter takes up an exploratory study of the case of antimafia activist Francesca Morvillo, one of Italy's first female judges and the wife of Giovanni Falcone. How does Morvillo's Facebook page articulate particular affective investments that resonate with the common, everyday understanding of invisible, forgotten figures and the ways in which memory and the memorable are taught?

Chapter Two

"Eccentric Subjects": Female Martyrs and the Antimafia Public Imaginary

Being killed is terrible, but being forgotten is even worse. It's like dying twice.
– Giovanna Terranova, president of the *Associazione Donne Siciliane per la Lotta contro la Mafia*

"Have you heard of Francesca Morvillo?" was the question I asked most frequently during my research on the antimafia movement in Sicily. No one seemed to know much beyond that Morvillo was the wife of antimafia magistrate Giovanni Falcone; that her brother Alfredo, an attorney in Palermo, continues to work as an antimafia activist; and that she was killed with Falcone and their escorts on 23 May 1992 in a deliberate explosion. As Morvillo, her husband, and their escorts travelled the highway from the Palermo airport to Raisi for a weekend of rest, five hundred kilograms of plastic explosives were detonated via remote control by mafia member Giovanni Brusca. "All hell seemed to be opened up before us in a second," recalled a driver following the convoy.[1] The explosives had been placed in a drainage tunnel under the freeway a few days earlier. When they exploded, Morvillo was severely injured and Falcone was trapped in the car. He was pronounced dead shortly after arriving at the hospital, and Morvillo died later that evening.[2]

Despite her dedication to the antimafia movement, Morvillo's memory remains stunningly absent from the Italian public imaginary. Leading Italian newspaper headlines reporting on the deadly explosion list only Falcone by name. Locating photographs of Morvillo is remarkably difficult, and her name was conspicuously absent from conversations I had with antimafia activists and students working in Corleone and Palermo. Although her name appears on three official Italian monuments in Palermo alongside her husband and escorts, I found no traces of memories of Morvillo among the extensive archive of testimonies, photographs, and legal transcripts housed in the antimafia museum in Corleone. Typically represented in this history are the mothers, sisters, and daughters who lost their sons, brothers, and fathers to mafia violence or who have lost their freedom and homes when working with the state against the mafia. While feminist protests such as *Il Comitato dei lenzuoli* and *Le Donne del Digiuno* commemorate the heroism of Falcone and Borsellino, Morvillo's name is subsumed in their commemorations under the category of "escort."[3]

In this chapter I examine the curious silence surrounding the memories of antimafia activist Francesca Morvillo, one of Italy's first female judges, who worked with incarcerated youth in Palermo. I explore the struggles and challenges of representing those figures, particularly women, who played critical roles in the antimafia movement and brought to light, named, and transformed a system of oppression but are barely remembered. That Morvillo is barely remembered within the Italian cultural and historical imaginary is one of my abiding concerns.

Given that Morvillo was neither a mother nor a betrayed wife, the absence of her memory from the antimafia landscape suggests a different kind of antimafia story, one set apart from the discourses of maternal self-sacrifice and wifely devotion most prominent in the official archives circulating among antimafia public culture.[4] What emerged in my search for Morvillo's memories is not only an archive of a different sort, one strikingly mainstream in its visibility, but an archive that contains traces of what Deborah Puccio-Den describes as a new antimafia iconography that makes use of political hagiography to commemorate antimafia activists who lost their lives in the process of working to dismantle the violent secret organizations that compose the Sicilian mafia.[5] With the rise of moral consciousness among Italian citizens who have come to recognize the mafia as a secret association with criminal goals, the concept of justice, argues Puccio-Den, has been transformed, as discussed in Chapter 1, into a quasi-religious ideal that expresses itself in the language of martyrdom and acts of religious-like devotion that combine to create a kind of "antimafia religion." This religious-like discourse uses political hagiography to create a new political era in Sicily that involves an ideological and global project of transforming civil society, culture, and the economy.

I did find a growing collection of images, newsfeeds, and letters posted on a Facebook page dedicated to Morvillo, initially curated by Stefania Gargioni and Stefania Bianchi.[6] Currently, the site is run solely by Gargioni, who at this writing is a doctoral student in history at the University of Kent. Gargioni stated that she had created the page for Morvillo because she wanted people to remember her not only as Falcone's wife but also as one of Italy's first female judges.

"She is remembered," notes Gargioni, "just as Falcone's wife. She is not re-membered for her own life."[7] In this chapter, I situate the memorial landscapes created on Morvillo's Facebook page as an archive of feelings that works si-multaneously as a public pedagogical project that questions, challenges, and at times protests the absence of her memory from antimafia public culture. For this chapter I define *public pedagogy* as the visual and written texts produced on Facebook and the reception of them by viewers, audiences, and Facebook friends who are active producers of their meaning. The public pedagogi-cal project taken up on Morvillo's Facebook page is set apart from neo-liberal ideologies that are driven by market-based identities with the aim of cultivat-ing an "entrepreneurial self" devoted to transparency, mastery, and easy-to-understand information.[8] One of the presuppositions underlying the digital memorial landscapes rendered on Morvillo's Facebook page assumes equality to be, in the words of Jacques Rancière, "a point of departure, not ... a destination."[9]

Within this framework, there are no masters – no subjects presumed to know. Rather, all individuals are assumed equally intelligent, invited to remem-ber Morvillo, contribute stories, pose questions, and post news, invitations, and YouTube clips. The time writers spend on Morvillo's Facebook page might be understood as analogous to the example offered by Rancière of nineteenth-century workers who refused to divvy up their time according to convention. As daytime was owned and controlled by their employers as work time, many workers set aside time in the evening, their leisure time, to pursue ideas and critique their social positions through discussion, reading, and writing rather than using this time solely to recuperate from the day's labour. Rancière elabo-rates on the ways in which labourers replaced sleeping with emancipatory ac-tivities. They were able "to give themselves the time that did not belong to them in order to enter into a world of writing and thinking that was not 'theirs.'"[10] Rancière argues that this "enunciative potential" reconfigures the boundaries of what can be said, how it can be spoken, and to whom it can be addressed. In the context of the antimafia movement, citizen writers are using Facebook, as well as other digital media, to reconfigure who, and what, will be remem-bered. Consequently, they claim and exert a form of pedagogical agency that has the potential to challenge conventional, nationalist narratives about mafia history and antimafia activism through what Marie-Laure Ryan describes as the "novel of proliferating narrativity." The approach to narrative replaces the grand climactic plot structure with multiple "little stories" that invite personal user involvement and, at the same time, links them with a larger social field.[11]

How does Morvillo's Facebook page – this archive of feelings – articulate particular affective investments that resonate with the common, everyday un-derstanding of invisible, forgotten figures and the ways in which discourses of memory and the memorable are taught? Public pedagogical projects, such as Morvillo's Facebook page, offer us a means through which to address these questions, for they hold broad educational implications for remembering, both formally and informally, in multiple public spheres.[12] Moreover, they articulate forms of the public good that serve as calls to identify with particular gender, racial, ethnic, class, sexual, and national bodies/minds politics.[13] Morvillo's Facebook page joins with an ever-growing assemblage of social networking projects that are used to create what Rancière understands as "emancipatory possibilities," by drawing attention to "a thing in common" – a tradition of antimafia history and contemporary antimafia movements that, while wrought with conflicting interests and investments, is part of a shared history.[14]

We might think of Morvillo's Facebook page, and others like hers, as a series of texts that coordinate and organize the meanings of citizenship that function to challenge the zones of inclusion/exclusion that political philosopher Giorgio Agamben delineates as "zones of exception."[15] Zones of exception target new racialized and gendered subjects and exclude them from political status, sovereign protection, and biopolitical power. This term, used by Agamben to describe the damaged lives that are stripped of their political significance, exposed to murderous sovereign violence, and treated as expendable targets of exclusion, is, in part, constructed by an invisible hierarchy for human rights struggles.[16] While Agamben uses the concept of zones of exception to represent the loss of biopolitical power, political significance, and sovereign protection among vulnerable living subjects, this chapter considers, after Agamben, how zones of exception target the memories of new racialized, gendered subjects after they are dead, consequently destroying potential legacies. Why does the figure of Morvillo follow a different trajectory after death than that of her male comrades? The figure of Morvillo stands on the threshold of humanity, she remains socially dead in the Italian public imaginary as nameless, invisible, as *pro nullo*.[17] Thus, unlike her male comrades, she suffers a double death – both biological and social – thereby foreclosing on the lessons and legacies that might circulate among future generations. Her Facebook page, as a public pedagogical project, attempts to revive her memory and mobilize particular meanings about the bodies that matter.

Archives of Feeling

The ephemeral materials collected on Morvillo's Facebook pages are not funded by state or national initiatives but by volunteer efforts and dedication, which, as noted by Ann Cvetkovich, pose challenges to conventional methods for cataloguing history and represent "far more than the literal value of the objects themselves." Such archives, argues Cvetkovich, "are composed of material practices that challenge the traditional conceptions of history and understand the quest for history as a psychic need rather than a science."[18] The emotional, psychic yearning for historical insight is especially salient in the context of protracted social, cultural, and personal trauma exacted by the mafia. Trauma leaves few visible traces, posing challenges to conventional, mainstream archival practices, which call for legal documents, material objects, personal correspondence, letters, and so forth. The activism, intimacies, love, and losses, not only of lovers, friends, and family but of public space and civil life, demand a radical archive of emotion that captures more than legal documentation, legislation, or formal police records can contain. Like other archives of trauma that commemorate, for example, the Holocaust, slavery, or gay and lesbian histories, archives created to remember the trauma inflicted by the mafia must expand the traditional archives and, as Cvetkovich explains,

> should enable the acknowledgement of a past that can be painful to remember, impossible to forget, and resistant to consciousness. The history of trauma often depends on the evidence of memory, not just because of the absence of other forms of evidence, but also because of the need to address traumatic experience through witnessing and retelling. Central to traumatic memory is what Toni Morrison, in the context of remembering slavery, has called "emotional memory," those details of experience that are affective, sensory, often highly specific and personal.[19]

Coupled with the silence the mafia demands of its victims, a public archive potentially runs the risk of jeopardizing the lives of its curators and friends. Yet the psychic need for remembrance presses on and is made manifest in the project of retelling the life stories attached to Sicily's traumatic past. Morvillo's Facebook page creates a dynamic, common space that holds fragments of memories, news clips, personal photographs, letters, oral histories, ephemera, stories, projections, and perspectives that stand apart from the place of proper antimafia narratives that have silenced Morvillo's memory.[20] Read as a public pedagogical project, Morvillo's Facebook page initially works to open a posthumous communication about her life, and then invites public discussion about the mafia's hold on civil society.[21]

Yet while Morvillo's Facebook page works both as an archive of feelings that infuses documentary records of the decades of antimafia activity after the 1980s with affect and as a revelation of the emotional impact of abusive criminal power, it eventually overshadows her memories in much the same way she is overshadowed in more mainstream antimafia public cultures. Thus, Morvillo's Facebook page can also be read as a place of struggle that partially displaces her memory with iconic images of antimafia history steeped in patriarchal institutions and practices that commemorate masculine histories and, at times, relegates her, once again, to a figure who lacks political significance worthy of remembering. The displacements of her memory pose specific challenges to sustaining Morvillo's legacy and raise important questions in the post-feminist moment about what, in 1990, Teresa de Lauretis describes in the following passage as the "non-being of a woman":

> the paradox of a being that is at once captive and absent in discourse, constantly spoken of but of itself inaudible or inexpressible, displayed as spectacle and still unrepresented or unrepresentable, invisible yet constituted as the object and the guarantee of vision; a being whose existence and specificity are simultaneously asserted and denied, negated and controlled.[22]

The paradoxical quality that characterizes the "non-being of a woman" is useful for considering the limited memories of Morvillo circulating within the Italian public imaginary specifically, and the implications this limitation has for imagining a feminist antimafia identity more generally.[23] What meanings can we ascribe to the ideals of self-sacrifice and martyrdom that eventually fill the archive created in Morvillo's name, specifically with respect to a feminist antimafia consciousness? What do these discourses teach the public about sacrifice, self-sacrifice, and the destruction of the female figure? What stories fail to be taken and told about the life of Francesca Morvillo?

Touring the Spaces of Morvillo's Facebook Page

On 9 September 2009 with Morvillo established as the interlocutor with whom friends on Facebook speak, streams of discourses began to circulate and drift, challenging the established absence of Morvillo from official antimafia discourses. Posted on her page in the upper left corner is a profile photograph of Morvillo with her husband, Giovanni Falcone. The photo is accompanied by a general, chronologically structured biographical narrative that presents Morvillo's place and date of birth – Palermo, 14 December 1945 – as well as details of her education and the circumstances of her death. We learn that Morvillo graduated from the University of Palermo with honours in 1967, that her first marriage ended in divorce, and that she and Giovanni Falcone wed in secret. The early postings begin to form a small but traditional plot-structured narrative of Morvillo's literal and figurative journey from her origins in a family of lawyers to a martyr who is remembered as a unifying subject of the law, devoted to her statesman husband and the antimafia movement. Initially posted, as noted earlier, by Stefania Bianchi and Stefania Gargioni, the more recent contact information for Morvillo's Facebook page is linked solely to Gargioni.[24] Threaded throughout the site is an introductory refrain that describes the site as "a small homage to a female attorney, the special wife of a special man your heroism will live on and not be silenced."[25] From this point on, Gargioni takes on the persona of Morvillo, as if Morvillo becomes Gargioni's avatar. When asked why she chose this performative style, Gargioni attributed the move to the format offered on Facebook for fan pages.[26]

As a story-taker, Gargioni plays with fictional and historical boundaries by borrowing elements from both. She takes on the fictive voice of Morvillo to call attention to contemporary news events Gargioni imagines Morvillo would be drawn to. For example, Gargioni posts a news item about a protest against the 'Ndrangheta in Liguria and lists, under the "Likes" category, organizations Morvillo might endorse, such as the non-profit antimafia group *Ammazzateci Tutti* and *Parole di Lulu*, a foundation dedicated to supporting the education and medical care of children in Chiulo, Angola. The digital hypertext format of Facebook infuses the principles of collage, hybridization, and pastiche with a renewed energy given the possibilities available to interlink documents of all types.

Morvillo begins to accumulate a following rather quickly. On 9 September, two people clicked like on Gargioni's introductory post. By 10 September, 36 people had posted comments. By summer 2010, this number reached 618. Early posts speak of the importance of Morvillo's memory. Mary Ciraci writes that Morvillo "is a special woman whose memory should not be kept in the shadows." In addition to posts that attest to the "quiet courage" of Morvillo, the early days of her Facebook page included entries from people who knew Morvillo personally or who have relatives who knew her, such as Raffaella Apple dal Lago who posted a note on 19 July 2010 that read:

> She had taken as her vocation – and with fortitude – a continued pursuit to combat the injustice she saw every day. Francesca was the cousin of my grandmother. My grandmother has many memories of her and she too believes it would be a great failure not to commemorate her. Today I think obviously of her and, in particular Paolo Borsellino on the anniversary of his death. Thank you all for all you have done.

By the second day after Morvillo's Facebook page is created, Angela Tommasino questions why there are so few interviews available with Morvillo and why there is such a scarcity of documentation and images to remember her by: "Why are there so few images of Francesca Morvillo? No interviews, documentaries, so little to remember her by ... This site makes it possible to honor her."

Tommasino insists that we must keep company with her memory and all that she accomplished. Tommasino's recognition that Morvillo has been absent from public memory is echoed in other posts and captured most saliently by Alessia Guerriero on 19 September 2009. Guerriero expresses gratitude for what she describes as the virtuous gesture of creating this site and shedding light on the memory of Morvillo, who, she notes, worked in the name of justice.

On Public Pedagogical Participation

The extensive online commenting, responding, and dialoguing on Facebook signals that people have seen, noted, passed through, or linked objects and ideas. On 4 November 2010 Morvillo's persona shared a link remembering the death of Giovanni Falcone, which was "liked" by 21 people. On 6 February 2011, 21 people tagged a photograph, posted by the Morvillo persona, of the public steps in Piazza della Memoria in Palermo, which includes Francesca Morvillo's name alongside Falcone and their escorts (one of the few sites that mark her memory). Marking posts stands as an important process of appropriation that has pedagogical implications for participants on Facebook. Not only do the processes of posting, commenting, liking, and tagging indicate elected involvement and allow people to choose connections to other groups, events, and people, but they also establish individual experiences that eventually lead to an emergent and collective project of assigning meaning to the memory of Morvillo as an accomplished person who was more than Falcone's wife. Early posts include the persona of Morvillo posting newsreels of interviews with Falcone,[27] websites for antimafia rallies and seminars, footage of the funeral for Falcone, Morvillo, and their escorts, and newsreels of resistance marches, one specifically in Rome in 1992.[28] Recent posts made by the Morvillo persona also link to newsfeeds and YouTube clips reporting on the Red Diary March (*La marcia delle agende rosse*), a procession organized in Palermo in July 2009 to commemorate the murder of Paolo Borsellino.[29]

Consumers and cultural users of Facebook use tagging and posts in everyday life to introduce, and to mark as present, Morvillo's contributions to the larger antimafia project. The quotidian realm of Facebook encompasses a site for the production of social meaning whereby the social subjects who participate construct "public identities" that in turn interact with the larger system of social and historical signs.[30]

Within days of the page's creation, a series of micro-stories and fragments of narratives began to circulate and create a field for what Michel de Certeau describes as a miniaturized (rather than nationally scaled) narrative that extended memories and feelings previously denied legitimacy.[31] Among these fragments are continued posts of gratitude for bringing Morvillo's memory forward and a stream of posts attesting to Morvillo's humility, courage, and modesty. On 10 September 2009 a testimony given by Morvillo's colleague Marisa Ambrosini is posted via YouTube commemorating Morvillo's life and her work. This post, introduced with a photo of Falcone, opens with Ambrosini's memories of Morvillo's dedication to antimafia work and the youth of Palermo. Thus, having entered the realm of the visible, Morvillo's memories take occupancy in images of a virtuous, humble woman dedicated to justice. Just how do these images and memories affect the antimafia social imaginary mapped out on Morvillo's Facebook page? In what specific ways do participants build the necessary social capital to strengthen civil society in Italy? Does Morvillo's Facebook page produce a new female social subject as well as acts of story-taking within the context of the antimafia movement?

Certainly, the range of posts announcing lectures, new books, protest marches, institutes, and YouTube clips suggests a process of active interpretation that has implications for social action and personal, emotional experiences. There is an announcement, for example, of the lecture "*Donne, mafia e antimafia*" based on Anna Puglisi's 2005 book of the same title, held at the University of Milan. On 31 May 2009 Bianchi takes on the persona of Morvillo and writes:

> I believe in this moment we cannot give up fighting against the delinquency of the mafia. In this moment, like in the past, the mafia works to thin out memories of dissent against them.

Bianchi emphasizes that the mafia is indeed not a phenomenon of the past, but continues to present serious threats to civil society in Italy. The concepts of citizenship and civility brought forth throughout Morvillo's Facebook page do not tolerate mafia violence and corruption. This intolerance is captured in the slogan "*Fuori la mafia dallo stato*" ("Get the mafia out of the state") and is chanted throughout a newsfeed posted on 1 October 2009. This newsfeed consists of images from *La marcia delle agende rosse* (the Red Diary March), which took place on 26 September 2009 in Rome. Mafia involvement in the state is understood as a continuing contemporary threat to society and citizenship. Leoluca Orlando, former mayor of Palermo and friend of Falcone and Morvillo, argues that "the new and winning mafia still seeks to control both heads and purses, but no longer does so by invoking and distorting the traditional cultural values associated with honor and family. Rather, the new mafia evokes and distorts notions of liberty and success, which constitute the emerging values of Italian culture."[32]

Many of the posts on Morvillo's page do not offer lessons in emancipation, citizenship, or the forms of civility that are so highly valued by Orlando and antimafia organizations, such as the Sicilian Renaissance Institute. Rather, following the work of Rancière, these posts tell stories, recite the utterances, and recall the actions of antimafia leaders. The posts on Morvillo's Facebook page do not, in other words, explain, but they tell stories that work, according to Rancière, to "verify the equality of intelligence" and depart from the practice of lessons that presume a master who knows and students who are ignorant. "The question," observe Simons and Masschelein in a reading of Rancière's work, "of 'who teaches who?' loses its pertinence: The lessons are not teaching or explaining something, but are making something public, making it present so that we can relate to it, or not: 'It sufficed only to announce it' ... The lessons then, are untimely and improper lessons in intellectual emancipation."[33]

The range of protest marches, conferences, books, seminars, and documentary newsfeeds that are made public are emancipatory insofar as they indeed claim and practise a way of thinking, speaking, and living that brings together unqualified, ordinary people, people who have, from the point of view of the sovereign social order, few competencies or qualifications for educating the public. The public pedagogical value exemplified on Morvillo's Facebook page corresponds to the value Rancière places on bringing together not experts but common people. As a collective the members of Morvillo's Facebook page sustain a deliberative struggle for the meaning her memory holds. Emancipation is not, argues Rancière, tied to a tradition of spectacular acts, rather, it is shaped by the search to create new forms of the common that stand apart from those established through consensus.[34] The dissensus introduced on these pages challenges the loss of Morvillo's memory, thereby undoing the apparent naturalness of the social order that contributes to the conditions of this loss.

The opening posts on Morvillo's Facebook page combine to tell stories of her as virtuous, dedicated to justice, and humble, thereby re-marking her rhetorically and imagistically as present within antimafia discourse, endowing her with value, and securing her memory as meaningful among her Facebook friends. The rhetoric of virtue and humility that emerges in these early postings corresponds to the saintly qualities Puccio-Den describes as a new genre in antimafia discourses, that of a political hagiographic model represented by Santa Rosalia, a medieval hermitess and Palermo's patron saint. Most relevant to understanding feminist antimafia discourses is the way in which the political hagiography of Santa Rosalia frames key figures – male and female – in the antimafia movement as simultaneously self-sacrificing and set apart, by necessity for reasons of safety, from the realm of daily existence. In Puccio-Den's discussion of Palermo mayor Leoluca Orlando and his identification with Santa Rosalia soon after the massive Palermo murders in spring 1992, she speaks of the ways in which central antimafia activists came to embody the hagiographic model represented by Santa Rosalia, most specifically their secluded, austere, and solitary existence; the sacrifice of their private life in the name of an ideal; and the stunning motif of the acceptance of death as an ineluctable fate. By confronting the mafia, Falcone and Borsellino continue to be cast and referred to as "martyrs of justice," and often, when they were alive, referred to themselves as "walking corpses."

The qualities of self-sacrifice in the name of an ideal are placed in relief in a collection of essays edited by Renate Siebert and dedicated to women affected by mafia violence. In her discussion of Morvillo, Siebert underscores the extent to which Morvillo accepted what Siebert describes as a "siege life" of the most extreme form imaginable.[35] Not only did she and Falcone live separately and decide against having children, out of fear, as Falcone told his sister Maria, for "bringing orphans into the world," but Falcone and Morvillo, along with antimafia judges and their families, were also denied the simplest pleasures of eating out, visiting friends, or shopping without protection. During the 1986–7 maxi-trials, Morvillo and her mother lived with other antimafia judges and their families in the high-security prison at Asinara in isolation and with secure protection from mafia attack. Self-sacrifice, humility, devotion to the state, a secluded existence, and the acceptance of death combine to create images of altruism and asceticism that are fused throughout the civic and judicial practices that have come to characterize the religious, selfless character of justice at the heart of the "antimafia religion." Yet while these features work to elevate the male protagonists in the war against the mafia to the status of saints, they in fact function to delete figures such as Morvillo from antimafia public discourses. In the early posts on Morvillo's Facebook page, the language of self-sacrifice, humility, and devotion works to compose a memorial site that sustains her memory in the public's mind. By 11 September 2009, however, the posts take an odd turn as Falcone begins to be more centrally drawn into the narrative spaces of Morvillo's Facebook page. Franca Giardiello writes: "a fantastic woman who remained forever by her man's side" ("*donna fantastica che è rimasta accanto fino all'ultimo al suo uomo!*"). Also on 11 September 2009 a newspaper article is posted with the headline: "Francesca, the fairy tale of a wife with courage" ("*Francesca, Fiaba di una moglie Coraggio*"). By 12 September 2009 the persona of Morvillo begins more consistently to commemorate not Francesca Morvillo but her husband and his comrades. Although her photographs are posted throughout the Facebook page, before the year is out, she paradoxically begins to fade beneath the persuasive speeches of resistance and protests against the mafia state, thus sustaining the antimafia movement as primarily a masculine project and casting Morvillo as a devoted wife who sacrificed herself for the good of the nation.

Tracing Morvillo's Disappearance

By 8 October 2010, the posts on Morvillo's Facebook page are primarily dedicated to commemorating the memories of Falcone, Borsellino, Rocco Chinnici, Claudio Dall'Acqua, Salvatore Barresi, and Sergio La Commare, to name a few. Morvillo once again appears to be deleted from the Italian imaginary. How can we understand this shift in focus resulting in Morvillo's exclusion from history, culture, and the antimafia imaginary landscape? What are the public pedagogical implications of an "antimafia religion" that places a high value on self-sacrifice and martyrdom for the good of the nation and commemorates primarily male martyrs? The problem of how Morvillo is represented in the public imaginary more generally and on her Facebook page more specifically is made manifest in the curious process through which her "friends" worked to unstitch what was, at the creation of her Facebook page, a more cohesive collection of her memories. This shift in status, as noted earlier, marks what de Lauretis describes as the "non-being of a woman":[36] someone who is both held captive and rendered absent in discourse. Morvillo's absence from antimafia memorial discourses represents aspects of this state of non-being.

As I traced the eventual disappearance of Morvillo from the discursive fields of her Facebook page, the words of Simone de Beauvoir returned to me vis-à-vis de Lauretis. In *The Second Sex*, de Beauvoir wrote: "Humanity is male and man defines woman not in herself but as relative to him; she is not regarded as an autonomous being ... He is the Subject, he is the Absolute – she is the Other." And then, Emmanuel Levinas, who, as de Lauretis observes, betrays a masculine and Eurocentric bias, argued that

> Otherness reaches its full flowering in the feminine, a term of the same rank as consciousness but of the opposite meaning ... Is there not a case in which otherness, alterity (*alterité*) unquestionably marks the nature of a being, as its essence, an instance of otherness not consisting purely and simply in the opposition of two species of the same genus? I think that the feminine represents the contrary in its absolute sense.[37]

Thus, argues de Lauretis, for Levinas, woman represents the absolute state of otherness – a site of radical alterity – necessary to man for her sex and offspring.

The posts that mark the transition of Morvillo from the subject of her Facebook page to a dedicated, "fairy-tale wife" who "will now always remain with her man" indeed resonate with the problematic descriptions of the feminine other that invoke feminine alterities in almost exclusively erotic, maternal, and domestic contexts – homemaker/domestic, selfless, self-sacrificing, devoted to family and husband. Before her memory is subsumed by male martyrs, her Facebook page represents her as a fuller subject, or what de Lauretis might describe as an "eccentric subject," thereby displacing these binaries, if only briefly. de Lauretis proposes that the position of eccentric subject is "excessive to, or not contained by, the socio-cultural institution of heterosexuality."[38]

Citing the work of Cherríe Moraga, Mary Louise Pratt, and Gloria Anzaldua, de Lauretis elaborates on the ways in which the eccentric subject courageously leaves or gives up all that is apparently safe, "that is 'home'" – sacrifices that are indeed experienced by Morvillo and so many of her comrades – forgotten and commemorated. Such loss is experienced, explains de Lauretis,

> physically, emotionally, linguistically, epistemologically – for another place that is unknown and risky, that is not only emotionally but conceptually other; a place of discourse from which speaking and thinking are at best tentative, uncertain, unguaranteed. But the leaving is not a choice: one could not live there in the first place. Thus, both aspects of the displacement, the personal and the conceptual, are painful: they are either, and often both, the cause and/or the result of pain, risk, and a real stake with a high price. For this is "theory in the flesh," as Cherrie Moraga has called it, a constant crossing of the border ... a remapping of boundaries between bodies and discourses, identities and communities – which may be a reason why it is primarily feminists of colour and lesbian feminists who have taken this risk.[39]

Morvillo's sacrifice of conventional notions of home, family, and matrimony, her dedication to civility and reparative justice, to Falcone, yes, and to her constituencies, her students, and the young men and women she defended in the courts of Palermo, called on her to take an excessively critical position at the time. She attained these positions through practices of political and personal displacements across boundaries between communities, discourses, sociosexual expectations, and identities. The term offered by de Lauretis suggests a more generative way of understanding the work of female antimafia activists not as martyrs but as eccentric subjects of history devoted to a material civility rooted not above or outside but within civil society.[40] The promotion of detachment from the world, self-sacrifice, and practices inspired from the religious spheres that value martyrdom have grave implications when applied to female antimafia activists, for martyrdom plays out differently across gendered lines. To promote the language of martyrdom for women is to unwittingly promote images of female activists/martyrs as silent and passive, both condemned to suffering and forgotten after their death. The martyr's discursive formation is always, and only, afforded by her death, and it is only in death that her social status is confirmed. As made evident on Morvillo's Facebook page, the danger inherent in the political hagiography of the antimafia movement for women is that the female martyred subject becomes an emblematically silenced and forgotten subject, while male martyrs of justice are commemorated long after their death. Educators concerned with antimafia studies will do well to remember that when the female martyr of justice speaks, the "I" that we might imagine she inhabits may not in fact be a literal, singular "I" at all, but rather a body of contradictory discourses that compete for our attention. Of course, this requires that studies of the new antimafia religion that intend to work towards making female martyrs speak reflect on the rhetorics of commemoration and memory used to educate a new generation for civility and justice.

Conclusion

How, then, can a public pedagogy of remembrance hope to create spaces for female antimafia activists to speak? One might argue, given the privatized interests of Facebook, that the work of a critical pedagogy of remembrance was doomed to failure from the start, particularly if we take as a central principle, as discussed in Chapter 1, the belief that a public pedagogy of remembrance takes place apart from state and private interests. Critics of social networking sites, such as Facebook and Twitter, have long argued that social networking functions to depoliticize social landscapes and offers a mere ersatz experience of social commitment and transformation. To what extent do the rhetorical constraints on Facebook undermine the initial intentions to keep Morvillo's memory alive? To what extent do social networking systems offer a far too conventional and limited set of rhetorical categories of expression to provoke the sense of conceptual, affective, and epistemic dissonance that de Lauretis so highly values? While each of these questions are important to pursue (and will be pursued in upcoming chapters), in closing this chapter, I would like to reflect on the specific commitments that characterize the public pedagogy of remembrance inspired by Francesca Morvillo's Facebook page.

First, the public pedagogy of remembrance initially represented on Morvillo's Facebook page directed its attention to sustaining memories of figures who cannot be contained by the sociocultural institutions of heterosexuality and are thus vulnerable to being forgotten. This commitment puts the concept of "zones of exception" to work by calling attention to the ways in which subjects left unprotected by the state and marginalized by society and culture can be cast into the oblivion of historical forgetfulness, thus depriving future generations of the value of their memories and legacies. This is the commitment Don Luigi Ciotti speaks of when he writes, "Along with the right to obtain reparation and justice, the right of victims is precisely to be remembered. Remembered in all their uniqueness and individuality. In their work and the results achieved. In their everyday humanity. And first of all, in their name."[41] In specifying a public pedagogy of remembrance that underscores the importance of remembering the dead confined to zones of exception, the case of Morvillo's Facebook page exposes the complex tensions that emerge when attempting to recover memories within transitional societies that have a proclivity to render narratives of martyrdom and victimhood rather than resistance. A public pedagogy of remembrance would begin by recasting the figure of Morvillo as an eccentric subject of history.

Second, the initial project of remembering taken up on Morvillo's Facebook page used storytelling and story-taking in ways that established an equality of intelligence among "friends" and dissolved distinctions between the one who learns and the one who teaches. The early memories generated on Morvillo's Facebook page were intended to represent the dilemma of Morvillo's absence from the antimafia memorial landscape and to position followers of her Facebook page to think from within this dilemma. In this sense this public pedagogy of remembrance invited a form of storytelling that is a form of situated critical thinking that is required when we are called on to think collectively, to use Arendt's words "without banisters"[42] – that is, without conventional categories and formulas. Unprecedented, traumatic events cannot be understood in terms of familiar categories, consequently, and here I follow Arendt, to understand acts of totalitarianism and unspeakable violence, one must begin not with categories but with acts of storytelling that capture the specificity of lives and histories. The opening posts of Morvillo's Facebook page indeed begin to address the crisis of memory she represents. Yet this pedagogical commitment was undermined by a failure to provoke followers of her Facebook page to sustain an engagement with the complexities of her life story as an eccentric figure of resistance rather than a martyr of justice.

The term *eccentric* is intended to echo the term *ex-centric*, indicating the spatial figure of an "elsewhere" that is also very much present. According to de Lauretis, the eccentric position expresses a critical, distanced, self-critical, and self-displaced set of perspectives that exceed the conventional category of woman. For a public pedagogy of remembrance to be relevant to societies in transition, it is crucial that narratives of agency and resistance are brought to the fore as the starting point of memory work. As if in response to the critics of social networking, I believe Morvillo's Facebook page takes on a set of important questions that begin to reveal the conditions necessary for a pedagogy of remembrance to unfold in transitional societies.

Chapter Three

"Children of the Massacre":
Public Pedagogy and Italy's Non-violent
Protest against Mafia Extortion

Vibrant democratic cultures and societies refuse to live in an era that forecloses on hope. Such societies embrace hope not as some utopian dream or privatized fantasy, but as a way of anticipating a better world in the future, by combining reason with a gritty sense of reality and its limits, and realizing your potential as full human beings.

– Henry Giroux, Convocation Speech, University of Santiago de Compostela, Spain

The Mafia is a system of power, articulation of power, metaphor of power, pathology of power. The Mafia becomes the State where the State is tragically absent. The Mafia is an economic system, forever implicated in illicit activities which bring profits that can be exploited methodologically. The Mafia is a criminal organization that uses and abuses traditional Sicilian values. In a world where the concept of citizenship tends to be diluted and the logic of belonging tends to be strengthened, where citizens with their rights and their duties give way to the clan and to patronage, the Mafia appears as an organization with an assured future.

– Giovanni Falcone and Marcelle Padovani, *Men of Honour: Truth about the Mafia*

Introduction

In March 2014 the Italian foreign ministry reported that Italy's mafia had a larger annual budget than the European Union, generating profits of close to $180 billion a year. This chapter explores the work of activists who campaign to resist mafia extortion. These activists, who grew up amid the mafia violence of the 1980s and 1990s, have become influential teachers, journalists, attorneys, and social entrepreneurs. Drawing on extensive interviews with the founding members of one of the leading anti-extortion groups in Italy, Addiopizzo, I explore the radical public pedagogical methods they use to educate local and global communities about resistance against mafia extortion, and the cultural and social conditions necessary to create and sustain a more ethical economy.

In January 1991 textile manufacturer Libero Grassi wrote a short letter to Palermo's local newspaper, *Giornale di Sicilia*, that began, "*caro estortore*" (Dear Extortionist). In his letter, Grassi described the steady stream of requests he had received from the mafia to pay extortion fees to provide for their "poor friends in prison." "With the very first contact," wrote Grassi, "I said no." In response, the mafia warned him to "watch your son, watch the warehouse, watch yourself."[1] Refusing to comply, Grassi reported the names of his would-be extortionists to the police, a move that resulted in five arrests in March. On 11 April 1991 Grassi appeared on nationwide television and spoke openly about the devastating impact the mafia had on businesses throughout Palermo. Despite police protection, his shop was broken into. The only thing stolen was the precise amount of money demanded by the Cosa Nostra. Soon after, his workers were threatened.

Local shopkeepers and business owners chose not to stand with Grassi. In fact, they openly criticized him for damaging the image of Palermo and "washing dirty clothes in public." Catania judge Luigi Russo continued to maintain that the payment of mafia bribes was not a crime, and Salvatore Cozzo stated in an interview in *L'Ora*, published on 11 April 1991, that "Grassi is undermining the image of the businessman." This publicity and the threat of mafia retaliation compromised him financially and instilled enough fear in many of Grassi's customers that they kept their distance from him and from his business.

Then, at 7:30 in the morning on 29 August 1991, as Grassi walked to his car on the Via Vittorio Alfieri in Palermo, mafia member Salvatore Madonia shot him in the head three times. Not one witness came forward.

Eighteen years later, I am sitting on Grassi's terrace in Palermo. I am speaking with his wife, Pina Maisano Grassi, about her anti-extortion activism. The July heat begins to lift as Pina serves small glasses of apricot juice and a bowl of roasted peanuts. Together with Edo Zaffuto, I listen to Pina's story of her husband's lonely protest against the mafia. Pina believes that the mafia is not solely to blame for Grassi's death. Also to blame, she explains, is the silence of the business community, the absence of state protection, and the absolute indifference of citizens and residents of the city. The crowds that poured into the city squares days after Grassi's murder to honour him offered little comfort to Pina and her son and daughter. There was little consolation, continues Pina, for the sense of abandonment and acute danger Libero was subjected to by neighbours and colleagues who dared not speak in the name of *omertà*. Not only does *omertà* function as an imposed code of silence that prohibits cooperation with state authorities, even in the case when one has been a victim of a crime, but *omertà* is also, in effect, a code of silence that isolates and terrorizes by forbidding communication with the outside world. Perhaps this is why Donatella Mauro equated speaking with death: "I don't know how far *omertà* goes when you realize that speaking means dying."[2] Renate Siebert describes this quality of silence in the following way:

> *Omertà*, silence, heralds this message of deathly narcissism: it is not mere chance that we talk of being silent as the grave. He who does not speak estranges himself from shared subjectivity, from dialogue: as a concrete flesh and blood subject he is already dead."[3]

In refusing to speak with the state, those who abide by *omertà* and keep the secrets that unite the fraternal, homosocial members of the mafia defend an inside world idealized as the uniquely good mother – and turn away from the larger social field associated with the father. The mafia, also called *mamma-santissima*, a "holyholy mother," is, explains Renate Siebert, "an object of love and hatred for whose defense and for whose possession the brotherhood was born."[4] While the membership of the Cosa Nostra is confined to men who repudiate women, the face of the Cosa Nostra is ironically feminine.[5] Siebert further explains this radical ambivalence:

> So this is a group made up of men only and marked with a radical ambivalence in relation to the feminine: a union between brothers on the one hand in the name of attachment to the mother, and, on the other, in the name of fear and contempt for the feminine. An exclusive group. An esoteric group.[6]

Grassi stands as one "martyr of justice" who refused to remain silent, in part, by sustaining dialogue with the public and with the state. Yet the silence of those around him, the very lack of solidarity with him, is emblematic of a fractured social body that struggles to reconcile inner worlds with the world outside.[7]

Looking at Zaffuto, Pina expresses how moved she was when, in 2004, she heard about a group of seven young university graduates who wanted to open a bar in Palermo but refused to put aside money for the *pizzo*, or extortion fee, each month. This group of graduates, who call themselves "children of the massacre," came of age during the 1980s – a time of intense conflict between a group of mafiosi from the interior town of Corleone and Palermo's mafiosi or "families." They warred over drugs, real estate, and construction contracts.

Rather than capitulate to the Cosa Nostra by offering them a budget line in their business plan, they decided to organize against the mafia by using a set of non-violent tactics not used before. Their intention was to use transitional justice to build a coalition of businesses and consumers that refused to participate in extortion activities and to put an end to the traumatic impact generations endured in the grip of *omertà*. The group of friends chose to frame the demand for extortion money made by the Cosa Nostra as a pedagogical provocation rather than an act of intimidation. They did so by working on a set of strategies to educate civil society about the profound economic, cultural, and psychic costs that come with extortion. To start, the group did something quite simple.

Towards a Public Pedagogy of Remembrance: Non-violent Protests against Extortion

In the middle of a July night in 2004, Edo Zaffuto, Francesca Vannini Parenti, Laura Nocilla, Raffaele Genova, Vittorio Greco, Ugo Forello, Daniele Briguglia, and Francesco Bertolino launched a poster campaign of black-and-white stickers designed to look like an obituary notice throughout the city. The stickers stated, "A whole people who pays the *pizzo*," or extortion money, "is a people without dignity" ("*Un intero popolo che paga il pizzo e un popolo senza dignità*"). "This was a call to arms against the *pizzo*, a way to grab attention," states Genova. "Initially, we didn't think we would succeed so well. We simply wanted to open the debate."[8]

The media attention came fast. Three days after the stickers appeared, Pina Grassi received a phone call from reporters asking if she knew who was responsible for the sticker campaign. "Who are they?" asked the reporters. "I said, 'Who knows? I haven't got a clue ... but they see things the way I do.'"

Edo Zaffuto, one of Addiopizzo's founding members, describes Addiopizzo as a grassroots civic movement similar to a non-governmental organization (NGO) with a tight horizontal structure, somewhat akin to fair trade. "Some people think of us as a fluid movement, like a campaign without a structure, but we have, since 2005, had to create an association with an infrastructure – a president, board of directors, someone to oversee the budget, et cetera, but we share leadership roles ... this was an important idea from the very beginning ... it's not important who plays the roles of the president or director, because the central idea is that it would be a shared leadership. Unlike *Libera*, which was the idea of one person, Don Luigi Ciotti, Addiopizzo was the idea of many."[9] In cooperation with other antimafia organizations, such as *Libero Futuro*, Addiopizzo directs its attention specifically to extortion.[10]

"And," notes Zaffuto, "when we address the *pizzo*, of course, we address the mafia in particular."

The term *pizzo* is Sicilian dialect for the beak of a bird. In mafia slang, the term *pizzo* works metaphorically to capture the image of a bird going about the countryside getting his beak wet by taking a sip of water here, nectar from a flower there, eventually quenching his thirst. "For as long as anyone can remember," notes Philip Jacobson, "the Sicilian mafia has dipped its beak in the pocket of big corporations, restaurants, shops, and hotels, even humble street vendors."[11] Zaffuto explains that the *pizzo* is essentially a progressive tax imposed by the mafia on businesses. The more you earn, the more you pay. Mafiosi traditionally use this money to assist the families of mafia members who are in prison and to pay for the legal fees of mafia members. The implications of extortion in southern Italy are profound, particularly given that the lack of growth in value added of southern Italian business caused by the pervasive presence of mafia extortion is estimated to be 7.5 billion euros per year, or 2.5% of southern Italy's gross domestic product (GDP). Zaffuto draws on data from *Indagine Cenis*[12] to explain that if there were no *pizzo* in southern Italy (from Naples to Sicily), between 1981 and 2001 the area's per capita GDP would have reached that of northern Italy. "If you consider these payments," argues Zaffuto, "and add to this the fact that the mafia uses extortion to eventually take control of businesses by dictating who will be hired and which suppliers owners can use, you conclude that there is no free market or free competition in Sicily because the market is controlled by the mafia. In Sicily, the capacity to make a living is tied to criminality."

In an interview with *Frontline*'s Carola Mamberto, journalist Alexander Stille maintains that "no healthy, sane business could invest in Southern Italy under the kind of conditions that prevail there. Why would you open a factory or start a business, even though labor costs are low, knowing that you're soon going to be pressured by this person or that to use a particular supplier? An enormous number of your profits are going to be siphoned off on that and it's just not worth it."

Addiopizzo, meaning "goodbye *pizzo*," holds the promise and the hope, notes Zaffuto, for future generations to live free from extortion and to break the grip the Cosa Nostra has on generations of what he describes as underdevelopment in Sicily. Addiopizzo's collaborations with educational and cultural institutions and the law focus on creating a culture for those who refuse to pay extortion fees but to do so must "pass through the law." And to pass through the law safely, Addiopizzo offers protection, what Zaffuto describes as "protection through solidarity with others," as well as legal counsel and consultation with the police.

"We have learned," continues Zaffuto, "from older anti-racket organizations in Sicily, how important it is to work in association with others."[13]

Addiopizzo's collective opposition to the mafia works on several levels. At the level of the law, Addiopizzo works with attorneys and the police to establish anonymity and safety when businesses initially report extortion. This is a period described by Addiopizzo as a necessary "low-profile moment." "When the police receive a report from a business owner about extortion," explains Zaffuto, "they come to us because in that moment, the best guarantee for the safety of the shopkeeper is to be inside a network – a protective shield – of other people." Later, Addiopizzo offers solidarity in public when the businesses go to trial against mafiosi. During the trials Addiopizzo members join the plaintiffs in court. Zaffuto describes this act of solidarity as one in which Addiopizzo creates "a community where the economic actors rebel or fight the mafia ... in part by working within the framework of a legal economy.[14] Once the trial arrives, it is necessary to be loud, to go public, to talk, to speak up, and to team up: "We invite people to come to the courthouse – to offer support, to wear the Addiopizzo shirts."[15] Among the most striking acts of solidarity is the way in which Addiopizzo "plays plaintiff" for shopkeepers who are afraid to sue for damages. In such cases Addiopizzo represents members of the society in ways similar to a class action suit. They effectively stand in for those who have been damaged by extortion and sue for damages. "We encourage the shopkeepers to sue because they will receive payment back. But, when they are too afraid, we are advised by our attorney, Ugo Forello, to stand in the place of shopkeepers and consumers who don't want to pay extortion money ... the basic idea is that the public has been damaged and should be compensated and that Addiopizzo 'stands in' for the social body at large."

Another vital level of activity taken up by Addiopizzo's team of volunteers is curating online narratives on its website that work to educate the public about critical consumerism and ethical tourism. The website, written in over 13 languages, includes their founding story and a range of materials, including articles and links to documentary films, lectures about anti-extortion activity, and books and interviews with antimafia activists and scholars. Most recently, Addiopizzo has begun to use e-commerce by creating a portal on the website so visitors can easily purchase *pizzo*-free goods. In 2009 the foundation Addiopizzo Travel was established as a formal tour operator. In cooperation with restaurants, hotels, shops, and agricultural businesses that have stopped paying extortion fees, Addiopizzo Travel works to prevent the mafia from practising extortion in the tourism industry by leading tours that support these *pizzo*-free businesses.[16]

In her economic analysis of Addiopizzo, Chiara Superti describes it as an organization that exploits "all the resources that the market and public institutions provide," and in turn synchronizes "the efforts of consumers, business, and institutional entities toward the same goal."[17] Superti continues:

> This coordination of disparate parties with aligned interests in fighting the Mafia has revealed itself to be a winning tactic. Furthermore, the organization works exhaustively to develop a more favorable environment for the flourishing of its initiative by educating and informing civil society.[18]

In the last few years there has been growing evidence from pentiti that Addiopizzo's approaches are effective as a deterrent to mafia harassment.[19] In his September 2014 report for *Newsweek*, Jacobson[20] disclosed that mafia boss Giovanni Di Giacomo was videotaped by state prosecutors from prison as he raged against Addiopizzo's bold campaign to shut down the Porto Nuova clan's significantly lucrative extortion rackets. Jacobson writes, "'It's a fucking disaster,' Di Giacomo lamented during the bugged jail conversation, complaining, entirely without irony, that the Addiopizzo campaign makes it much harder to earn a dishonest living."

Yet despite Addiopizzo's winning tactics, mafia activity continues to thrive in Italy. Recent calculations reported by the *Confesercenti* (an association representing small and medium enterprises in retail, tourism, and services) show that the mafia is the main enterprise in Italy, with annual profits of close to 30 billion euros. In 2007 extortion generated 10 billion euros.[21] In March 2014 Italy's foreign ministry claimed that Italy's mafia groups have a larger annual budget than the European Union.[22] Add to this the fact that the unemployment rate for young people continues to climb and the percentage of working adults continues to slip.[23] Forty-six per cent of 15- to 24-year-olds are unemployed, which accounts for 46% of the country's and 60.9% of the south's unemployment. The correlation between joblessness and mafia employment is not news and stands as one example of how the mafia functions as a surrogate state when legitimate state security fails. In the words of Padovani and Falcone, "the mafia becomes the state when the state is tragically absent."[24]

In collaboration with teachers and antimafia cultural organizations, such as *Libera* and the *Centro Siciliano di documentazione "Giuseppe Impastato"* in Palermo, the curriculum designed by Addiopizzo and Addiopizzo Travel educates youth and residents about the importance of addressing extortion, in the words of La Torre president Vito Lo Monaco, "as the most primitive, primary method of accumulating wealth" and as destroying democratic life. To what extent can a relatively small group of concerned citizens and residents successfully protect business owners who refuse to participate in extortion activities in a society in and of transition? To what extent does Addiopizzo create a political space for freedom from extortion? What is the promise and what are the limits of such an organization given the force of mafia infiltration into government, politics, and the global economy?

Public Pedagogy and Mafia Terrorism

Because Italy continues to transition from a history of mafia violence while simultaneously experiencing that violence, an antimafia group such as Addiopizzo faces particular challenges as it engages in a public pedagogy of remembrance that focuses on cultivating critical consumerism. As Dana Renga astutely points out in her study of trauma, gender, and Italian mafia cinema, the mafia is paradoxically one of the newest and oldest forms of domestic terrorism:

> The Mafia has terrorized the Italian populace in a much more long-term, widespread and systematic manner than, say, Italian terrorist organizations did some thirty to forty years ago during the *anni di piombo* ["the leaden years," approximately from 1969 to the early 1980s]. Moreover, unlike terrorism during the *anni di piombo*, which was arguably overcome, Mafia terrorism has transcended the historical boundaries that customarily delineate national traumas. Thus, its ongoing effect might constitute the Mafia as a cultural trauma comparable with or even more extensive than that of terrorism in Italy during the *anni di piombo*. In this way, paradoxically, it is the newest and the oldest form of Italian terrorism.[25]

Renga argues that Italy has yet to experience a period of post-mafia dormancy necessary for generating a trauma narrative of mafia violence.[26] Following Bernhard Giesen, Renga maintains that "collective traumas require a time of latency before they can be ... spoken about, and worked through."[27] Both Renga and Giesen believe that this historical void undermines the possibility for both a trauma discourse to emerge and a subsequent national mourning to take place, and renders impossible the nation's capacity to recognize and alter the mafia's social, political, and economic causes to "prevent its recurrence as well as enable forms of renewal."[28] The analysis made by Renga is particularly relevant when studying societies in transition. Not only does Renga imply that societies in transition are not yet able to claim cultural trauma when that trauma persists, but she also gestures towards an observation made by Roger Simon in his study of Allen and Littlefield's collection of lynching photographs. The staging or representation of commemorative events does not necessarily mark the end of a collectively perceived trauma and signal "we have moved beyond the violence of past times."[29] Simon emphasizes that it would be a mistake "to reduce every practice of public remembrance of unjust violence and its consequent loss to these terms."[30]

Given that Italy does not yet exist in a post-traumatic state – despite educational, legal, and cultural projects directed at transitional justice – precisely because the Italian mafia continues to traumatize individuals and communities, how can transitional narratives cultivate forms of cultural renewal? Is it indeed possible to compose transitional narratives of ethical remembrance given that the trauma of mafia violence continues to evolve? What ethical discourses are used by Addiopizzo to cultivate critical and alternative consumer practices, and in what ways do these practices inform an ethical pedagogy of remembrance? These questions are pivotal to my study of public pedagogy and the difficult knowledge that is carried by traumatic events that persist in communities committed to transitional justice.

What is striking about the storytelling and story-taking practices of Addiopizzo is the way memories circulate throughout their practices of pedagogical remembrances. Unlike, for example, the repetitive, melancholic narratives of remembrance associated with the Falcone Tree and Francesca Morvillo's memorial Facebook page, the narratives curated by Addiopizzo come closer to a form of remembering that fulfils the work of mourning while retaining traces of the impact of the trauma of extortion. At the centre of Addiopizzo's public pedagogy is a practice of storytelling and story-taking about extortion in Sicily that is driven by a desire to give form to political and cultural transformation. Critics of Addiopizzo claim the group uses the mafia to market and profit from images of a "new Sicily" and that Addiopizzo has had an insignificant impact on the ways in which the Cosa Nostra continues to operate throughout its territories; I argue that Addiopizzo affects the mafia through a series of strategic narrative practices that shatter the complex homosocial project of *omertà*.

The group's use of story-taking and storytelling consistently strives to replace estrangement, isolation, fear, and silence with shared subjectivity and natality – that is, a hope for new beginnings. Hannah Arendt introduces *natality* as a moment "when one is born into the political sphere and where acting together can create the truly unexpected ... and demonstrates how the unexpected might arise within this sphere of freedom."[31] The concept of natality offers a productive ground for theorizing Addiopizzo's entrance into the worldliness of pedagogical action. Its narrative practices combine to form a provocative ethical pedagogy of remembrance that plays out in the public sphere and is primarily directed at a new generation of citizens and residents. As a principle contingent on rather than separate from human action, the principle of natality that finds expression in the public pedagogy of Addiopizzo emerges in the particularity of the life stories the members tell, as well as in their ceaseless capacity to initiate new action that supports a public sphere where plurality and open conversation remain possible.[32]

The Paradoxes of Natality: Plurality and Belatedness

Writing in 1958, Arendt established natality as "the central category of political ... thought ... the miracle that saves the world."[33] Arendt uses the term *natality* as a shorthand for human ingenuity and establishes it as the very aim and essence of education.[34] In the following excerpt, Arendt establishes the quality of action that locates, sustains, and renews the body politic. This crucial project of action establishes conditions for a practice of remembrance that Arendt equates with history:

> Action, insofar as it engages in founding and preserving political bodies, creates the condition for remembrance, that is, for history. Labor and work, as well as action, are also rooted in natality insofar as they have the task to provide and preserve the world for, to foresee and reckon with, the constant influx of newcomers who are born into the world as strangers. However, of the three, action has the closest connection with the human condition of natality; the new beginning inherent in birth can make itself felt in the world only because the newcomer possesses the capacity of beginning something anew, that is, of acting. In this sense of initiative, an element of action, and therefore of natality, is inherent in all human activities. Moreover, since action is the political activity par excellence, natality, and not mortality, may be the central category of political, as distinguished from metaphysical, thought.[35]

Here, Arendt identifies natality as the central category for political action. Working against any tendency to act as if the world were impervious to change or no longer in need of alteration, Arendt casts the political actor as one who initiates unexpected activities that result in new ways of being, and generates self-discovery as well as social understandings.[36]

The human condition, argues Arendt, "is conditioned existence" – we are born into a history that is not of our making.[37] Consequently, the political actors who initiate new ways of being must do so amid conditions that both precede and constitute them. In her study of Arendt's concept of natality, Natasha Levinson explores what she identifies as the paradoxes that characterize this complex form of human initiative: belatedness and plurality. Levinson observes that while we are heirs to a specific history, we are also new to it; hence, we experience ourselves as belated, as arriving a bit too late. While the experience of

belatedness has the potential to generate an awareness of the complexity of on-
tological, political, and social problems, it also has the potential to paralyse us
and to undermine our capacity for generative, transformative social action. "In
this way," notes Levinson, "belatedness not only conditions natality, it has the
potential to act against it."[38] Levinson observes that people may feel so weighted
down by history and social positioning that they see no point in attempting to
create new social realities.[39] In other words, a sense of belatedness might very
well provoke us to disavow our implications in the history that precedes us.

When historical inheritances include the weight of racism, corruption, terrorism, and acute poverty, we may be more vulnerable to disavowing our place
in history. We can hear traces of repudiation in claims made by youth who feel
lost in the cycle of poverty and corruption that is born, to quote Falcone and
Padovani one more time, "where the state is tragically absent," when state support and protection breaks down and the "state of exception" becomes the rule
of law. This form of resignation turns away, argues Arendt, from the promise of
natality: the capacity to establish new relations and to generate new social realities through our words and deeds.[40]

Equally challenging is the second feature that constitutes the paradox of natality: plurality. The transformative ideas we develop must inevitably be de-
bated in public spheres where our beliefs and values are met with criticism and
open to debate. We can never know the outcome of our actions in advance – or
if in fact we will make any difference at all. "All this is reason enough," writes
Arendt, "to turn away with despair from the realm of human affairs and to hold
in contempt the human capacity for freedom, which by producing the web of
human relationships, seems to entangle its producer to such an extent that he
seems much more the victim and the sufferer than the author and doer of what
he has done."[41] Faced with continual economic, political, and social challenges
to initiating new ideas into the political sphere, it is easy for resentment to seep
in and undermine the potential for natality to emerge.[42] Natality requires a particular form of resilience, one that understands both history and the strategic
practices that keep historical narratives alive so historical memories can thrive.

Arendt very well might have recognized Addiopizzo as a social movement,
comprising unique actors who exert agency despite the presence of historical
forces that are out of their control, despite living in a society in and of transition
where trauma hovers and can erupt at any time. Exactly what does teaching
for natality look like within a society in and of transition? Exactly how does
Addiopizzo negotiate the delicate tension between a sense of belatedness – having arrived as heir to a history of violence – and a sense of plurality that asks
that we "live with other people, strangers, forever in the same world, and makes
it possible for them to bear with us"?[43]

Addiopizzo's tactics of storytelling and story-taking work as a process of re-signification. The stories told include memories of human fallibility and an unstaunched history of specific injustices – the forging of sociality not after social breakdown, given that mafia terrorism continues to exist, but within trauma's interstices. In the following section I bring Arendt into conversation with psychoanalytic and educational theory in an effort to outline a notion of public pedagogy that understands the working through of trauma in transitional societies as an interminable psychic process of reconstituting social life through our capacity to re-signify history even when the threat of social breakdown persists.[44]

A Walk in the City with Addiopizzo Travel

In 2011 Addiopizzo Travel won the prestigious TODO! Award for socially responsible tourism. In 2013 the organization became a cooperative and most recently celebrated with a cascade of festivities and press releases for being recognized as a tour operator.[45] Founding members of the cooperative include Dario Riccobono (credited with the original idea), Francesca Vannini Parenti, and Edo Zaffuto, all co-founders of Addiopizzo. Three different kinds of tours are offered: *viaggi studio* (study tours), *escursione e vacanze* (vacation excursions), and *turismo sociale* (social tours). Addiopizzo Travel describes *pizzo-free* tourism as

> a new frontier for the ethical tourist, support[ing] those who rebel against the mafia. We offer you a land of extraordinary cultural and artistic heritage; an experience which balances beauty with social duty. This is an opportunity to understand, first hand, the most important moments, people, and places of the antimafia movement.

On Addiopizzo Travel's website,[46] you will find confirmation that Italy continues to suffer the impact of domestic terrorism while maintaining a commitment to engage students in citizenship education. Framed as a "new kind of study trip," the description on the website in July 2015 read:

> Through Addiopizzo's long experience in working with schools and universities, we have developed a package especially for students: a tour which combines an in-depth examination of the mafia phenomenon with a powerful lesson in citizenship. The history of mafia and of the antimafia movements is relived through the first-person narration of our protagonists, while visiting the most important locations and hearing about the stages of a battle that is still being fought. This is a

study tour which provides cultural awareness through first-hand experience of a living revolution.

What rhetorical strategies are used to compose this "first-person narration of our protagonists," and what locations are selected as "most important" in the "stages of a battle that is still being fought ... a living revolution"?

For seven days and six nights, members of Addiopizzo Travel usher students through the streets and hill towns of a Sicily that deliberately defies the stereotypic images generated by American gangster films or Coppola's mafia trilogy. Students and teachers eat in *pizzo*-free restaurants and *agriturismos* (tourists board at farms or in rural villages and experience farming up close). They sleep in *pizzo*-free hotels and bed and breakfasts. As students walk through the ancient outdoor markets in Palermo, they are introduced to the myth of the *Beati Paoli*, a sixteenth-century secret sect believed to be precursors to the mafia. Students are led down streets that have been renamed to commemorate "martyrs of justice," and they gather around the plaques cemented on stone buildings and fastened to trees that create a record of mafia terrorism. Students meet with leading antimafia figures, such as Giovanni Impastato, Umberto Santino, and Anna Puglisi, and participate in the making of antimafia television news in Partinico, *Tele Jato*, owned and hosted by esteemed Italian journalist Pino Maniaci. Coffee is served at a *pizzo*-free bar in Corleone's newly named Piazza Falcone and Borsellino before students walk a few blocks to the antimafia museum that holds an archive of documents from the maxi-trial and an extensive collection of photographs by Franco Zecchin, Letizia Battaglia, and Shobha Battaglia.

On the surface, this "ethical tour of Palermo" may appear to be no more than a variation of a walking reality tour that profits from a history of extortion and brutality and protects participants from encounters or entanglements with people, places, and politics.[47] Framed as "study tours" that last from one to seven days, they generally attract elementary, middle, high school, and university students, faculty, and financially privileged tourists. Tours are continually being designed and revised, and members of Addiopizzo Travel often custom-design tours in collaboration with faculty and antimafia activists.

However, a closer analysis of the storytelling and story-taking practices composed by Addiopizzo Travel offers evidence of narratives circulating in public spaces where participants engage in first-person conversations with contemporary antimafia activists who introduce an often neglected history of antimafia dissent. These conversations make visible the symptoms of transition into democracy: betrayals, corruption, and violence, to name some of the central themes that emerge in Addiopizzo Travel's public pedagogies of remembrance.[48]

Following a narrative pattern similar to that outlined by historian Michael Rothberg and legal scholar Ruti Teitel, the narrative signature of Addiopizzo's storytelling practices follows a distinct process of re-symbolization that includes (1) composing "mini-narratives that are situated within the state's pre-existing national story," (2) building on existing legacies of dissent against the mafia, and (3) refusing to "let go of the past" in the name of a happy ending.[49] Taken together, these approaches to storytelling work against the narrative fetishism described by Eric Santner that we explored in Chapter 2 in the discussion of the Falcone Tree. Santner argues that narrative fetishism emerges in "the construction and deployment of a narrative consciously or unconsciously designed to expunge the traces of the trauma or loss that called that narrative into being in the first place."[50] While a fetishistic narrative that emerges out of a traumatic situation may recognize the fact of trauma, it disavows the persistent impact of trauma on the present.[51] The challenge facing transitional narratives that resist sliding into consoling narratives, as I noted earlier, is to retain the traces of the trauma's impact. Consequently, what I understand as ethical pedagogies of remembrance must recognize past disavowals as well as how ongoing disavowals are sustained and reproduced in culture and society.

In the following section I offer a closer analysis of two representative study tours led by Addiopizzo Travel that capture the central public pedagogical principles of natality under discussion and the narrative practices of story-taking and storytelling they use to educate the public about critical consumerism. I will consider the ways in which these narratives work within the context of a country working towards transitional justice while still experiencing the continual threat of mafia violence. I begin with a tour near Capaci through the city centre of Palermo where Sicilian culture is offered on the way, through markets, piazzas, cathedrals, and historic sites of tragedy.

Another Sicily: Situating Mini-Narratives within the State's Existing National Story

Dario Riccobono, one of the founders of Addiopizzo, grew up in Capaci, a town often associated with the bomb that blasted the bulletproof sedan of prosecutor Giovanni Falcone. The explosion, strong enough to register on local earthquake monitors, killed Falcone; his wife, Judge Francesca Morvillo; and their escorts, Rocco Dicillo, Antonio Montinaro, and Vito Schifani. Part of the official story of Falcone's murder holds that the assassination was intended as payback for all the mafiosi Falcone had put behind bars. Although this is partly true, official accounts rarely address the extent to which Falcone was abandoned and left unprotected by the state. During a recent antimafia tour, Riccobono began by introducing students to what Addiopizzo Travel terms the "symbolic places of the antimafia." Riccobono leads a group of students from Pavia (a city in northern Italy about 35 kilometres south of Milan) up a hill alongside the motorway in Capaci where Falcone was killed.[52] On the way, they stop along the culvert under the motorway where the explosives were released and where a tall state-sponsored obelisk stands commemorating Falcone, Morvillo, and their escorts. Riccobono details the release of explosives: mafia experiments with the explosives days before, how the explosives were set on a skateboard and rolled under the motorway, and the champagne glasses raised by mafia leaders after the murders. He continues to lead the group up the hill. "This is a special place," he explains, "because from here, Giovanni Brusca detonated the explosives under the motorway. The explosives left a huge crater." Standing alongside the site is a large blue sign, created and maintained by the people of Capaci, that reads "No Mafia!" It is one of the first signs visitors see as they drive from the Falcone-Borsellino Airport into Palermo. Riccobono describes the Capaci motorway after the bombing as a war zone, a scene you might see in a Hollywood gangster movie or in footage from Afghanistan or Iraq:

> Yes, a war, and I have seen it in my village. These experiences mark you forever. Yet, I believe that this is the place where everything starts again. Where this, my village, is born again. A fantastic place where the cliff dramatically falls into the sea ... this village is famous all over the world for a mafia slaughter. I can't accept it. I want to show you its real face ... for you to get to know another Sicily.

Riccobono explains to the students that he and his colleagues will introduce them to the island of Sicily through the eyes of Sicilians. "We want travelers to discover not only our beautiful places but also our very interesting people and their stories ... We promote the beauty of our land, talking about Sicily without ignoring the mafia problem." The commitment to introduce what Addiopizzo Travel describes as "the real face of Sicily" makes emotional life a basis for politics by paying particular attention to affects that are not traditionally thought of as political – shame, anger, despair. Riccobono refuses to accept that Capaci is remembered for a mafia slaughter and little more. His introductory narrative begins to transform a public site of loss, stigma, and violence into a public site of cultural renewal and remembrance. While Riccobono looks to the past, he does not recount the brutal massacre in Capaci as a story that is completely or securely set in the past. Rather, he recognizes his village as both marked by mafia violence as well as being the very site "where everything starts again," where the village of Capaci is "born again" despite the continued recurrence of state terrorism.

In what they describe as a cultural revolution, Addiopizzo Travel consistently traces sites throughout Sicily where bombs were placed and people murdered not, as they state, "as symbols of death, but of the rebellion of civil society against the violence of the mafia. Not sterile memorials, but places of living memory and focal points for the renewal of the collective energy for justice and truth."[53] In each encounter with witnesses, sites, and objects of significance, Addiopizzo Travel works to bind intellectual and affective life in an attempt to secure memorial legacies that are social in character, vibrant, alive, and open to new insights and understandings. These remembrance practices depart from practices associated with "sterile memorials," which, as we saw at the Falcone Tree, tend to slide into repetition and disavowal.[54] Furthermore, these practices stand apart from a pedagogy structured solely in melancholia, precisely because they direct their teaching not to loss and mortality alone, but to articulating new beginnings in the context of a living history. Although the loss expressed in Addiopizzo Travel's pedagogies of remembrance speaks to what is lost in the face of the mafia's domination and oppression, this loss is expressed in part by recognizing rather than naturalizing the injuries of extortion. In this way, the traces of trauma's impact are retained, while at the same time, the practice of remembrance takes up the work of mourning and renewal. Let me further explain by once again examining Freud's reflections on mourning and melancholia.

Disentangling from Loss

Throughout Freud's writings about grief, he drew attention to the relationship between what he describes as the "normal affect of mourning" and melancholia.[55] Both are reactions to the loss of a love object. Freud describes melancholia as "a profoundly painful dejection, cessation of interest in the outside world, loss of the capacity to love, inhibition of all activity."[56] Freud finds similar reactions to the loss of someone or something loved in cases of mourning. "The mood of mourning is a painful one," observes Freud. The person in pain does not easily turn to a new love object, even if a substitute is readily available. One of the distinguishing characteristics between the two forms of grieving, however, is that while mourning is finite, melancholia remains unresolved. Lost in this state of psychic stasis, the melancholic is incapable of articulating what he or she has lost in himself or herself, suggesting that melancholia is associated with the loss of an object that is withdrawn from consciousness and cannot be articulated or represented.[57] "In mourning," writes Freud, "the world has become poor and empty; in melancholia, it is the ego itself."[58] He goes on:

The patient represents his ego to us as worthless, incapable of any achievement and morally despicable; he reproaches himself, vilifies himself and expects to be cast out and punished. He abases himself before everyone and commiserates with his own relatives for being connected with anyone so unworthy.[59]

Not only does the melancholic refuse to love again, but the lost love object is also devoured by the ego where it sets up house and continually berates itself and demands to be punished. Consequently, the loss is compounded. There is the loss of the love object and the loss of the ego. The drive to love is lost – and with it, speculated Freud, all attachment to natality and what inaugurates the expansive domain of the ego: love, being loved, being in love, and loving. In other words, the melancholic is incapable of simultaneously holding remorse, anger, and sadness while turning to the world and risking love again. Arendt might argue that the melancholic cannot take on the responsibility for renewal or for saving the world from ruin, because the melancholic cannot invest libidinal energy in the world, a project she eloquently articulates at the conclusion of "The Crisis in Education":

Education is the point at which we decide whether we love the world enough to assume responsibility for it and by the same token save it from that ruin which, except for renewal, except for the coming of the new and young, would be inevitable. And education, too, is where we decide whether we love our children enough not to expel them from our world and leave them to their own devices, nor to strike from their hands their chance of undertaking something new, something unforeseen by us, but to prepare them in advance for the task of renewing a common world.[60]

As a collective, Addiopizzo Travel expresses a love for the world strong enough to assume responsibility for it and for "undertaking something new, something unforeseen by us." Addiopizzo Travel confronts the complex challenges of creating and sustaining an ethical economy in the very midst of mafia terror with the intention of "renewing a common world." It is in this sense that Addiopizzo works within trauma's interstices, not after social breakdown, as I noted earlier, but in its midst. Addiopizzo introduces a different sort of protagonist to participants on this ethical tour, a protagonist who not only speaks publicly against mafia violence but also introduces imaginative, spontaneous, non-violent practices of protest against mafia infiltration amid state terrorism.

Rather than seeking individual solutions to the social, political, and economic challenges the mafia poses to democratic life, Addiopizzo Travel seeks to establish faith in acts of solidarity and embraces a principle of communal responsibility that promotes the values of a social state. Esteemed sociologist Zygmunt Bauman describes a social state as one that promotes the "principle of communally endorsed, collective insurance against individual misfortune and its consequences."[61] Bauman's description precisely captures the fundamental value Addiopizzo places on working in solidarity with communities in the name of a social state with an eye towards dismantling the homosocial order of *omertà* and its antipathy for shared subjectivity:

A state is "social" when it promotes the principle of the communally endorsed, collective insurance against individual misfortune and its consequences ... And it is this same principle that lifts members of society to the status of citizens. It makes them stakeholders as well as stock-holders. They become beneficiaries, but also actors, responsible for the creation and availability of benefits. They become individuals with an acute interest in the common good, which is understood as the shared institutions that assure the solidity and reliability of any state-issued "collective insurance policy." The application of this principle may, and often does, protect men and women from the plague of poverty. Most importantly, however, it can develop into a fertile source of solidarity, able to recycle "society" into a common, communal good. It provides defence against the twin horrors of misery and indignity, and against the terrors of falling, or being pushed, overboard from the fast accelerating vehicle of progress. A defence against condemnation to "social redundancy" or consignment to "human waste."[62]

The principles of communally endorsed collective insurance against individual misfortune and "human waste," as well as the creation of shared institutions that can be trusted to ensure solidarity and reliability of the state-issued "collective insurance policy," are embedded in the testimony offered during Addiopizzo's ethical tours and resonate throughout the pedagogical discourses that structure Addiopizzo Travel's curricula. In the second part of Riccobono's ethical tour, students are introduced to what Addiopizzo Travel describes as "Sicilian antimafia strategies" through the teachings of specific "protagonists," in this case, testimony given by Orazio De Guilmi, a close friend and collaborator of Italian activist Danilo Dolci (1924–97). This part of the tour is designed, in their words, to

increase students' knowledge of the mafia phenomenon in its complexity directly in the field, and to discover the most efficient strategies to contrast the Cosa Nostra that are being carried on in Sicily by the state and the civil society. During this part of the tour, students work with experts involved in the fight against organized crime, including historians, attorneys, members of the law enforcement, journalists, and relatives of mafia victims. Situated in the western part of Sicily, the tour retraces the story of the mafia by exploring the socio-cultural context in which the mafia formed and developed and by visiting the symbolic places connected to the successes of the antimafia movement.[63]

Once students settle in, De Guilmi offers testimony to Dolci's mission and the non-violent education and grassroots planning that involved thousands of people in hunger strikes, marches, a public radio station, and public accusations of the local mafia and nepotistic system. Known throughout the world as the "Sicilian Gandhi" for his approaches to non-violent work to overcome violence and poverty in post-war Sicily, Dolci was trained as an engineer and an architect in Switzerland. After World War II, at age 26, Dolci decided to take time off from a professional career and work in southern Italy with a priest, Don Zeno Saltini. Saltini had recently opened an orphanage for three thousand abandoned children in the location of a former concentration camp near Modena. Unemployment, hunger, illiteracy, and lack of sanitation, water, and electricity were prevalent throughout western Sicily, and the mafia maintained control over just about every aspect of civic life. Students come to understand the vital role this rural area of Sicily has played and continues to play in antimafia activism.

Introducing himself as "one of Dolci's most trustworthy friends, the only one of Danilo's friends who remained here," De Guilmi explains to students the concept of the reverse strike: "Hundreds and hundreds of farmers and builders with shovels and pickaxes went to fix the roads for free." As students walk the roadway the people built during the reverse strike of 1955, Dolci's colleague describes the social and political conditions that provoked two hundred jobless citizens in Partinico to begin rebuilding the road that had been destroyed by an overflow of rainwater, a road the government had refused to fix. "A reverse strike," he explains, "is both constructive and resistant at the same time." The citizens were met with almost four hundred police officers and *carabinieri* (military police), heavily armed with tear gas and clubs, who ordered the men to stop working. The men responded, "You have no authorization – it's occupation of public land." Dolci, joined by Carlo Zanini, Salvatore Termini, Ciccio Abbate, and Ignazio Speciale, spoke with authorities and the men were then arrested.[64] Later, when Dolci accused the government of collusion with the mafia, he was arrested and imprisoned for libel. He responded by broadcasting his views on a private radio station, which was promptly shut down. Eventually, because of his tireless campaigning, dams were built, bringing irrigation, energy, and new jobs to the region. Dolci negotiated with the government to bring new industry from the north, and he continued to criticize the mafia, again being threatened with prison and death. It is a source of wonder to local people that the mafia never seriously retaliated against Dolci; the speculation was that he was so popular that the mafia feared mass reprisal.

Students' encounters with antimafia history, this history's protagonists, as well as a repertoire of antimafia non-violent strategies demonstrate the ways in which Addiopizzo Travel re-signifies a half-spoken history of dissent using narrative strategies associated with societies in and of transition. Walter Benjamin might describe the public pedagogy of Addiopizzo as part of the work of the "angelic historian," who, in Benjamin's words, "regards it as his task to brush history against the grain."[65] The view of the angelic historian is to illuminate the excess in history, that is, all that resists representation, all that resists being incorporated into a homogenous national narrative that is driven by a process that "piles wreckage upon wreckage."[66] The persona of Benjamin's "angelic historian" offers educators a powerful lesson about teaching in the midst of catastrophes that undermine democracy and potentially give rise to brutal forms of authoritarianism. To teach against the grain of history is both to render a historical narrative and to make apparent the events that cannot be written or spoken. To brush against the grain of history is to reveal alternative, often overlooked sides of an apparently stable history and to revive lost, ignored, and faded voices that extend well beyond the classroom walls. As the heirs to a history not of their own making, Addiopizzo works in the tradition of a long history of antimafia dissent, a tradition that values solidarity and a turn not away from but towards the world.

Conclusion

Addiopizzo and Addiopizzo Travel offer public pedagogy scholars a rich, living archive of material for understanding the educational experiences people have outside school but that are too infrequently studied by educational scholars. Grounded in the principle of natality, and distinguished by rhetorical practices of re-symbolization, the public pedagogy of remembrance practised by members of Addiopizzo broaches critical areas of inquiry for considering the extent to which their anti-extortion methods and narrative tactics substantially cultivate an antimafia culture that has the capacity to impact mafia violence. In fact, one of the central issues that emerge among critics of Addiopizzo is that despite its anti-extortion campaigns, the mafia continues to be financially lucrative and powerful, and penetrates all levels of public and private life in Italy as well as outside the country's borders. Where, then, can we locate the material transformative potential in their public pedagogy of remembrance?

Members of Addiopizzo are careful to distinguish their public pedagogy as a project of cultural renewal and collective memory formation. In this sense their work addresses the social phenomenon of the mafia while recognizing the limited impact their work can have on the criminal activity of the Cosa Nostra. Given the international scope of the mafia, as well as its skill at penetrating legal and illegal enterprises, it would be naive, as noted earlier, to conclude that an organization such as Addiopizzo can alone destabilize mafia criminality. To fully assess the impact that Addiopizzo has on mafia activity, it is crucial to understand that the mafia is a social and not only a criminal phenomenon. The work, of Addiopizzo – both its anti-extortion campaigns and its study tours – engage in projects of social renewal that open up spaces of possibility in relation to a traumatic past that persists in the present by using narrative to negotiate traumatic injury and in turn to restore, rather than to forget, a history of resistance against the Cosa Nostra, one that the Cosa Nostra, as with so many totalitarian regimes, would prefer be obliterated. The focus on narratives of resistance and victimization make an important contribution to understanding how societies in transition use narratives to mourn and to work through traumatic injury. Storytelling, or the weaving of a narrative out of the actions and commitments of individuals, is in part constitutive of the meaning of their lives, and, given the distance from the events they describe, narratives can provide further insight into the motives and values of history's protagonists. This is why Arendt placed such a strong emphasis on the power of storytelling. She believed that remembrance and the retelling of actions as stories could save the lives and actions of social actors from the oblivion of historical forgetfulness. The political function of artists and historians, and I would add educators, is to preserve the memory of past actions and to make them a source of insight for the future. Through acts of story-taking and storytelling, Addiopizzo takes up the pedagogical impulse of transitional justice by creating open spaces where organized remembrance can take place.

The use of storytelling as a medium for cultural renewal is a significant undertaking. In closing this chapter I would like to underscore the vital importance natality plays in conceptualizing story-taking and storytelling projects as works of mourning. To turn towards the world in solidarity with others with the intention of engaging in and sustaining memories of resistance and victimization, particularly those that are obscured under the category of state secret, challenges the many ways in which the mafia and the state work to undermine possibilities for justice. Relevant here are, for example, the Massacre of Portella della Ginestra (1947), the death of activist Giuseppe Impastato (1978), and the murder of journalist Mario Francese (1979), cases we turn to in upcoming chapters and that figure in the public pedagogy of Addiopizzo. Addiopizzo's emphasis on what Jan Assmann describes as "counter memory" challenges official, national narratives that aim at establishing common ground and a unified national identity. Counter memory "explicitly contradicts another memory. You remember it this way, but I remember it differently because I remember what you have forgotten."[67] Unlike the repetitive, idealized, melancholic narratives appended to the Falcone Tree and posted on Francesca Morvillo's Facebook page, the narrative tactics of Addiopizzo take on the qualities of a mourning that remembers a difficult past silenced by normative memory formation and that refuses consolation or triumphant fictions. By turning to the world in an effort to address a history of catastrophic loss not of their own making, Addiopizzo and its public pedagogy of remembrance invites participants to dwell together in grief and reminds us of our vulnerability to suffering and to death and the value of collective life and forged solidarity in sorrow. In this sense Addiopizzo offers educators insights into the way in which a death-affirming politics of loss can be replaced with a life-affirming politics of natal pleasure that has the potential to create the conditions of possibility for new beginnings and requires resilience and the capacity to endure the failure that is inherent in human finitude.

The anti-extortion campaigns that Addiopizzo organizes on behalf of victims of mafia extortion are inspired by a life-affirming politics of natal pleasure as well. However, the actions associated with natality produce effects, according to Arendt, that are limitless and ultimately uncontrollable.[68] The collective opposition taken up with local and state antimafia authorities to pursue reparation for material and psychic trauma works to eradicate the fear among victims that the mafia uses to ensure their silence and cooperation. The work of pursuing retributions for harm from extortion, while not enough in itself to eradicate the Cosa Nostra, does in fact increase the profits of business owners and offers them the prerogative to choose their own vendors and be less vulnerable to relying on cheaper, illegal labour. As a generation that came of age when the island of Sicily witnessed one violent assassination after another of prosecutors, police, children, innocent bystanders, and mafiosi alike, this young group of activists – "children of the massacre" – takes symbolic and physical action to reject the mafia's sovereignty over their area.[69] At this writing in January 2016, over eight hundred businesses had joined Addiopizzo, each displaying a sticker on its door that indicates it refuses to pay extortion fees or protection tax. Add to this the fact that over 10 thousand residents of Palermo refuse to shop or eat where extortion fees are paid. These figures stand as a testimony to the credibility that Addiopizzo has developed since its first campaign in 2005.

Its label indeed symbolizes a commitment to standards of legality and assures consumers that they are taking part in socially responsible services. Following Cavarero, I would like to end this chapter by suggesting that while Addiopizzo does indeed successfully participate on several levels in educating citizens and residents of Sicily to be critical consumers, their public pedagogy of remembrance promotes a different cultural formation, one that manifests a desire for new beginnings by composing narratives of non-violent dissent to revive Arendt's question about who we are, as human beings, and to shift from a culture suffused with death to a culture that marshals the life drive.

Chapter Four

On the Road to a New Corleone:
Digital Screen Cultures and Citizen Writers

The duty of memory is the duty to do justice, through memories, to an other than the self.

– Paul Ricoeur, *Memory, History, Forgetting*

The suggestion that bringing in more magistrates and police will solve the problem of the Mafia is totally inadequate. If the Mafia pays you, finds and keeps you in work, helps you win contracts, get promotions or run your business, then you won't reject it. The solution to the problem of the Mafia is to make the state work.

– Paolo Borsellino, in *The Antimafia: Italy's Fight against Organized Crime*

Introduction

What is often called the Great Mafia War of 1978–92 is also known in Italian as *la mattanza* (Italian for "slaughter"), a term taken from the fishing industry. *La mattanza* refers to the annual ritual of brutally harpooning bluefish tuna, a practice Roberto Rossellini poignantly portrays in his 1950 film *Stromboli*.[1] Historian John Dickie offers this reference in the opening to his discussion of the Cosa Nostra's rise to power in the narcotics industry.[2]

By 1981 *la mattanza* was under the cruel and ambitious leadership of Luciano Leggio. Corleone, established as the central hub for the heroin industry between Asia and the United States, also became the headquarters for the Cosa Nostra's domestic marketing of heroin. Within the next decade, Italy's hardcore addict population reached epidemic proportions – exceeding two hundred thousand. As police and prosecutors worked to break the hold of the Cosa Nostra, they were murdered with increasing savagery and regularity. The regime of assassinations, habits of clientelism, extortion, and vote-rigging of

Italy's major post-war political party, the Christian Democrats, combined to create a pervasive mistrust of the state and its representatives. David Williams's astute observations of Palermo (about a 50-minute drive from Corleone by car) hold for Corleone as well, where, in Williams's words, people feel "a deep-seated fatalism and exhausted pessimism ... it seems traumatized, dismembered, weighed down by unresolved grieving ... its baroque shadow life fuelled by the conspiratorial suspicion and paranoia of dietrologia, a melancholic obsession with 'what lies behind' (dietro): behind surface appearances, received 'truths,' language, silence, history; behind cover-ups and 'walls' of all kinds."[3] Novelist Mario Puzo adapted the name of Corleone for his famous fictional crime family in *The Godfather*. Francis Ford Coppola perpetuated an image of Corleone as a corrupt and primitive village with his Godfather Trilogy.[4]

Today, however, the Cosa Nostra no longer holds Corleone firmly in its grip, and *Godfather* tours are offensive to the Corleonesi. Since 2002 activists, artists, educators, and politicians have worked to create new images of Corleone, once considered the "rural capital of the mafia." The contemporary collective project emerged from initial protests against the Afghanistan war and the desire among residents to repair Corleone's precarious infrastructure. The activism in Corleone inspired a form of spatial and cultural politics that in turn spawned unanticipated civic participation in the struggle to reclaim Corleone from the Cosa Nostra, as well as from stereotypic images that detract from Corleone's more complex antimafia history. Using the slogan "Another Corleone, Another Sicily," activists began to organize a lengthy cycle of oppositional actions that included imaginative interventions, such as what they describe as "ethical tours of Corleone," which is part of a larger project of responsible tourism that ushers visitors on tours of vineyards developed on mafia confiscated property, visits to cafes and restaurants that refuse to pay extortion fees (the *pizzo*), strolls through the renamed Piazza Falcone-Borsellino, as well as visits to the Laboratory of Legality and the International Center for Documentation on the Mafia. These "affective spaces" work to reclaim exiled histories of agrarian dissent against the mafia and to establish a sense of dignity and what antimafia activists and educators describe as *legalità* despite the persistence of mafia terrorism.[5]

Resonating with the global Occupy Movement's pursuit of direct democracy, spatial justice, and representative politics, the activism in Corleone also turned – and continues to turn – to a half-spoken history of agrarian protests that are missing from mainstream culture and education textbooks. This chapter extends the study of collective resistance against mafia violence through an inquiry into the work of citizen journalists in Corleone. I argue that the case of Corleone Dialogos, a digitally networked grassroots news association, contributes to illuminating principles of collective non-violent resistance that should inform education's understanding of public pedagogy and transitional justice. The citizen journalism practised at Corleone Dialogos provokes difficult questions about a public pedagogy that uses citizen journalism as a medium to generate collective memories of dissent and inspire non-violent action against mafia activity in transitional times.

The chapter situates the work of Corleone Dialogos and citizen journalists Giuseppe Crapisi, Cosimo Lo Sciuto, Maria Rosa Piranio, Annalisa Grizzaffi, and Mario Mattone in the larger context of the debates surrounding citizen journalism and places in relief the central principles guiding their work writing in a society in transition: (1) a commitment to what Michael Hardt and Antonio Negri describe as "the field of the commons," made evident in their reportage of the rich but little-known tangible and intangible cultural heritage of Corleone; (2) the use of citizen journalism to break the code of silence, *omertà*, and restore and sustain solidarity and public life; and (3) the commemoration of a history of dissent against the mafia that politicizes the social field and works to create new forms of solidarity and visions of justice by generating what Michael Rothberg conceptualizes as "multidirectional memory," an approach to understanding collective memory in transitional societies.[6] The lens of multidirectional memory has the potential to illuminate exiled histories of antimafia protest that inform the contemporary moment, and offers insight into the messy contingencies that characterize the history of the mafia and antimafia in rural western Sicily. These principles combine to shape an understanding of what Roger Simon described in *A Pedagogy of Witnessing: Curatorial Practice and the Pursuit of Social Justice* as a public pedagogy of ethical remembrance.[7] The insights provided in this chapter emerge in the tension between my research in Corleone and theoretical reflection. In the final section of this chapter, I consider the promise and the limits these principles hold for shaping an antimafia public pedagogy dedicated to social and cultural renewal in Sicily.

Defining Citizen Journalism

The practices characterizing Corleone Dialogos closely reflect, as described by Chris Atton in his study of citizen journalism, the "practices of decentralized, directly democratic, self-managed and reflexive networks of 'everyday life and solidarity' that Alberto Melucci finds at the heart of social movement activity."[8] Atton's analysis of citizen journalism is theoretically informed by Walter Benjamin's claim[9] that effective political propaganda must move beyond reproducing radical or revolutionary content to critically realigning the methods of production and rethinking what it means to be a media producer today.[10] The intellectual legacy and the social and financial resources used to support

Corleone Dialogos are provided by *Libera/Libera Informazione*, a digitally networked news organization founded in 2007 by Roberto Morrione, an RAI award-winning investigative journalist who also founded the network Allnews and Rainews. *Libera Informazione* provides news about legality and antimafia activity through a digitally networked agency that trains young editors, citizens, residents, and students to create decentralized, self-managed reports on the mafia and antimafia movements – *"informazione per legalità e contro le mafie."*[11] Morrione's vision was to offer geographically dispersed participants opportunities to debate issues and events, and to collaborate on global activist initiatives. Since its inception, Morrione's project has expanded to include independent transmedia projects, such as Corleone Dialogos. These projects extend the education of participants – writers and readers alike – and offer them opportunities to actively participate in reshaping their identities as Sicilians, as well as their social and cultural environment, despite the persistence of mafia-related crime.

The transmedia narratives composed by Corleone Dialogos typically take and tell stories across multiple media platforms with a focus on providing information to ordinary people about antimafia social movements and social cooperatives. In addition to publishing a monthly newspaper (*Oltre il muroi*, meaning "Beyond the Wall"[12]), Corleone Dialogos uses social networking systems, including Facebook, Twitter, blogs, flickr, YouTube, and texts sent to mobile phones. Corleone Dialogos is dedicated, as its mission statement says, to changing "the culture of our land" and to creating "the basis for new social and economic development."[13]

In a study of *Libera Informazione*'s use of web-based media to create counter-public spaces, Baris Cayli finds that members of organizations such as Corleone Dialogos use social media to exercise their commitment to democratic ideals of access, inclusion, deliberation, and participation in projects directed towards and engaged in social renewal. Collectives associated with *Libera Informazione*, argues Cayli, successfully renew contemporary culture through media channels in the public sphere by informing communities at the local and national levels and raising consciousness about the criminal-political nexus and activities of mafia groups. The story of *Libera Informazione*, concludes Cayli, is one of public engagement and participatory, reformist culture that challenges conventional journalism by introducing a counter-public sphere that exists apart from profit. Moreover, because journalists, when acting alone, continue to experience threats when exposing mafia activity, *Libera Informazione* offers protection through solidarity with others.[14]

The news reported by Corleone Dialogos includes a 2013 apology issued by the mayor of Corleone, Lea Savona, to victims of the mafia. In her apology

Savona announced that Corleone no longer belongs to the mafia and urged those who were involved with Cosa Nostra to turn themselves in. Also posted were an article announcing a presentation by filmmaker Alberto Castiglione about his documentary film *For That Breath of Freedom* (*quel soffio di libertà*), a film about Sicilian social movement organizer Bernardino Verro; the public announcement – and defiance of the law of silence *omertà* – among entrepreneurs in Corleone to refuse to pay extortion fees to the mafia; and the subsequent arrest of mafia members. Posted alongside news about mafia crime and resistance are articles about agriculture, crises in waste management, climate change, landslides in Corleone, labour disputes, and social gatherings that bring together activists throughout Italy to celebrate what they describe as "the lands of Corleone" by taking part in mountain biking expeditions. Add to this news items about conferences on migration and the rights of LGBT (lesbian, gay, bisexual, and transgender) residents.

Using what Dan Gillmor describes as "grassroots or open source journalism," the members of Corleone Dialogos are amateurs who produce material with less editing and less rigour than professional journalists.[15] While they sometimes select from, post, and riff off news from sources such as the BBC and *Corriere del Mezzogiorno*, this selection process is another way in which they insert themselves into the current news production process as curators of collective memory formation. As global media becomes increasingly privatized (since 1994, Silvio Berlusconi's media empire has taken a firm hold of Italian media systems), citizen journalists disrupt media monopolies and take on more significant roles in an informed citizenry, in part by creating a greater space in the media for news, policies, and information regarding the histories of antimafia non-violent dissent, mafia activity, antimafia legislation, cultural events, and memorial gatherings that commemorate Sicily's "martyrs of justice."

While scholars such as Bowman, Willis, Cayli, and Carr recognize citizen journalism as a form of participatory media culture, civic emancipation, and an emerging new humanism, other journalists, scholars, and citizens see it as little more than "opening the floodgates to unverified, de-professionalized gossip," and confusing front-line for arm-chair reporting. Since the Arab Spring, marked by its live tweeters detailing the protests and cameraphone videographers documenting violence, critics of citizen journalism have cautioned against romanticizing this form of newsmaking.[16]

Political theorist Jodi Dean raises serious concerns about the impact that any social networking project can have on social change. Given that global, capitalist communication networks are unavoidably and inextricably entwined with what Dean describes as the practice of communicative capitalism, their social impact, argues Dean, is substantially limited. "Just as industrial capitalism relied on the exploitation of labor," observes Dean, "so does communicative capitalism rely on the exploitation of communication."[17] Dean is sceptical of the extent to which social networking systems that create a profit for the few and produce severe economic inequality for the many can work to democratize social movements. Fantasies of activity and participation drive communicative capitalism and the belief, according to Dean, that "the values heralded as central to democracy take material form in networked communications ... ideals of access, inclusion, discussion, and participation come to be realized in and through expansions, intensifications and interconnections of global telecommunications."[18] In the process of using ever-more-innovative upgrades to creating a common public sphere for deliberation and open participation, social networking systems, such as Facebook and Twitter, not only fail to provide democratic ownership of their platforms but also, as Dean observes, create an ersatz sense of political engagement. "Busy people can think they are active," observes Dean:

> The technology will act for them, alleviating their guilt while assuring them that nothing will change too much ... By sending an e-mail, signing a petition, responding to an article on a blog, people can feel political. And that feeling feeds communicative capitalism insofar as it leaves behind the time-consuming, incremental and risky efforts of politics ... It is a refusal to take a stand, to venture into the dangerous terrain of politicization.[19]

The "low-risk" political involvement Dean describes is also critiqued by Malcolm Gladwell and Evgeny Morozov, both of whom speak to "slacktivism" as a form of what Morozov describes as "feel-good online activism that has zero political or social impact."[20] Slacktivism gives those who participate in "slacktivist" campaigns an illusion of having a meaningful impact on the world without demanding anything more than joining a Facebook group. Morozov characterizes online activist activity as ideal for what he describes as a lazy generation. "Why bother," he asks, "with sit-ins and the risk of arrest, police brutality, or torture if one can be as loud campaigning in the virtual space?"[21]

Many of the critiques of digital media, including Gladwell's and Morozov's concerns about slacktivism, assume a traditional practice of citizenship modelled on the image of the dutiful citizen engaged in traditional forms of political participation, such as voting and face-to-face protests. More contemporary concepts of citizenship highlight civic action through community work, unconventional political action, and digitally mediated forms of political expression. Contemporary concepts of citizenship also take into account the way in which social media is used to mediate acts of social renewal.

Is it possible to use social networking to create a political sphere of communication that has emancipatory potential for cultural and social renewal given its ties to the exploitation of labour and neo-liberal markets? Do the social networking practices associated with the work of Corleone Dialogos significantly affect public consciousness about mafia violence and serve the commons? Or does Corleone Dialogos's use of social networking systems serve as a clear case of the insidious ways in which antimafia digital platforms promote a kind of slacktivism and actually displace attention from the profound inequalities produced and amplified by global financial networks, many of which are tethered to mafia profit and prosperity?

The following section considers the ways in which citizen journalists at Corleone Dialogos use social networking to extend the memories of an agrarian history of antimafia protest to contemporary antimafia activism. Tracing their approach to public pedagogy to a theory of the commons that resonates with the scholarship of Hardt and Negri, I argue that the citizen journalists at Corleone Dialogos present a compelling challenge to claims made by sceptics of citizen journalism that new media practices, such as blogging, posting, and Facebooking, function to neglect organization and revolt. Corleone Dialogos's commitment to the commons and its active, physical, political engagement in cultural renewal casts its use of social media and citizen journalism in public pedagogical terms that have significant educational import. How are collective histories of victimization remembered in transitional societies? Rothberg's concept of "multidirectional memory" offers a lens through which to consider a series of important questions: Does the remembrance of one collective history, asks Rothberg, "erase others from view?"[22] When collective memories, for example, of mafia brutality, emerge alongside memories of multiple traumatic pasts tied to economic devastation and gender violence, must a competition of victims ensue?[23] Must collective memory of state-sanctioned mafia violence be understood as a part of a history, a culture, and an identity that combines to form, in W.E.B. Du Bois's terms "a separate and unique thing" to establish efficacy? Following Du Bois, Rothberg sets out to comprehend the danger inherent in making claims about the uniqueness of a trauma, even when grounded in history, given that such claims potentially render narratives that are depoliticized and ahistorical. In my estimation, the citizen journalism of Corleone Dialogos has the potential to challenge a model of competitive memory by locating, in Rothberg's words, "competition within a larger spiral of memory discourse in which even hostile invocations of memory can provide vehicles for further, countervailing commemorative acts ... and cut across and bind together diverse spatial, temporal and cultural sites."[24] This approach to composing transitional narratives holds promise for creating complex acts of solidarity in which historical memory serves as a means through which to create new communal and political identities and recognizes that all memory opens up and ropes off communication with the past.[25]

Corleone Dialogos's Facebook page and social media activity mix to form an archive that holds the multidirectional flows of influence, silences, anxieties, and marginalized memories that collective memory provokes. The abundant cross-referencing between legacies of mafia corruption and agrarian dissent against the mafia are too often effaced or rendered insignificant in part by presenting Sicily as Italy's wound, an unlovable region traumatized, as writer George Scialabba aptly points out in his introduction to Leonardo Sciascia's crime novel *The Day of the Owl*, by an apparent "unbroken history of rule by irresponsible elites – landowners, the Church, and the Bourbon monarchy." Collectively, argues Scialabba, they left the island "without civil society or the virtues it makes possible: no solidarity, no trust, no enterprise, no public spirit, not even simple honesty."[26] The evidence that counters these claims is available, but it requires a form of comparative thinking called forth by a multidirectional memory that persistently renews its commitment to justice and the "field of the commons."

Heritage Sites, Multidirectional Memory, and the Field of the Commons

The citizen-driven news movements exemplified by Corleone Dialogos are committed to what Hardt and Negri describe as the "field of the commons."[27] They use this term to describe the production and liberation of a diverse multitude, to make suspect or illegitimate claims to private property, and to challenge the continual movement throughout the modern period to privatize land, water, air, and space. According to Hardt and Negri, the commons includes not only the air, water, and fruits of the soil that all humanity has inherited, is entitled to, and should share, but also the production of languages, knowledge, information, emotional, cultural, and social life safe from the threat of coercion.[28] Citizen writers at Corleone Dialogos share an abiding concern with the multitude, or the working poor, as well as a belief in the labouring class to create an alternative world apart from that given by capital. For the members of Corleone Dialogos, this commitment to the commons includes developing and expanding resources for citizens and residents of Italy, not only to free society from the grip of mafia corruption but also to support those who are marginalized in society because of poor health, unemployment, underemployment, restricted citizenship, and disabilities. By reporting, for example, on public services, women's public protests against sexual harassment,[29] and workshops for citizen journalists conducted by professional Sicilian journalists on transparency in news production, as well as mafia and antimafia activities, Corleone Dialogos works against the privatization of media and the limiting of what counts as newsworthy.

One of many examples of Corleone Dialogos's commitment to "the field of the commons" includes using enriched multimedia content (music, videos, photographs, etc.) to compose what it describes as "narrative paths" that retrace the history of Corleone through the actions of citizens and place in relief the "rich but still little known tangible and intangible cultural heritage" of their province. Attached to their reportage are, as I noted earlier, a series of touring projects. Select passages from a tour of what the citizen journalists at Corleone Dialogos describe as "the other Corleone," follow:

> The route starts in the Villa Comunale, in Piazza Falcone-Borsellino, in front of the bust of Bernardino Verro, the first socialist mayor of Corleone ... Past the Piazza Falcone-Borsellino, you will arrive in Via S. Leonardo, the site of the kidnapping of unionist Placido Rizzotto, killed in 1948 ... On the left of Via B. Boar, there is the headquarters of the Agricultural Cooperative Union of 1903 ... There will be a visit to the Piazza Garibaldi, where there is the bust of Placido Rizzotto, in order to remember the peasant movement of the occupations of land reform ... The tour continues with a visit to the Borgata Ficuzza, full of charm and natural interest and significant from the point of view of history ... We will arrive at the headquarters of Arci "Corleone Dialogos," and here we will present to you activities of the association, among them our bimonthly information about Corleone, and documentaries screened about the mafia.[30]

This ethical tour of Corleone is similar to the tours offered by Addiopizzo Travel (see Chapter 3). What distinguishes this work, however, is the way in which Corleone Dialogos uses ethical tourism to physically extend their journalism to what the members designate as the field of marginalized traditions, intellectual legacies, and heritage sites that challenge national stories and stereotypes of Corleone that the president of Corleone Dialogos, Cosimo Lo Sciuto, describes as "shameful." "What are the first words that come to mind," he asks me, "when I say the word *Corleone*?" "Inevitably," Lo Sciuto explains, "people say things like, *The Godfather*, Vito Corleone, Totò Riina, mobsters and corruption. It is as if there is nothing dignified about where we live. It is as if our history is nothing but shameful."[31] A sense of shame is consistently referenced in the citizen writing at Corleone Dialogos and in conversation with antimafia activists.[32] Different from grief, shame involves evaluative, reflexive, and social dimensions. "It is an emotion," notes Roger Simon, "rooted in critical judgments and their consequent feelings of inadequacy and unworthiness. Central

... is the realization of intense feelings of disgrace not only in regard to oneself, but also in regard to previously idealized particular assemblies and collectivities within which one is felt to be implicated."[33] In ways akin to the antimafia activists at Addiopizzo and Addiopizzo Travel, the citizen journalists at Corleone Dialogos have inherited a past not of their own making, a past felt as deficient and a mark of failure, a past they feel both implicated in and determined to recast.

The bust of Placido Rizzotto, the Piazza Garibaldi, the renamed Piazza Falcone-Borsellino, and the headquarters for the Agricultural Cooperative Union of 1903 stand as common possessions that summon up disputes and discords as much as consensus about a rural agrarian history of non-violent dissent against the mafia that extends to today. These tours – all given by volunteers – unfold against profit and stand apart from processes of commodification and reification that are enclosed by capitalist entrepreneurs. In this sense, Corleone Dialogos situates its reportage and cultural initiatives within the context of a set of social and cultural practices that investigate and restructure the conditions possible for shared social life.[34] The initiatives emerge as a response to the way in which the cultural and social life in Corleone has been appropriated by both the mafia and state-sanctioned corruption. This approach to the commons fulfils social needs by creating what P. Alonso Gonzalez describes as "social networks of mutual aid, solidarity, and the practices of human exchange that are not reduced to the market form."[35] Set apart from capital, the spaces written about and remembered by Corleone Dialogos stand as the locus of freedom and innovation among communities long silenced by *omertà*.[36] This shift in social life from one of silence to one of collective deliberation about memory formation is best understood in terms described by Rothberg as a "dialogical exchange between memory traditions" that keeps open the potential for a more just future of memory.[37]

Exactly what history of dissent is summoned by this walking tour through Corleone and the narratives activists write and reference as citizen journalists? To what extent does their work open the social field for more inclusive storytelling and story-taking about the legacies of dissent, violence, victimization, and a cooperativist history that dates back to the *Fasci Siciliani dei Lavoratori* (Sicilian Workers Leagues) of the 1890s peasant movement?[38]

Attention to the subtle historical points of reference made by the citizen journalists' campaign against the mafia illuminates the competing meanings, practices, and memories of the antimafia movements.[39] Tracing the biographical figures and sites of protest most often referenced in contemporary antimafia narratives – the 1947 massacre at Portella della Ginestra, the 1948 murder of Corleone's trade union leader, Placido Rizzotto, assassinated by mafia boss Luciano Leggio, and the 1978 assassination of political activist Giuseppe Impastato – leads to the concept and practice of cooperativism indigenous to western Sicily and tied to communalist worker-based agrarian and post-agrarian reform.[40] The link between a history of agrarian dissent against the mafia, mafia entanglements, and contemporary activists' activities emerges more clearly if one notes Corleone Dialogos's citation of Bernardino Verro's influence, including the fact that his portrait is used as the cover photo for its Facebook page. Between 2011 and 2015, over 50 articles were written and posted about Verro by Corleone Dialogos. Each summons memories of his position as the first socialist mayor of Corleone and the founder of the first cooperative *Unione Agricola*. Not only can Verro be read as the father of the new Corleone, but Verro's mafia ties also inflect and complicate antimafia discourse and public pedagogy within a society that continues to simultaneously experience transition and mafia violence.

Half-Spoken Histories of Mafia Entanglements

Western rural Sicily has an impressive history of social agrarian cooperativism that dates back to the 1890s and was revived in 1996 when the state of Italy began to confiscate land and other assets owned by the mafia and redistribute them to local agricultural cooperatives. Cooperativism works as both a trope and a signature practice for the contemporary antimafia movement, although its practice today is quite distinct from its practice during the late nineteenth century and into the 1940s.

In his ethnographic study of the antimafia social cooperatives in Alto Belice, located in the western part of Sicily about 20 kilometres from Corleone, Theodoros Rakopoulos describes the early peasant antimafia cooperativism as a "modular" notion, an idea he borrows from Benedict Anderson's approach to understanding nationalism, nationality, and nation-ness as cultural artefacts.[41] These artefacts come into being within very specific circumstances. Anderson describes them as modular precisely because they have the capacity to be transplanted, to merge and morph, and to take occupancy in a range of social fields within a wide array of political and ideological constellations.[42] "Anderson's account," observes Rakopoulos, "suggests a notion that, in turn, allows portability and distillation in new contexts. Contemporary Sicily, undergoing changes influenced by the ensemble of mobilizations dubbed 'the antimafia movement,' is an ideal site to explore how cooperativism relates to social change."[43] Thus, argues Rakopoulos, cooperativism, as a modular concept, works as an index to how the ideas of nationalism, nationhood, and collective memory formation cohere around the idea and practice of cooperativism within the contemporary Sicilian imaginary. Moreover, the link between cooperativism and a peasant mobilization in Italy that represents the "birth of the antimafia movement" challenges the limited vision of Sicilians as historically passive, lacking a capacity for civic life, backward, and, in the words of Risorgimento writers such as Carlo Cattaneo and Vincenzo Gioberti, clearly "other," impoverished, rude, and for Cattaneo, "a bourgeois nightmare," the spectacular opposite of his native Lombardy.[44]

The commemoration of dissent makes a significant contribution to memory in transitional times given how often memories of dissent are silenced within transitional justice frameworks. The commitment to investigate and report on themes of resistance among residents as well as among artists, journalists, and social entrepreneurs is evident in much of the writing and postings of citizen journalists in Corleone. News about the annual "waves of citizenship, waves of legality" – a commemorative ceremony that marked the murders of Giovanni Falcone, Francesca Morvillo, and their escorts – is ritualistically reported on by Corleone Dialogos (in spring 2015, however, Corleone Dialogos reported on the closing of this ritual). Articles and announcements about the gallery showings of the *pittore sociale* (social portraits) of Sicilian artist Gaetano Porcasi are often featured, as well as reports of newly confiscated property taken from the mafia for the public good. Add to this events such as marathons established in the name of *legalità*.[45]

What is often left as unproblematic within the context of human rights advocacy and truth commission committees working in the name of transitional justice is an implicit assumption, observes Bronwyn Leebaw,

> that in remembering political violence we have a dichotomous choice between avoiding the stories of those who cannot be characterized as passive victims in need of healing, or opening the door to vengeful Furies bent on poisoning the land with their grief and rage. To structure investigations of political violence in accordance with this perceived dichotomy is to condone the forgetting of those who took action in the name of solidarity and change. The stories of those who organize various forms of resistance are complicated for contemporary transitional justice institutions.[46]

Leebaw calls for a public pedagogy that learns from stories of those who resist systematic atrocities in an effort to evaluate the problem of complicity in the past and to establish new forms of solidarity, agency, and community in the future.

Rakopoulos located such stories of dissent in interviews with his oldest informants: men 60 to 80 years old who were sympathetic to the antimafia movement. Rakopoulos found that these men consistently referred to the *Fasci*

Siciliani dei Lavoratori (Sicilian Workers Leagues) of the 1890s peasant move-ment as "the ancestor of antimafia cooperativism."[47] Indeed, this was my expe-rience when interviewing Lo Sciuto about the founding of Corleone Dialogos. Part of the story Lo Sciuto and his colleagues at Corleone Dialogos tell of "an-other Corleone" includes the activism of Verro and the 1893 conference he hosted in Corleone to draft model agrarian contracts for labourers, sharecrop-pers, and tenants with the intent to deliver them to landowners. According to Lo Sciuto, under Verro's leadership, Corleone became the critical centre of the peasant movement and the strike wave. The story taken here rationalizes Verro's involvement with the mafia as strategic while creating a direct link be-tween Verro's project of dissent and the non-violent activism taken up by citi-zen writers at Corleone Dialogos.

In an 1893 article by journalist Adolfo Rossi for the liberal Roman daily *La Tribuna*, Verro is described as "a young man of twenty-seven or twenty-eight." Rossi writes, "He genuinely has a touch of the Arab in his face, his beard, and especially his large bulging eyes."[48] Clearly Rossi's description, inflected with prejudice, indulges his Italian readers in a sentimental image of Sicily that resonates with what literary theorist Nelson Moe describes as a "contrastive structure": a mixture of delight and disgust that begins to infiltrate Italy's own representations of its lower southern half.[49] Rossi describes Verro as a devoted *Fasci* leader, a "bear of a man, energetic and short-tempered."[50]

During his interview with Rossi, Verro responded to the journalist's questions about his leadership and work with the *Fascio* with enthusiasm: "Our Fascio has about six thousand members, men and women … Our women have understood the advantages of a union of poor people so well that they now teach their children socialism."[51] What Rossi did not know is that six months before this interview, Verro had been initiated into the Corleone cosca of the mafia.[52]

The story of Verro is a story Corleone Dialogos takes in an effort to rewrite a history imagined as shameful, to render for themselves a new face for Corleone. Not only is the common possession of Verro's memory used to confirm a com-munal identity that can contain the principles of *legalità*, but Corleone Dialogos also turns to memories of Verro in an effort to recast a community imagined in the words of Pasquale Villari and Leopoldo Franchetti as a cruel and exception-al place, which was "a threat to the political and moral integrity of the nation."[53] On the surface, it appears that Corleone Dialogos reaches for the story of Verro in ways that nations working through the process of transitional justice do. They reach for existing stories, build, in fact, on pre-existing political legacies, to recategorize central events from their past.

Yet the imperfect erasure of Verro's mafia affiliation resurfaces. This affilia-tion returns in the power configurations of the present-day cooperatives. The mafia continues to haunt antimafia efforts, in part by sustaining class divisions and hierarchies within the cooperative structure that separates rural from urban labour and administrative from temporary manual labour, and plays out along complicated gender lines. The discourse of community used to describe the antimafia cooperatives often reproduces, argues Rakopoulos, "unequal relations of power that reflect mafia rhetoric and practice," and potentially jeopardizes internal democratic work relations.[54] The language of a just state, used throughout the antimafia legislation associated with social cooperatives, makes claims to actively intervene in restoring confiscated land from the mafia to the common domain.[55] But how just are social cooperatives that pay very little to co-op worker members and impose a standardized, regulated wage employment framework that threatens their core value of curbing the mafia? Rakopoulos finds that while cooperatives in Sicily are driven by the ideal of equality among all the participants, they are in fact stratified. Although the notions of community and legality potentially enrich the cooperatives' social fabric, these notions also work to undermine their antimafia mission.[56]

The divisions and the tensions within the cooperatives are barely reported on or addressed by the public pedagogy of Corleone Dialogos. I believe these tensions are further obscured by Corleone Dialogos's desire to establish solid, unambivalent identities associated with their mission to pursue a life of *legalità* with particular affective investments.

A closer reading of the citizen journalism at Corleone Dialogos presents a complicated set of pedagogical and ethical questions that turn on the issue of competing memories and how to ethically address mafia infiltration into past and contemporary activist projects. What kind of public pedagogy is adequate for representing and recalling history's overlapping forms of violence?[57] How do we assess the impact of multidirectional memories and their ethical and political effects? Rothberg asks several important questions when assessing the value of multidirectional memory:

> Is the simple recollection of multiple histories indicative of the dynamic, productive interplay I have called multidirectional memory? ... Opening up our powers of comparison requires a framework that takes the wayward currents of collective memory seriously but can also make judgments that distinguish between different articulations of relatedness ... as soon as memory is articulated publicly, questions of representation, ethics, and politics arise.[58]

Verro's memory and the stories taken about his resistance provoke difficult knowledge about the ways in which mafia and antimafia exert their influence on each other within the context of rural and urban politics, and speak to the cross-cutting nature of public memories.[59] The protagonists remembered as martyrs of justice, such as Bernardino Verro, Placido Rizzotto, Giuseppe Impastato, Giovanni Falcone, and Paolo Borsellino, are, observes Rakopoulos, separated from their time's messy historical contingencies to compose a selective genealogy of names cast as figures who were sacrificed in the antimafia movement.[60] What is left out of this archive of collective memory are the complex ways in which contesting the mafia worked to shape the peasant movement as antimafia and in turn contributed to the establishment of contemporary local cooperatives that are structured hierarchically and persist in the exploitation of labour.

The public pedagogy of citizen journalists at Corleone Dialogos that commemorates Bernardino Verro brings traces of past events into the present that work, albeit unwittingly, to create a rupture in historical consciousness, a rupture that makes it possible for certain traces of the past to return in unexpected ways and alter the present and the possibilities for the future.[61] This is precisely the moment Roger Simon marks as a pedagogical and political event that casts remembrance as a form of difficult learning:

> The intention of such learning is not to shock in ways that arrest thought or mobilize a set of psychodynamics that serve to defend against changes to existing relations and practices. Rather this is a learning that seeks affirmation as a radical necessity, as an opening to the recognition and requirement that the present must be rethought ... On such terms, attending to traces of the past brings something new in the current moment in a way that helps remake it ... The past approached on such terms opens the present not merely to gaps in its knowledge, but to a radical reframing of what historical remembrance might accomplish beyond an awareness of things not previously known.[62]

Simon might read the imperfect erasure of Verro's memory as an opportunity to reopen the past to understand the present and future as something that is not yet complete. Drawing on Rothberg, Simon goes on to locate a bond among the past, present, and future to create a nexus in which to consider justice and new forms of action, and to establish, in Simon's words, a "singular sense of responsibility in and for the unfinished state of the present and its possible forms of futurity."[63] Verro's memory, called forth in an effort to foster a deeply felt understanding of the past, submits to a memorializing impulse that depends a good deal on the dynamics of identification with a heroic figure who apparently triumphs over mafia corruption and sacrifices his life in the name of justice and legality. The story taken here includes recognizable themes and comes close to foreclosing, as I noted earlier, on the "otherness" Ricoeur references in the epigraph to this chapter: "Duty to memory is the duty to do justice, through memories, to an other than the self."[64] By simplifying Verro's complicated history of mafia involvement, his memory becomes assimilated into an archive of triumphant narratives that keeps his memory at a comfortable distance from insights that might actually implicate our complicity in sustaining relations of violence, corruption, and oppression.[65] Remembrance alone, Simon reminds us, is not the secret of redemption.[66] Simon argues, and I agree, that a public pedagogy of remembrance that pursues justice must move beyond affective attachments; it must reconsider how justice is framed. It might begin with a set of guiding questions that complicate models of justice: Who is most fully recognized and fully represented within the antimafia's public memory? Who is counted as a subject of justice? What form does justice take and under what jurisdiction will justice be adjudicated? While Corleone Dialogos's citizen journalism creates a political sphere of communication that has emancipatory potential for cultural and social renewal, particularly within the context of a society in transition, it simultaneously remains uncritically identified with heroic narratives that consolidate the martyr status of little-known antimafia activists and glosses over the ways in which mafia and antimafia activities exert their influence on each other. These imperfect erasures are not due, I believe, to communicative capitalism's proclivity to depoliticize. Rather, I want to suggest that the mafia exerts a strange and haunting influence on antimafia public pedagogies that is made manifest in the exclusion of memories of complicity in the citizen journalism of Corleone Dialogos. Strangely enough, these exclusions sustain a normative order of historical memory that potentially cultivates a neat and tidy divide between mafia and antimafia histories and present-day activism. What would it mean for antimafia pedagogies to revisit and rewrite hegemonic sites of memory that collapse into what Deborah Puccio-Den describes as the antimafia religion, as discussed in chapters 1 and 2?[67] The concept of multidirectional memory offers a means through which to begin approaching this work precisely because it is contingent on recognizing the cross-cutting nature of public memories.[68] The view I advocate is one that more fully politicizes the partial and lost memories of complicities through memory work and political deliberation that sustains a critical relationship with existing norms for civility and justice.

Conclusion

To expand studies of the online spaces where antimafia protests take place and to engage the debates about what counts as civic engagement in the context of antimafia activity, my goal in this chapter has been to first provide an analysis of the citizen writer in Sicily. I explored the extent to which oppositional social groups, such as Corleone Dialogos, use media practices to rewrite the public articulation of collective memory. Not only do the citizen journalists at Corleone Dialogos use writing to insert themselves into the historical record as story-takers and curators of critical memory formation, but they also challenge claims made by critics of social media that new media practices, such as Facebooking and blogging, function to neglect organization and dissent.

Yet while citizen journalists at Corleone Dialogos present a clear case of what Baris Cayli describes as "public engagement and participatory reformist culture," they also present a clear case of antimafia activists' proclivity to compose a select genealogy of names that represent an unambivalent, unified antimafia identity.[69] This proclivity was also made evident in the analysis of the Falcone Tree and Francesca Morvillo's Facebook page, where proper names are turned into names-symbols that obscure the complex, ambivalent, competing loyalties, beliefs, emotional ties, and inner conflict experienced in the pursuit of transforming mafia territories into what Robin Pickering-Iazzi describes as "geographies of justice, constituted by civil rights and responsibilities."[70] My concern about an unambivalent antimafia identity tied to heroic, martyred figures is shared not only by scholars such as Pickering-Iazzi but also by Deborah Puccio-Den, Amy Boylan, Dana Renga, and Theodoros Rakopoulos. To memorialize singular figures as exceptions overshadows the ways in which they worked in solidarity with others, and, argues Pickering-Iazzi in her study of Rita Atria, a young woman who served as state's witness against the mafia, "obscure the unspectacular, yet meaningful, cultural practices of legality in daily living."[71]

Attention to the complexity of multidirectional memories that veer away from what Rothberg describes as "competitive memory" holds the promise to inspire more capacious transitional justice narratives of collective memory formation that question attachments to unified heroic figures and triumphant narratives.[72] What might such extensive, multidirectional narratives look like and how might they work to more fully politicize lost or partial memories of complicity within the antimafia imaginary?

For Pickering-Iazzi, these narratives would shift attention from abstract or universal figures of justice to what she describes as "distinctive ... un-reproducible expressions of subjectivity" that would generate varied understandings of testimonies in mafia studies.[73] Drawing on Cavarero's vocal phenomenology of uniqueness, Pickering-Iazzi proposes that narratives of collective memory value the "embodied singularity of each person, not as essence or abstract entity but as a social subject with a face and a name, who is at once multiply located in relation to such terms of identity as sex and gender, race, generation, and socio-economic class, yet also lives a life uniquely his or her own, bearing responsibility for it."[74] This would mean, for example, that stories not be subsumed under terms, argues Pickering-Iazzi, such as *pentito, martyr of justice, mafioso*, or *mafia woman*, to offer a few examples of terms that silence the singularity of the person who speaks. While recognizing that all narratives are indeed constructions, such an approach has the potential to represent the specific features of subjectivity and to offer more nuanced engagements with projects tied to legality and illegality.[75]

Rothberg might argue that in valuing the "embodied singularity" of the person who speaks, a public pedagogy of remembrance would also work to recognize multidirectional memory and the need for more memory of violent histories, not less. A public pedagogy of remembrance would do well to recognize that apparently distinct histories – for example, of slavery and colonialism – are not easily separated. Such is the case with histories, as illustrated by the figure of Bernardino Verro, legality and illegality, and mafia and antimafia. Bringing together histories that are ordinarily kept separate from one another would be a generative step towards composing more capacious narratives that have the potential to sustain a critical relationship with existing norms for civility and justice. Following Rothberg, I believe this calls for a critical genealogy of memory discourses. Such a genealogy might include critical readings of citizen journalism, moral solidarity with victims of diverse injustices tied to mafia crime, including victims with liminal status within mafia organizations, such as women and children, who, as Renga points out, have never committed an illegal act yet are bound to their clan and endure daily precarity. Finally, a pedagogy of remembrance that incorporates multidirectional memory would include an ethics of comparison that coordinates the asymmetrical claims of victims rather than pitting victims of mafia violence against one another in a logic of competition. Such an ethic would work towards increasing public remembrance, in part by showing how the awareness of an apparently unrelated event can actually increase attentiveness to other, remotely related events. This would include attention to what Rothberg describes as transcultural memory – an important project for a public pedagogy of remembrance to consider if it hopes to more fully capture the ways in which mafia criminality operates across generations, economies, societies, and national borders.[76]

Chapter Five

Reconstructing Memory through the Archives: Public Pedagogy, Citizenship, and Letizia Battaglia's Photographic Record of Mafia Violence

What isn't an archive these days? ... In these memory-obsessed times – haunted by the demands of history, overwhelmed by the dizzying possibilities of new technologies – the archive presents itself as the ultimate horizon of experience. Ethically charged, politically saturated, such a horizon would seem to be all the more inescapable for remaining undefined. Where to draw the limits of the archive? How to define its basic terms?

– Rebecca Comay, *Lost in the Archives*

I felt it was my responsibility, as a part of the Sicilian people, to fight ... And so, with my camera, it turned into a madness, a desperate life where in a single day I might see five men killed, men with families. And, despite the horror of it all, I tried to maintain a minimum of poetry within me.

– Letizia Battaglia, *Passion, Justice, Freedom: Photographs of Sicily by Letizia Battaglia*

Introduction

This chapter shuttles between the archive in its literal sense as a site of storage and in its figurative senses as a migrating, foundational concept that is fused with affect and speaks of memory and forgetting, disavowal and betrayals. I argue that a productive ground for theorizing the archive as a site of radical public teaching that sustains an engagement with difficult knowledge among contemporary communities traumatized by violence can be found in the public pedagogical projects of antimafia activists currently working in Sicily. I introduce the photojournalism of Sicilian antimafia activist Letizia Battaglia as an exemplary form of public pedagogy that works to promote plurality. Drawing on the early work of Henry Giroux and building on the work of Jennifer Sandlin, Brian

Schultz, and their colleagues, I use the concept of public pedagogy to refer to forms of public intellectualism and social activism taken up by individuals who are dedicated to cultural criticism as political action.[1] Battaglia's self-described "unintended archive" of mafia murders breaks silences and complicities with state and mafia corruption through storytelling and story-taking practices that operate apart from state control. The approach to public pedagogy represented in Battaglia's work does not seek to teach the public or to demand the public learn. Rather, her public pedagogy promotes plurality through experiments in activism that aim to represent alternatives to living under threats of violence, imposed silence, and corruption – that is, to imagine, to paraphrase Arendt – new ways of being together and to reclaim opportunities to work publicly, in solidarity and in difference.[2] In this sense, Battaglia introduces what Gert Biesta describes as "a pedagogy of demonstration ... that is entirely public, both in its orientation and in its execution."[3] Battaglia's early work, however, began by challenging a long-standing denial of mafia violence that can be traced as far back as 1898.

In his compelling portrait of organized crime *Cosa Nostra: A History of the Sicilian Mafia*, historian John Dickie introduces a restricted 485-page document housed in Italy's Central State Archive in Rome.[4] The document was submitted to the Ministry of the Interior in instalments between November 1898 and January 1900. Written by then Palermo chief of police Ermanno Sangiorgi, the report systematically describes the personal details of 218 mafia members, their initiation rites, and business methods, and how the mafia forged money, committed robberies, and terrified and murdered witnesses. Perhaps most stunning is that Sangiorgi's records corroborate, almost to the letter, the report given by informant Tommaso Buscetta to antimafia prosecutor Giovanni Falcone in the late 1980s. If Sangiorgi's papers had not fallen into the wrong hands, he might have exposed the mafia only a few decades after it emerged. Instead, the mafia has sustained generations of traffic in toxic waste disposal, environmental destruction, heroin rackets, and government-sanctioned assaults on Italian civil society.[5] Dickie identifies Sangiorgi's handwritten, brittle, yellowing record as a "riveting illustration of Italy's long-standing failure to see the truth about the mafia."[6] If the emergence of the modern state charged the archive with housing material to generate social solidarity and to make national memories, the story of Sangiorgi's archived reports are a painful symptom of a nation's insistence not to repress but to deny a history of violence and corruption. In *An Outline of Psychoanalysis*, Freud distinguishes between repression and denial by way of one's relationship with the internal and external world. Although repression is an important pathway of mental conflict that signals unbearable, shameful, or difficult internal instinctual demands, denial (or disavowal), directed towards the outer world, is a process through which the ego defends against an intolerable external reality.[7]

"Whenever we are in a position to study [disavowal and repression]," writes Freud, "they turn out to be half-measures, incomplete attempts at detachment from reality."[8] Thus, while the Italian state may have disavowed the presence of systematic mafia infiltration into civil society, this disavowal cannot be contained. Not only does Dickie find in Rome's Central State Archive written evidence of the state's failure to protect its people, but he also locates a destructive psychic disturbance and abuse of state power that, in the words of Christopher Bollas, "trades in denial" by exploiting the human need to believe in state protection as it pursues its destructive end. Bollas describes such "trading in denial" as an attack on the earliest and most profound of human relations and assumptions: the relation to the parent. Each state is a derivative of the parenting world that exists in the mind of its citizens, and a terrorist regime will exploit the unconscious relationship to obtain a denial of its terrors among the citizens, who will support the denial.[9]

Italy is not alone in its refusal to recognize the truth about organized crime and its lasting and sorrowful global presence. Archives, for example, in Argentina, Chile, Uruguay, and the United States house evidence of human rights violations tied to organized crime that raise important questions about contested memories and what happens when human rights violations are denied by citizens because of fear of retaliation, or when the perpetrators of such violations are protected by the many faces of impunity – political, judicial, and cultural.[10] The traumatic legacy of Sangiorgi's document burns with the kind of fever Jacques Derrida had in mind in *Archive Fever*, a *mal d'archive* – an inability, according to Derrida, to recognize that the archive is "unrealizable," that its structure is spectral, neither present nor absent "in the flesh," neither visible nor invisible, and most certainly not stable.[11] The archive is in fact positioned, according to Derrida, between absence and presence; an indeterminate entity that is persistent in its resistance to categorization and in its destruction of memory. Derrida casts the archive as a site of amnesia precisely because it destroys memories in the very process of selecting (and hence excluding) what will be remembered. In response to the question "what is an archive?" Derrida responds:

> The archive, if this word or this figure can be stabilized so as to take on signification, will never be either memory or anamnesis as spontaneous, alive and internal experience. On the contrary: the archive takes place at the place of originary and structural breakdown of the said memory.[12]

"There would be no archive desire," argues Derrida, "... without the possibility of a forgetfulness which does not limit itself to repression."[13] Stitched into this archival forgetfulness are desire, longing, anxiety, and denial. Housed in the archive in Rome are secrets concealed by the state, artefacts of private betrayals, and unthinkable histories. Scholars, journalists, educators, and activists such as Dickie, who burn with the desire to know, to make known, and to unearth early evidence tied to present trauma, emerge on the other side of disavowal, reaching, as they do, beyond the stasis of the physical archive to represent half-spoken, traumatic memories that perhaps can never fully be understood or remembered.[14] Taking place at the structural breakdown of memory, this kind of archival work potentially creates, I argue, a social matrix which psychically and physically protects communities that have suffered societal trauma by expanding the arc of remembering.

In her study of cumulative societal trauma, Elisabeth Young-Bruehl uses the concept of a "social protective shield," elaborated on by D.W. Winnicott[15] and Masud Khan,[16] to describe the social matrix protecting communities from a violent breach, rupture, or break that compromises their health and psychic well-being.

"A social protective shield," she writes, "could be defined as a relational network of people and institutions that grows up to enwrap basic social units – like families, but also states – in customs, programs ... that prevent the unit's failure and remedy their ills medically and psychotherapeutically. Social shields of all sorts develop in societies as different needs and 'social ills' are discovered and addressed."[17]

Social protective shields may develop spontaneously or from political movements that build on civic participation and emphasize human rights as we see, for example, with the mothers of the disappeared in Argentina and the United Nations (UN) Convention on the Rights of the Child.[18] The Central State Archive in Rome houses documents, letters, ephemera – lost lives – that might otherwise be forgotten and can be read, following Derrida, as an illustration of how the archive occurs at the very moment when there is a structural breakdown in memory, when something traumatic has occurred, causing a kind of feverish sickness. In a restricted file protected from public access, Dickie discovers a malice in the archive. Wrapped up with documentation presumed to be lost or kept secret, Dickie breathes life into a story previously denied, a story that contains evidence of harm tied to traumatic, unthinkable societal experiences. In the act of recovering this story, Dickie also bears witness to the catastrophe of memory traces that call out to be reworked and re-storied.

Dickie's work, however, is no longer that of a solitary or privileged scholar. Standing on the other side of state and national archives are the ever-expanding, capacious, globalizing archives made possible through social and digital media, digital recording, and storage technologies. The sheer volume of recordable archived materials and the possibilities these technologies present to ordinary residents call into question what constitutes legitimate knowledge, what can and should be archived, and opens up spaces for calling into question the security and the meaning of the nation-state. The question posed by Rebecca Comay in my epigraph "What isn't an archive these days?" is a pointed question – where does the archive begin and end? What is included and what is excluded? What happens when previously privileged materials, such as the documents Dickie comes across in a restricted folder, are made publicly accessible? What is altered when, for example, the archive is housed in a photojournalist's apartment? Or on Facebook? On a blog? Or when an archive is provided a GPS coordinate, an idea set forth by Elizabeth A. Povinelli and her colleagues in rural northwest Australia, so that it can be accessed only in a certain place with a specific piece of technology?[19] What can we learn from the archive – both literal and figurative? In what ways can the archive work as a social protective shield, most especially among communities working through the trauma of war, climate disasters, and the terror of mafia-related crime?

Based on an analysis of interviews with Battaglia, online circulations of her images, her 2013 exhibit to celebrate International Women's Day, and newspaper coverage of her work, I argue that Battaglia's archive of photographs contributes to prompting a renewed cultural formation of the female speaking subject by creating, over time, a different narrative of female rebellion against the mafia. I consider the extent to which her archive challenges a culture that has, for too long, been suffused with death and martyrdom and suffered at the hands of what feminist philosopher Adriana Cavarero[20] describes as "the inadequacy of male justice."

The moving emotional force found in Battaglia's archive of photographs of mafia violence, specifically of women, is the desire of what Cavarero[21] describes as "the narratable self" that longs for and gives, "receives and offers, here and now, an unrepeatable story in the form of a tale." Cavarero inspires educators to enliven the stories housed in the archive, but not by imagining that one can objectively settle on how things were in a distant past. Rather, the material housed in the archive must be continually, ritualistically re-storied through the work of narrative transformations that compose and reorder what communities find meaningful. With these ideas in mind, I focus on select photographs of Battaglia's that are reproduced digitally on various online antimafia social networking sites and that were exhibited in March 2013. I use these photographs to place in relief three pedagogical principles that might serve as a guide for educators interested in creating or working with archives that aim to represent marginalized histories or to challenge the lure to trade in denial in the face of difficult knowledge:

1. Battaglia's archive of photographs sustains a search for lost or neglected objects, lost stories, subjugated knowledges, and excluded socialities.
2. Battaglia's portable archive of photographs does not simply preserve a past but re-elaborates and re-inscribes history in ways that expand, disturb, and ultimately reconstitute traumatic memories so they can be worked through.
3. Battaglia uses her photographic archive to create a "social protective shield" that offers members of her community an existential sense of belonging, political union, and a source of expression.

An Unintended Archive

Married at 16 with the hope of establishing her freedom from what she describes as Sicily's "macho society," Letizia Battaglia left her husband 19 years later, having realized that marriage left her feeling isolated, depressed, and alone. "I grew up first surrounded by a family that was afraid ... of a culture where things can happen to a young girl who was too free ... they kept me in the house."

"My husband turned out to be worried about my safety ... so I still didn't have any freedom. For a few years, I couldn't go out alone, my husband was so fearful ... It was a culture of fear ... my parents, my husband – they were crushing me ... I fell ill. I was confused ... and then I had the luck to meet a splendid Freudian psychoanalyst in Palermo, Francesco Corrao, whom I will never forget. He told me ... 'You are strong ...You can rebuild your life and save yourself.' I went into psychoanalysis, and after two years I had the strength to leave my husband."[22]

Soon after leaving her husband at a time when divorce was still illegal in Italy, Battaglia began to write for newspapers to support her three young daughters, first in Palermo and then in Milan. In 1974 Battaglia was inspired by a theatre piece she saw in Venice, *Apocalypsis cum Figuris*, directed by Jerzy Growtowski, one of the most influential theatre directors of his time. Growtowski was recognized for what he termed a "theatre of participation" or "parateatre" that, among other things, broke down the division between actor and audience. When first asked to join his ensemble, Battaglia refused. Months later, when asked again, she agreed to participate with the group. There Battaglia met Franco Zecchin, also a participant in Growtowski's ensemble at the time. They would become lovers and, over the next 19 years, political and artistic collaborators. He was 22; she was 40.

In 1975 after working for three years in Milan, Battaglia received an invitation from Vittorio Nistico to direct photography at the newspaper *L'Ora*,

Palermo's Communist daily newspaper. Under Nistico's leadership, *L'Ora* was known as the "great school that defied the mafia." The paper dedicated itself to investigative reporting, and committed itself to exposing the mafia that dominated public life in Sicily. Known for skillful reporting that refused to settle on reports from the police or official explanations distributed from the corridors of power, the work of photojournalists such as Battaglia and Zecchin would eventually mark a tradition of journalism as public service that stands starkly apart from the contemporary media conglomerates associated with the private empires of figures such as Silvio Berlusconi.

Battaglia recently described herself to journalist Carlo Ruta as knowing very little about the mafia during her early years at *L'Ora*:[23] "I was a girl of about forty, lively, generous with libertarian ideals and vaguely communist ... but then drugs arrived and youth began to ruin their lives ... I began to understand a little bit more." In 1975, Battaglia began to photograph the convulsive mafia executions that erupted throughout the streets of Palermo. "I was bare-handed except for my camera," recalls Battaglia, "against them with all of their weapons. I took pictures of everything. Suddenly, I had an archive of blood. An archive of pain, of desperation, of terror, of young people on drugs, of young widows, of trials and arrests. There in my house ... surrounded by the dead, the murdered. It was like being in the middle of a revolution."[24]

After 1977 Palermo descended into what journalist Alexander Stille describes as "the long night of one of the most bloody and tragic periods any European city has known since World War II."[25] Between 1978 and 1992, approximately one thousand people were murdered or made to disappear as the mafia established a booming heroin industry that, by 1984 would bring Italy's hard-core addict population to more than two hundred thousand.[26] Battaglia, Zecchin, and their assistants were present at almost every major crime scene throughout the city. In 1980 they were joined by Battaglia's 27-year-old daughter, Shobha. Together they covered the brutal murders of the chief of detectives, the head of the fugitives squad, three chief prosecutors, and Italy's two most important and beloved mafia prosecutors: Giovanni Falcone and Paolo Borsellino; in politics, the head of Sicily's leading opposition party, the head of the leading government party and two former mayors of Palermo. The Battaglias and Zecchin used what have now come to be iconic antimafia images to create antimafia exhibitions in schools and on streets where no one could avoid seeing them.

Over 20 years, of which 18 were spent without even a zoom, only a wide-angle lens separating her from the death and degradation that surrounded the city, Battaglia documented the criminal activity committed by the mafia on the streets of Palermo.[27] Together with Zecchin, Battaglia created a photography school and gallery in an effort to introduce the world to the Sicilian mafia, tragedies understood at the time as marginal and exclusively local.[28] The role northern Italy and Europe at large played in mafia crime went unnoticed. In the face of so much crime and its attendant poverty, it was never a question, recalls Battaglia in an interview with Melissa Harris, "of making beautiful photographs. It was a question of standing up to these people and saying 'we are here and we are against you.'"[29]

For Battaglia, the photograph works as a means to engage the public pedagogically. Growtowski's influence can be felt in the way in which Battaglia used photography to create a direct encounter between the people of Palermo and the mafia. Recognized for his belief that the theatre should have a therapeutic function for people in present-day civilization, Growtowski[30] argued that actors should co-create the event of theatre with its spectators – intimately, visibly, "in direct confrontation with him and somehow 'instead of' him." Growtowski suggests that the actor may at times find it necessary to make contact with difficult aspects of society on behalf of the spectator, so that, in turn, the spectator is able to recognize an aspect of society previously denied. The art of confrontation characterizes Battaglia's public pedagogy insofar as she uses her camera to make contact with the criminal activities of the mafia and state political corruption. On behalf of the people of Palermo, she, Zecchin, and their colleagues curated antimafia exhibitions in public spaces, apart from state control and without profit. Battaglia's photographs began to challenge students, shopkeepers, and ordinary residents to recognize what for so long had been disavowed – that there was a mafia. Her photographic lessons, composed in black and white, interrupt the pull to deny the infiltration of organized crime into just about every sector of civic life in Palermo and the surrounding areas. In a 2013 interview I had with Marina De Carlo, a former shipyard director in Palermo who resigned from her position because of the daily stress of mafia threats (De Carlo was pressured to smuggle drugs into the cruise port of Palermo), she emphasized that "yes, Battaglia's photographs woke up our city, but we knew deep inside there was a mafia ... Most important," recalled De Carlo, "her photographs provided evidence to the world that there was a mafia and it was not simply a Sicilian problem."

Battaglia's photographs, exhibited in what I would describe as portable pop-up spaces throughout the city, stand outside state control and describe the precarious conditions or what Giorgio Agamben designates as "zones of indistinction" that produce "states of exception" that render citizen rights irrelevant. These zones demonstrate, argues Agamben,[31] the ease with which governments can shift categories of people from those who have rights to those who do not. And while many residents of Palermo were ostensibly protected by a formal citizenship, their right to state protection from mafia violence as citizens was denied. The lives portrayed in Battaglia's photographic archive are seen as devoid of value by the sovereign government. Battaglia used her wide-angle lens to reframe, in the words of Dora Apel,[32] "the reality of the visible and bring into focus the invisible." Moreover, her photography functions according to the critical principles laid out by Ariella Azoulay[33] in her study of photography's civil contract: "to contest injuries to citizenship" in the form of "photographic-complaints."

In her interview with Harris, Battaglia went on to express the acute sense of abandonment the people of Palermo felt in the face of the Italian state during this time:

This war began in 1975, one against the other – in a "civilized"' society. War had broken out against the men and women of the institutions, war against the honest judges, politicians, policemen, and journalists. The biggest civil war that could happen in a city began, because the mafia had gone too far and the bloodshed extended beyond their own family vendettas.[34]

Housed in *The Guardian*'s archive entitled "Shooting the Mafia – in Pictures" is the 1976 photograph of Vincenzo Battaglia's murder.[35] This photograph stands as a statement of horror that declares the extreme conditions in which the people of Palermo lived, confirming what so many viewers knew but preferred to keep silent out of fear of retaliation from the mafia. At any moment a resident of the city could be murdered, caught in cross-fire, mistaken for someone else, or used to set an example. These conditions of fear and denial structure the position of what Azoulay terms the civil addressee or the viewer of the photograph. On viewing the photograph, the civil addressee is called on to deviate from the side to which she or he may be wedded – that of silence or *omertà* and address the emergency claims being made by taking action.[36] This can produce a shift from looking at the emergency claims made in a photograph as a generalized statement of horror – in this case, "the Sicilian misery" that does not implicate me – to a specific civilian discourse that provokes a shift in the viewers' awareness by altering how they routinely see a photograph and that urges them to demand an intervention. Battaglia's photography shifts awareness, in part, by framing not only the direct victims of mafia crimes but also their families. Standing in an alleyway, barefoot, alone in her grief, her legs splattered in blood, a woman leans forward, as if in a desperate prayer, towards her dead husband's body. He was killed on his way to the bakery to buy cannoli.

In the 8 August 1980 photograph of a woman crying out in grief in front of the Hotel Costa Smeralda, a woman, also barefoot, mistakenly believes that her son has been murdered. In the grip of imagined loss, she falls into the arms of police and male bystanders; this photograph captures the anguish of residents sentenced to silence and left unprotected by the state.[37]

The trauma of mafia violence erupting throughout the city breached the shield of existential belonging, social care, and service that Khan and Winnicott believed was so essential for a community's well-being.[38]

Stille notes that when citizens' basic rights – to physical security, health care, housing, even a place in the cemetery – are turned into privileges that can be granted or refused, as they have been in Palermo since time immemorial, people tend to turn for help to extralegal authorities, such as the mafia.[39] Such illegal turns – for example, to drug trafficking, tax evasion, and black markets – can be understood as a traumatic response – transmitted to future generations – to a cumulative social erosion, deterioration, and failure of the state to care for its people over time. A societal trauma, notes Young-Bruehl, inflicts harm on social relationships and this harm is compounded in the person and the society it harms (as well as in the perpetrators). These traumas accumulate, are passed on, and interfere with thinking – including the kind of sound political judgment that is contingent on freedom of mind, imagination, and a capacity to speculate about multiple causes of and outcomes to events.[40] Societal trauma undermines a thoughtful unity in which communities might flourish by cultivating a form of fundamentalism described by Young-Bruehl as embracing a pre-existing thought system with a fundamental event that explains all of history, polarizing all humankind into all-good and all-bad. The thought system also plots an endpoint at which ultimate judgment is delivered by a forgiving or punishing deity, ruler of the macrocosm who is outside the macrocosm, transcendent.[41]

Battaglia understands these conditions well and uses her photography to transform a negatively attained unity formed in the face of fear into a thoughtfully chosen, flourishing unity that inspires democratic life and creative living.[42] Battaglia's public pedagogy complicates the disavowal of societal trauma by inspiring, along with a range of grassroots Sicilian antimafia organizations, forms of social activism that can sustain a thoughtful unity in the face of unthinkable experiences through a combination of public work, organized resistance, and artistic expression.

After 19 years in Palermo, Zecchin left to live in Paris. Letizia Battaglia continued to photograph, in black and white, the brutalities of mafia crime, and her photographs have become part of a larger antimafia project organized by educators, activists, artists, and social entrepreneurs to challenge the mafia and to cultivate democratic life, an ethical economy, and civility in Sicily and Italy as a whole. Her collection of photographs continues to serve as an "unintended archive" that documents a history of violence as well as, I believe, a desire for radical hope and renewal. Battaglia's images are those, notes photographer Lorenzo

Linthout, of a photographer who "participates and who witnesses the profound need for justice and beauty."[43] Her photographs are described by Antonio Negri as capturing the faces of men and women that "speak to the heart ... and their unresolved demand for humanity."[44]

In the following section I move in closer to two photographs of women in Battaglia's archive that migrate, via digital and social media, into the discourses of contemporary antimafia activists. I use these photographs to explore the pedagogical and aesthetic practices Battaglia uses to "re-story" a cultural record that creates shared political spaces of action for narrating the lives of persons ordinarily rendered non-existent by history. "A life led in the absence of a space of exhibition leaves behind no life-story," argues Cavarero.[45] Battaglia's images, read as historical documents, make lives legible and present and insist on re-storing civil relationships and forms of being together that imagine a future apart from violence and corruption. In Azoulay's terms, Battaglia's pedagogy uses photography to support community and, notes Apel, "to build an oppositional public sphere so that people may, ultimately, act on the rights they do not have, and by enacting those rights, bring them into being."[46]

"Make Your Skepticism a Lever for Knowledge"

Also housed in *The Guardian* archive is the iconic photograph of Rosaria Schifani, the 22-year-old widow of bodyguard Vito Schifani, taken by Battaglia in May of 1993, one year after Rosaria's husband was assassinated with antimafia prosecutor Giovanni Falcone; his wife, Judge Francesca Morvillo; and two other bodyguards in an explosion in Capaci. Over the last 20 years this photograph has taken on the symbolic weight of a nation's grief and sustains memories of the upsurge of organized revolt against the mafia emerging at this time.[47] The photograph almost always invokes memories of Falcone's state funeral at the basilica in the San Domenico Church. And each year, on the anniversary of the assassination at Capaci, the photograph migrates across Facebook sites and antimafia blogs and recalls the words of Rosaria Schifani standing at the podium in the San Domenico Church. Schifani continues to be remembered for spontaneously departing from a speech prepared with a priest and moving an entire nation when she announced, with a lucid desperation, "Without justice, I cannot die ... There are mafiosi in here, too ... too much blood, there's no love here, there's no love at all ... I forgive you, but you have to kneel." Her grief erupted, observes Renate Siebert,

> like night thoughts moving into the clear prayer of daylight ... like breaking a ta-
> boo ... Standing at the podium; she expressed a longing for her husband in a

physical way, she misses his beautiful legs. "Nobody had the right to destroy his body. This is what I always think, simple as can be, without thinking about it at all in a clever way." It is the pagan despair of someone with the painfully reached understanding that never again really means never again.[48]

For the last 20 years, this photograph has continued to move from antimafia websites to magazines and newspapers, art exhibits, and book jackets. Circulating around this photograph are narratives, letters, and testimonies that speak of Schifani's courage to break the code of silence (*omertà*) and publicly address the mafia, to challenge state and church complicity in mafia violence, and to refuse the position of female martyr.[49] In one of many letters written to Schifani soon after she spoke at Falcone's state funeral, Giovanna Giaconia, widow of Judge Cesare Terranova, murdered by the mafia on 25 September 1979 wrote: "What I really appreciated in your prayer at San Domenico was the mistrust woven into those words, 'the state, the state.' Well done, Rosaria, make your skepticism a lever for knowledge. And remember this is a state that signed a blank cheque for the mafia."[50]

The black-and-white portrait of Rosaria Schifani, half exposed by light, is considered one of the most important in Battaglia's archive. It has been described by photographer Lorenzo Linthout as "a deathmask, split between light and shadow."[51] Battaglia took this photograph at the home of Felice Cavallaro, for the cover of a 1993 biography he published of Rosaria. Her grief composed, her eyes closed – this photograph expresses the reclusive, guarded life that is forced on those who combat the veiled civil war that is the mafia.[52] Not only is the particular life of Rosaria Schifani represented in this photograph, but the digital, film, and print-based circulation of this image suggests that it works as a powerful provocation for women who know intimately of mafia violence to tell a story of their own, attesting to the power of Battaglia's photography to engender the reciprocity of storytelling and to work as a social protective shield by creating political union and existential belonging. The testimony and portrait evoke each other – taken together, they continue to inspire women to speak publicly and to share their grief, anger and memories, practices that, in part, fuse the joint political activism that has, for generations, been taken up by women in the antimafia movement. In letters to Schifani written weeks after her husband's funeral, Rita Bartoli, widow of state prosecutor Gaetano Costa, wrote, "I advise you always to ask for justice because it is not pointless. And I advise you also to speak, to speak a great deal. Don't think only of forgiving. Ask, claim justice and speak most of all to those who live in this place."[53] Another letter, written by Marina Pipitone, widow of Michele Reina, Christian Democrat Party secretary in Palermo, after Schifani spoke at San Domenico reads:

> The words I heard you speak on TV, Rosaria, are the same words I spoke then. I saw myself in your image. I saw myself as a very young woman, struck in the face by the monster. Be strong, Rosaria. And strengthen others because it really seems to me that you have it in you to give hope to people.[54]

And from Giuseppina Zacco, widow of the Sicilian Communist Party secretary Pio La Torre,

> Speak, speak, speak, dear Rosaria. For years I stayed at home refusing to take part in meetings and debates. I didn't feel ready. Then one day I found myself in Bologna involved in a demonstration. I spoke. The words I said were simple. But they were effective. Word got around and from that day on I got invited all over the place, even to consulates abroad. I have even written a biography.[55]

In a recent documentary about Rosaria Schifani directed by Fabio Vannini, *Ho Vinto Io* (I Won!), Schifani returns to Palermo after 20 years away. And while she describes how the support from the larger antimafia community taught her that grief could be turned into "a springboard for collective pressure," for social change, she does not believe that the mafia will ever repent – "they are," she states, "in a death spiral, without hope."[56]

The Re-elaborations (*Rielaborazioni*)

On 23 May 1992, the day Schifani's husband Vito was murdered, hours before Falcone and Morvillo died along with their other escorts, Antonio Montinaro and Rocco Dicillo, Battaglia stopped taking photographs of mafia massacres. In a recent interview about a European retrospective of her work in Venice, Battaglia recalls the shock she felt on hearing of Falcone's death and her consequent refusal to take another photograph of the dead:

> I sat watching a documentary on the television with my mother, her hands in mine. I would usually see him [Falcone] on a Sunday afternoon, but this time I was unable to do so. At a certain moment my programme was interrupted by the news that something had happened to Falcone on the motorway. We were unable to move for a few seconds, then panic hit me ... The only thing I could do was to telephone my studio and to warn Franco and Shoba. I wasn't about to go to the motorway, in fact, I was never again to take photographs of the dead and all that goes with it. Eighteen years later, I realized that I had taken photographs of just about everything I could have done, in Palermo, for my then newspaper, *L'Ora* ... But most of all, I took pictures of misery, of dead bodies, of those being arrested, of bombs,

of court cases, of litter, of the wounded, of fascists, of children, of women of dem-onstrations and of the humiliated ... on that fateful afternoon whilst holding my mother's white and soft hands, something inside me died and I took the decision to never take another photograph of another dead body, of any more pain and certainly of no more Mafiosi. Today, exactly twenty years later, I can only deplore my weakness or indolence or whatever you want to call it. It blocked my courage. It was my duty to resist, to take more photographs and to consign them to a future memory. These photos, which I never took, actually hurt me more than those that I did.[57]

After the murder of Falcone and then, weeks later, the murder of Paolo Borsellino, Battaglia ended her 20 years of photographing crime scenes. In the aftermath of these tragedies as well as the closing of L'Ora, Battaglia created her own publishing house and turned to politics full time.[58] In 2004, still feeling disgust at all Palermo had lost, she was examining a large photograph of a mother with her three poor children huddling together in a bed because of either cold or hunger. In that moment, Battaglia recalls feeling the need "to destroy it [the photograph] ... That is," she explains to Ganci, "to make it into something else, I could give it a new life. So, from 2004 on were born le Rielaborazioni (the re-elaborations) and I started to turn my reportage shots into something different." Battaglia continues to re-story the old shots, by using them as background for something else. In front of a dead body, she inserts into the foreground what she describes as a positive image, such as a young woman, for example, to breathe new life into it. The photograph Tre Donne (Three Women), featured at the Workshop in Venice between 20 April 20 and 18 May 2013 to celebrate International Women's Day, and as of this writing in 2016, in an exhibit of Battaglia's photography in Rome, captures how Battaglia uses juxtaposition and montage to interfere with chronological planes, to look towards the future, and to re-story the violent history of Palermo. Tre Donne juxtaposes the lit portion of the portrait of Schifani, whose face is in the far background, against little more than a profile of the face of Francesco Laurana's stone bust of Eleonora of Aragon, which floats behind the face of Martha, Battaglia's 14-year-old granddaughter, as if to create historic resonances. What histories are cross-referenced in this portrait of three women? What pedagogical implications are inherent in Battaglia's reworkings?

Spectral time suggests that the past inhabits the present. "The ghostliness of time," writes Nicoletta Di Ciolla, "is not only enacted through the incursions of the past into the present, but also through infiltrations in the opposite direction: as the past casts a shadow on the present, the present similarly unfolds into the past," introducing education to a synchronic idea of history.[59]

Also called forth is Arendt's and Cavarero's concept of natality. Recall that in Battaglia's discussion of her re-elaborations, she explains the moment when, feeling disgust at all that Palermo had lost, she realized she could transform the photograph of the mother and her hungry children into something else – "I could give it [the photograph] a new life." Her re-elaborations create, I believe, an imperishable memory of loss and destruction that looks to birth and to life rather than to death as a central pedagogical category.

Called forth in these images are the unrepeatable and singular lives of Vito Schifani and Eleanora of Aragon. Also called forth are the unique lives of Rosaria Schifani and the young Martha. Cavarero uses the notion of uniqueness to indicate a person's irreplaceability. In each of these lives, in the unique response of each person to her historical and social particularities, is a concrete location for natality, a spot where newness can enter the world. Rather than premising her work on mortality and death, Battaglia joins Cavarero in turning to the category of birth and, in turn, departs from the narratives of martyrdom that are so prevalent in the antimafia imaginary.[60] The turn to new beginnings creates an ethos of hope and renewal that strengthens the social protective shield through an act of imagination that invests an unthinkable past with a reparative promise. Winnicott (1958) might describe Battaglia's urge to juxtapose past images against present images as a "spontaneous gesture" that offers access to lived experience in the present and is met by the people of Palermo with a sense of feeling alive.

Conclusion

Housed in Battaglia's apartment in Palermo is an "unintended archive" of over six thousand photographs that exposed the corruption and anti-democratic practices of the state and challenged the world to understand organized crime as far more than Sicily's local problem. The documentary practices of Battaglia draw on pedagogical and artistic traditions that, in the words of Apel,[61] "claim the frame for the rightless" by making her stance apparent, and by making visible the social and political conditions that make her photography possible. The spaces of violence and vulnerability captured by Battaglia over the course of 20 years continue to be in urgent need of representation. Contemporary antimafia activists, teachers, and journalists who use narrative and photography, such as journalist Roberto Saviano and the citizen writers of Corleone Dialogos, have inherited from Battaglia a civil contract that Azoulay describes as being produced from documentary photography. This civil contract creates a new kind of citizenship that is based on spectators' relationships with and duty towards one another rather than to the state and creates a civic refuge for those robbed of citizenship and for those who, although citizens, are denied state protection. The photographic complaint, which can more easily migrate via digital technology, can produce grievances and claims that otherwise, argues Azoulay, would not be made and might not be so easily seen. Battaglia offers education important lessons in how the photographic archive can serve as a social protective shield for communities traumatized by mafia criminality. Her photographic archive continues to expand the arc of remembering by challenging the state repression of memory and its practice of trading in denial.

I want to underscore that this aesthetic expansion of remembering loss and unspeakable violence looks to life, rather than death, as a central pedagogical category. In ways akin to Addiopizzo, Battaglia's photographic archive, combined with her contemporary process of re-elaborating older photographs, marshals the life drive by re-symbolizing and hence revitalizing the discourses of martyrdom that obscure the complex and singular histories of the antimafia imaginary. This is one way in which Battaglia's photojournalism extends a pedagogical tradition associated with social documentary and biography. Her reconstruction of mafia archives breaks silences and complicities with violence through storytelling and story-taking practices that work towards reimagining a complex history and its impact on the present and the future. This break in silence and the composition of diverse sets of images that span timescapes, city scenes, and historical figures combine to create what Pickering-Iazzi describes in her study of the urban imaginary of Palermo as an enactment of "diversified discourses" that "contribute to the thoughts, fantasies, and fears forming the 'Palermos'" that "articulate a protean irreducibility of the urban sense of place."[62] It is in Battaglia's capacity to use her re-elaborations to generate multiple meanings and discourses that challenge images of Palermo as a city without hope. Such excesses of meaning undermine the binary narrative of the antimafia and work as a provocation to imagine a Palermo transformed, complex, and represented as a complex sociopolitical field through multiple narrative voices and registers. Among these voices and registers are not only victims but also activists, citizens, and residents of the city who work to restore agency to the social process of transitional justice through ordinary practices of daily living.[63]

Chapter Six

"The Duty to Report": Political Judgment, Public Pedagogy, and the Photographic Archive of Franco Zecchin

The reason why each human life tells its story and why history ultimately becomes the storybook of mankind with many actors and speakers and yet without any tangible authors, is that both are the outcome of action.

– Hannah Arendt, *The Human Condition*

Snatched out of repression and impressed in life stories, memory is instead the narrative modality in which the questioning of the inexplicable resurfaces and is preserved.

– Adriana Cavarero, "Narrative against Destruction"

Introduction

On Franco Zecchin's website at http://franco.zecchin.book.picturetank.com is "The Duty to Report," an archive of photography and written documentation from the time he spent photographing the effects of mafia violence for the *L'Ora* newspaper with his partner and then-lover Letizia Battaglia. Zecchin traces the early years of his antimafia photojournalism to 1975 when he settled in Palermo. Although his activism began in Palermo, his social and geographical interests had progressively widened to the island of Sicily. From the very beginning, Zecchin felt the imperative to challenge the stereotyped vision of the mafia as something confined to the south of Italy. On the afternoon of 9 July 1976, Zecchin first experienced the aftermath of a mafia killing, the murder of Benedetto D'Atola in the Zisa neighbourhood of Palermo. New to photojournalism, Zecchin did not take any photographs at the time, rather, he intently watched Battaglia photograph the crime scene, noting which images the newspaper wanted. He recalls:

The photographer must get a clear image that bears witness to, and narrates, what has happened; in the fraction of a second he must have the right light, a good composition, the image in focus, and must know the exact moment to snap, when a face turns, when a gesture is most expressive. He must succeed in reconciling these demands, that are strictly photographic, with the need to tackle all the obstacles that crop up while ... working.[1]

This chapter takes its title from Zecchin's archive entitled "The Duty to Report," in which he situates his early education as a photojournalist in Palermo within the context of the mafia intimidation, murders, and drug trafficking that escalated from the mid-1970s to 1992. Zecchin finds early in his work as a reporter that even a newspaper as apparently radical as *L'Ora* was bound to the interests of public security officers, police superintendents, and the state, all of whom too often interfered with the "duty to report" mafia violence. Writes Zecchin,

The photographer has no control over the use that the mass media make of his pictures; he is only the first link in a chain of information, the first necessary link-up with reality; his is a raw and immediate interpretation, immersed in the event that has happened. After him, there will be someone who will decide how to reduce this immediacy, manipulating it to construct proofs that support his own version of the truth or that desired by the political and economic interests of the publisher.[2]

Zecchin marks the harrowing 1978 death of antimafia activist Giuseppe Impastato as the point at which he and Battaglia committed themselves to using their photojournalism to provoke a shift in political and social consciousness and to work apart from privatized interests and state control. In an interview with me in 2015, Zecchin explained that Impastato's murder affected him on several levels. Not only did this murder alter his way of practising photography, but it also provoked him to use his photography on both a political and a social level. He joined Anna Puglisi, Umberto Santino, Battaglia, and a small group of militants and left-leaning intellectuals to create the Giuseppe Impastato Sicilian Centre of Documentation.

Impastato, founder of *Radio Aut* (1976) and the newsletter *L'idea socialista* (in 1965), and a member of the left-wing Italian Socialist Party of Proletarian Unity (PSIUP), was born into a mafia family in 1948 in Cinisi, a province of Palermo. On 9 May 1978, when Impastato was 30 years old, he was murdered by the order of mafia boss Gaetano Badalamenti, a close friend of his father, Luigi. Former prime minister Aldo Moro's body was found folded into the trunk of a red Renault on Via Caetani in Rome on the same day. The discovery of the body of Moro, then president of the Christian Democratic Party, killed by the Red Brigades after 54 days in captivity, overshadowed the assassination of Impastato. By the time Zecchin arrived at the scene where Impastato's body had been tied to the Palermo-Trapani railway line and blasted with dynamite, the rails had been repaired and no evidence was left of Impastato's assassination – only accusations that Impastato had committed either a failed terrorist attack or suicide. These claims, notes Zecchin, were supported by the press as well. The conservative Milanese newspaper *Corriere della Sera* ran a brief story with the headline "Leftist fanatic blown apart by own bomb on railway track."[3]

Disillusioned with photojournalism, Zecchin and Battaglia felt what he describes as "the pressing need to find other channels to bring people information that was free and uncorrupted by obscure political and economic interests."[4] Taking as their point of departure the photographic exhibit "Mafia and Territory" organized by Impastato before his death, Zecchin and Battaglia joined Santino, Puglisi, and Impastato's comrades to produce information that disclosed that Impastato did not commit suicide. First, they reconstructed the exhibit "Mafia and Territory." Initially, their exhibits were confined, as was Impastato's, to neighbourhoods in Cinisi. Later, Zecchin and his colleagues developed a wider conception and presented material about mafia-related crime throughout Sicily, with the intention of showing the connection between criminality, politicians, economic power, and social conditions. They began to claim public attention by setting up provocative pop-up galleries in schools and on street corners in Corleone and Palermo depicting murder after unspeakable murder. They integrated images of the latest mafia activity and extended their pop-up galleries throughout Italy and Europe. Curating without profiting, Zecchin and Battaglia asked ordinary citizens and residents to participate in active, social forms of recognition and remembering by using photography to break what Zecchin describes as a "widespread culture of resignation, submission and *omertà*."[5] For Zecchin "the duty to report" included an imperative to challenge the literary and romantic stereotypes of a good mafia that defended vulnerable members of society and offered them the protection denied by the state. For Zecchin "the duty to report" implied an ethical obligation to use photography as a medium through which to call attention to the very real presence of mafia infiltration into government, society, and all aspects of civil life – a reality at that time that was stunningly disavowed.

In her analysis of the legal principles that established the mafia as a criminal organization, Deborah Puccio-Den draws attention to the fact that despite the increasing number of assassination attempts and murders, "the theory of the mafia expounded by folklorist Giuseppe Pitré (1841–1916) continued to prevail."[6] This view held that the mafia was not the same as criminality; the mafia was simply understood as a way of being, feeling, or behaving. It was characterized as a psychological attitude or temperament linked to "Sicilian-ness."[7] Puccio-Den offers a few axioms to capture these perspectives:

> The Mafia is neither a sect nor an organization; it has neither rules nor statutes; a Mafioso is neither a thief nor a criminal; the criminal Mafia is not the Mafia but criminality, and criminality should not be confused with the Mafia, as the latter is simply a way of being, feeling, or behaving, a psychological attitude or temperament linked to "Sicilian-ness."[8]

Equating the mafia with "an exaggerated sense of honor," Sicilian prime minister Vittorio Emanuele Orlando stated in a 1925 speech,

> if by Mafia ... they mean being furiously intolerant of bullying and injustice, and showing the generosity of spirit needed to stand up to the strong and be understanding toward the weak; if they mean having a loyalty to your friends that is stronger than anything, stronger even than death; if by Mafia we mean feelings like these, attitudes like these – even though they may sometimes be exaggerated – then I say to you that what they are talking about are the distinguishing traits of the Sicilian soul. And so I declare myself a Mafioso and I am proud to be one![9]

In the context of so much denial, complex political and juridical challenges emerged as it became necessary to prove that the mafia was not a cultural code or temperament but a criminal phenomenon that had a negative impact on society from several perspectives: corruption, degradation, poverty, and violence.[10]

Inherent in Zecchin's commitment to report and to challenge the denial of mafia criminality is, I believe, an ethical imperative to use photography as a response to the mafia's intent on eliminating life stories along with lives themselves. In the midst of mafia terrorism, Zecchin believed it was necessary to use photography to revisit the narratives of victims to ensure that their story, beginning with their names and personal data, can become a part of the larger historical narrative that might restore the human status of uniqueness to victims of mafia crime.[11]

At the same time Zecchin recognizes that the excess of horror remains. "Horror does not get resolved in a frame that articulates or explains it," as Adriana Cavarero reminds us. "Actually, it is preserved in the life stories that hold its trace. Rather than being forgotten, and therefore erased, inexplicability thereby assumes a different intensity that interrogates us even more categorically."[12] Traces of inexplicability interrogate the viewer of Zecchin's photograph of Antonio Scardina, murdered by the Cosa Nostra on 10 July 1983. Zecchin's photograph registers the death of one among many children murdered by the mafia for witnessing a crime. Taken minutes after Antonio's murder, the photo serves as a request, an appeal to take action against mafia terrorism and to remember the life of an 11-year-old child whose living traces, while housed among family, are barely evident in the public realm today. This photographic act, whose impact cannot be predicted or measured, embodies the definition of action Arendt offers to distinguish it from labour and work. The photograph acts in ways we cannot know in advance, and in turn it has the capacity to make others act on behalf of one another, all of whom are bound by an ethics that exceeds national definitions of citizenship. Antonio Scardina is dead. He can no longer act. We do not know who stands beyond the frame of this photograph, although we can imagine police, family, neighbours, bystanders – all terrified to report. The spaces where they live, controlled by mafia terrorism, impose fear and eradicate the possibility for plurality to thrive. The death of Antonio Scardina is a message to the people of Palermo that they in fact are non-citizens, and their access to any space of action is restricted if not entirely denied. The photograph of Antonio Scardina's traumatic murder restores the conditions of plurality to the space of action by undermining, in the words of Ariella Azoulay, "the apparently stable conditions of domination."[13] In the midst of the traumatic grip of mafia violence, Zecchin did not waver from a duty to photograph crime and to make a defiant effort, along with his colleagues, to restore and sustain civil conditions.

Another picture included in Zecchin's archive captures what Cavarero understands as Arendt's relational politic. This relational politic is a form of action that responds to the ethical claim made by the exposure and vulnerability of the other. This claim breaks the walls of silence and demands engagement, thought, and negotiation, particularly in the context of a society where speaking out against injustice can lead to death.[14] On 7 October 1986, during the maxi-trials in Palermo, 11-year-old Claudio Domino was murdered by a mafia gunman outside his school while playing with friends. Witnesses reported that the killer approached the school slowly on a motorbike and shouted towards a group of boys leaving the school: "Hey, Claudio! Come here for a minute." As Claudio approached, the gunman pulled a pistol from his jacket and shot the boy between the eyes. *The Chicago Tribune* reported that Claudio's murder was an act of retaliation against his father for refusing to do a favour for several of the mafiosi on trial. Investigators speculated that Antonio Domino, who operated the company responsible for cleaning the courtroom where the trial was being held, may have been asked to pass on a message and refused. Terrified after the murder of his son, Antonio Domino again refused, this time to cooperate with police in the investigation into the death of his son.

In the portrait of Claudio, taken by Zecchin at the boy's wake, he lies in his coffin dressed in a suit. His left eye is open, a bandage covers the fatal wound near his swollen right eye. The photograph counters the code of *omertà* by bringing the story of Claudio's life and death into a political, public space – a shared, albeit precarious space of interaction set apart from state control.[15]

Only one year earlier, the mafia had murdered six-year-old twins Giuseppe and Salvatore Asta and their mother, Barbara Rizzo Asta. They were killed by a bomb intended for Judge Palermo at Pizzolungo on 2 April 1985. This was no mistake, reports Renate Siebert. "From where they were positioned, the mafiosi who activated the remote device to make the bomb explode were perfectly able to see the car driven by Signora Rizzo Asta with the children in it."[16] Hundreds of children have been murdered by the mafia. Their relationship with children operates within their management of terror, blackmail, and cheap labour and promotes *omertà*.[17] The death of children, continues Siebert, "feeds fear and terror and therefore serves the interests of territorial domination."[18] The portrait of Claudio Domino acts as a public record of the extent to which mafia will go to instil terror, silence speech, and dispossess vulnerable populations of public spaces in which to take action and express dissent. Moreover, this photograph serves as a public record of the way in which the mafia uses the death of children to sustain an image of Sicilian culture as a population that is socially dead, a term Orlando Patterson uses to describe the status of the slave, rather than a population very much alive and who takes action.[19]

To what extent do Zecchin's photographic exhibits offer educators lessons in how the photograph can re-humanize and redeem the meaning of human life from the ruins of mafia totalitarianism? In what follows I turn to my interviews with Franco Zecchin and his archives to establish his photographic exhibits as constituting a clear case of creating the necessary conditions for action that Hannah Arendt believed was contingent on active participation and deliberation in the public sphere. I consider the ways in which the photojournalism of Zecchin frames the diverse histories and messy contingencies that inflect historical narratives. In addition, I explore the approach to story-taking and storytelling practised by Zecchin that fulfils the promise of both Azoulay's civil contract as discussed in the previous chapter and the condition for action valued by Arendt. Arendt's theory of action (and her revival of the ancient concept of praxis), links action to freedom and plurality by articulating the relationship of action to speech and remembrance and distinguishing action from the more instrumental projects of labour and work. Speech, public speech, speaking out against mafia crime in solidarity has always threatened the mafia's grand designs. Arendt's understanding of action as a form of human solidarity and ingenuity suggests a form of participatory democracy that is contingent on a worldly practice experienced in the presence of others. Borrowing from Augustine, Arendt threads the theme of new beginnings, initiative, and natality throughout her understanding of action and offers important insights into the educative import of Zecchin's photography.

To prepare a context for an analysis of Zecchin's photography, I begin with a description of the political background in Sicily when Zecchin began to photograph mafia violence, and then move to a pedagogical analysis of select images curated for exhibitions set up in schools, streets, and other public spaces in Palermo and Corleone in 1979.

A "Paradigm of Complexity"

The Italian antimafia law (Law 646 known as the Rognoni-La Torre Law) established in September 1982 modified article 416 of the criminal code by creating the crime of "association of a mafia type" and extending existing powers – passed in legislation of 1956 and 1965 – to limit the freedom of movement and carry out surveillance of suspected criminals. In addition, it incorporated the asset-tracing, freezing, and confiscation powers of the 1965 law. The new law identified association with the mafia when it consisted of three or more members and, according to the law,

> when those who belong to it make use of the power of intimidation afforded by the associative bond and the state of subjugation and criminal silence which derives from it to commit crimes, to acquire directly or indirectly the management or control of economic activities, concessions, authorizations or public contracts and services, either to gain unjust profits or advantages for themselves or for others.[20]

Until 1982 no law recognized mafia activity as illegal or criminal. Sociologist Umberto Santino, founder (with Anna Puglisi) of the *Centro Siciliano di documentazione "Giuseppe Impastato"* in Palermo, offers a comprehensive definition of the mafia as well as the conditions that sustain it. Casting the mafia as a "paradigm of complexity," he writes:

> The mafia is a system of violence and illegality that aims to accumulate wealth and positions of power. It uses a cultural code and enjoys certain popular support. In this way, the mafia phenomenon is seen to be a complete unit with multifarious aspects: criminal, economic, political, cultural and social. In this view the actual criminal association is part of a network of relationships which is much vaster: a social block with an interclass composition that ranges from the lowest social levels to the highest (probably some hundreds of thousands of people in Sicily).

The Sicilian society is a society producing mafia (*società mafiogena*) for many reasons: many people consider violence and illegality like survival means and ways of acquiring a social role; violence and illegality are usually unpunished, the legal economy is too weak to offer substantial opportunities, the State and the institutions are seen as distant and foreign, approachable through the mediation of the mafiosi and their friends, the struggles against the mafia have been lost and the consequences for many people are the mistrust and the belief that it is impossible to change the situation, social life is lacking because of a crisis of political parties, an insufficient role for trade unions and civil society is too weak and precarious etc. Mafia is a form of totalitarian state and its peculiarity is the territorial control (*signoria territorial*) from the economy to politics, to private life. For the mafia rights don't exist, there are only favours.[21]

The mafia that thrives in Sicily today is described by Santino as "the financial mafia," a period he traces to the 1970s. The financial mafia has an international reach that allows it to take advantage of banking secrecy, tax havens, and "financial innovations" that also offer the possibility of avoiding controls on capital.[22] When Zecchin arrived in Palermo in 1975, the financial mafia was unencumbered by a mafia law and five years into a booming heroin industry that had its roots in the drug trafficking they'd engaged in since the 1950s. Freelance writer Alison Jamieson reports that between 1976 and August 1980, when the first heroin laboratories were discovered, the principal exporting collective – the Spatola-Inzerillo-Bontate families – is believed to have refined and exported an average of four to five metric tons of pure heroin annually, making US$600 million of profit per annum.[23] With the anti-terrorist fight absorbing the majority of Italy's criminal investigators and share of national resources to combat terrorist violence, which was concentrated mostly in the centre and north of Italy, the "heroin mafia" in Sicily was able to take up business with relatively little interference.[24]

During this time Giuseppe Impastato was active at *Radio Aut* and hosted a radio broadcast with Pino Manzella and Salvo Vitale called *Onda Pazza* (Crazy Waves). From their microphones, they would break the code of *omertà* by talking about the mafia – never refraining from naming names and making precise accusations about the links between the mafia and local politicians. Impastato's accusations clearly indicated he had an internal source of information.

In the face of strict codes of *omertà*, the radio show worked to create an experience of the polis Arendt might describe as "the most talkative of all bodies politic."[25] Impastato and his fellow activists used speech as a means through which to persuade their community to take action against the mafia rather than using militant tactics of force and violence.[26] Arendt argued for a quality of civic engagement that corresponded to "the human condition of plurality, to the fact that men, and not Man, live on the earth and inhabit the world."[27] Action is the site of politics, participation, debate, open-ended, and multiple. By breaking the silence of *omertà*, Impastato and his friends created a public space in which people could escape from the press of silence and fear that became strangely normalized by the mafia's presence. During the years the financial mafia was most active, the law of *omertà* imposed a radical isolation and breakdown in public life.

Omertà cultivates a particular quality of silence, argues Renate Siebert, one that identifies with a virile masculinity. It is a quality of silence that despises feminine characteristics in men and destroys shared subjectivity and communication. One might argue that Impastato and his friends feminized the public spaces of Cinisi by introducing a relational space that was based on what I would describe, following Cavarero, as a feminist need to radically criticize any proposition that eradicates bodily existence and difference. This notion of selfhood is based on an understanding of the constitutive dependency of the self on the other.[28] As well, this notion of selfhood requires a unique "who" that emerges in the context of a narrative relation grounded in relationality and reciprocity and as Sharon Todd argues, "addresses, and articulates ... the political aspects of conflict that plurality gives rise to."[29]

Using humour and satire, Impastato often mocked mafiosi, particularly mafia boss Gaetano Badalamenti, calling him *Tano Seduto* ("Sitting Tano"). "We're on the outskirts of Mafiopolis (Cinisi)," Impastato announces. "The buildings commission has met. On the agenda is the approval of Project Z 11. The great capo Tano Seduto will be circling the square like a sparrowhawk." Also active in the Che Club, Impastato joined young people from Cinisi and the surrounding areas to publicly call out the betrayals they felt towards the Communist Party for collaborating with the Christian Democrats who profited from mafia alliances. The Che Club found inspiration from the extreme language of Maoism, the Civil Rights Movement in the United States, and protests against the Vietnam War. In his exceptionally well-documented biography of Giuseppe Impastato, historian Tom Behan observes that the political activity in western Sicily at the time, particularly in the area of Cinisi, was evidence that

> young Italians in particular were made aware there was an alternative to the luke-warm opposition that the Communist Party had led against the Christian Democrat government. Some activists drew direct parallels between national liberation struggles in other countries and government repression in the south of Italy ... Peppino [a nickname for Impastato] and others were beginning to provide a more tangible focus ... It was his friend and fellow activist Salvo Vitale who remembers

that "Peppino managed to give our group strength and coherence, forcing us out-wards and into contact with real problems."[30]

In addition to fighting for decent water supplies, the Che Club turned their attention to the controversies surrounding the Punta Raisi airport behind Cinisi. Each week a Boeing aircraft would set off from Palermo to New York smuggling heroin on the third runway made possible by the mafia expropria-tion of land from Cinisi peasants. Impastato had taken on a significant lead-ership role in the peasant protest, first against building the airport and later against building this third airstrip.

Days before his assassination, Impastato was prepared to stand as a candi-date for the Proletarian Democracy. In one of his earlier articles, "The Mafia – a Mountain of Shit," Impastato spelled out his beliefs: "A dramatic situation of gang warfare must be avoided in our country. Mass struggles must become the driving force of social transformation."[31] Days after his death, Impastato was elected as a local councillor with an unprecedented number of votes for the Proletarian Democracy list in Cinisi.

The death of Impastato received very little national attention. In fact, not until 2002, 24 years after Impastato's murder, was his reputation cleared and Tano Badalamenti convicted of ordering Impastato's death. "The murder of Giuseppe Impastato was the beginning of a shift," remembers Zecchin, "to-wards a political and social use for our work." At Impastato's funeral, Zecchin recalls what he describes as "a great show of emotion and almost a sense of blame for having abandoned the struggle and the social commitment in order to devote ourselves to our private lives. Peppino was killed because he had been left on his own." Together with Letizia Battaglia, Zecchin donated many of his photographs to the *Centro Siciliano di documentazione "Giuseppe Impastato"* (Giuseppe Impastato Sicilian Centre of Documentation), founded by Anna Puglisi and Umberto Santino. Today the Centre continues to be recognized as the finest research institution in the world on mafia crime.

Soon after the death of Impastato, Zecchin and Battaglia took as a pretext, as noted earlier, his "Mafia and Territory" and began to set up similar public pho-tographic exhibitions of their own in schools and streets where no one could avoid seeing them. The exhibitions created by Impastato and his friends, mount-ed along the *corso* in Cinisi in 1976 and during spring 1978, included dozens of panels half a metre by one and a quarter metres in size that illustrated and ex-plained in great detail the local council's corruption and collusion with the ma-fia.[32] In the archives of Giuseppe Impastato Sicilian Centre of Documentation, you will find a photograph of three men, including Badalamenti, walking through the 1976 exhibition. The 1978 exhibit was removed one day before Impastato was murdered.

How far removed is the *corso*, or street, from state control? In what manner is the *corso* embedded in the larger social sphere of mafia politics, corruption, and intimidation? To what extent can we assume that the street is a gathering space, open and accessible to all – a site Arendt might describe as the public realm where, in her words, "the central concern of all citizens was to talk with each other"?[33] The public pedagogical turn taken by Impastato fulfils the duty to report insofar as it mobilizes documentation, images, and graphs that ask viewers to recognize present acts of injustice, violence, and corruption. The exhibit can be understood as offering a form of testimony that opens up for consideration the destructive force that a long history of mafia violence has on social life. Certainly there is ample evidence that Impastato and his friends intended to use their documentation panels to provoke an affective force that would compel viewers to take action against the pervasive corruption in Cinisi that extended itself to the larger global sphere. And they did make an impact on social consciousness and cultural life, as made evident in the posthumous election of Impastato as town councillor to the Proletarian Democracy. Yet it is important to keep in mind that the *corso*, like any street, is not set apart from state control, although it may be, but not necessarily, removed from private interests. The photographic exhibits set up by Zecchin, inspired by Impastato, fulfil a duty to report by calling forth difficult narratives that sustain life stories rendered meaningless by the state, and they do so in the very presence of dangerous state politics that dismisses far too many citizens and residents as unworthy of protection or entitled to little more than precarious living conditions.

In her reading of Arendt's discussion of the Greek narrative as a remedy for the fragility of action, Cavarero underscores the value Arendt placed on how biographical narratives bestow meaning and secure the memory of a singular life that might otherwise be reduced to "an erasure without any residue of the uniqueness of the one who has lived."[34] The totalitarian methods of the mafia direct attention to eradicating uniqueness and eliminating all residues of humanity. Among the most important lessons education can learn from Arendt is the value of recovering and remembering the specificities of lives lost to a wretched totalitarianism – this is, in her estimation, the importance of storytelling. Writes Cavarero,

> After the experience of the extermination camps, it becomes necessary for Arendt to revisit the narratives that ensure a story, not so much of the heroes of ancient times, but of the victims of the Lager, whose existence, starting with the erasure of

their names and personal data, was being obliterated, so that having lived in the world, they could not become part of a story, nor of history: "The status of the inmates in the world of the living, where nobody is supposed to know if they are alive or dead, is such that it is as though they had never been born."[35]

In what ways does the photojournalism of Zecchin recover the memories of mafia victims and perpetrators to "ensure a story" and a place in history? In the next section of this chapter, I bring together Arendt's understanding of action with theories of storytelling to analyse select photographs Zecchin included in two 1979 street exhibitions, one in the central piazza of Corleone and the other in Palermo. The open-air photographic exhibits, entitled "The City and the Power" ("*La Citta e Il Potere*"), were curated to challenge *omertà* and to cultivate awareness and a sense of agency among communities terrified to speak of or to take action against the Cosa Nostra. Together with Battaglia, Zecchin displayed images of mafia violence fastened on boards within the central plazas. In Corleone, the images were displayed outside the central church. When the congregation came out, they looked at the harrowing images for a few moments and then fled. Within five minutes, not a soul was left in the square; such was the danger of being seen to be looking at these images. But the photographs had been seen – if only momentarily. The photographs by Zecchin, shot in black and white, staged and invited participation in social, historical, and cultural memories that are shocking, empowering, mobilizing, and traumatic. Building on the arguments presented in previous chapters, I conclude by arguing that Zecchin's photography recovers difficult knowledge and narratives of protest within the context of transitional justice, and, as a form of public pedagogy, they work towards cultivating action and collective resistance in response to state-sanctioned atrocity.[36]

Photography, Public Pedagogy, and the Failure of Remembrance

The pedagogical impulse animating Zecchin's curatorial approach when mounting open-air pop-up exhibits was to confront viewers with difficult images of ever-escalating violence. The very act of confronting these images was, in Zecchin's estimation, an important form of resistance. In ways similar to the exhibitions created by Impastato, the street exhibitions Zecchin set up with friends and colleagues interrupted the practice of distancing the public from information. Zecchin recalls that "no one believed that photographs could be a weapon in the battle against the mafia ... Our idea was just to put up photographs everywhere ... in piazzas, in schools, in the streets ... The mafia had always been so absolutely sure of its own power ... They did not expect that a collection of photographs could have such a powerful effect. The people of Sicily had been living for so long in a state of terror, everyone was desperately afraid of naming names."[37]

The photographic project Zecchin speaks of here carried forth Impastato's project of challenging *omertà* by creating public spaces that inspired collective deliberation and solidarity – a space, that is, where meaningful action could take place, not out of force but voluntarily. "Our weapon was information," recalls Zecchin, "and we used it to break the transmission of a widespread culture of denial, submission, silence: the *omertà*. We showed young people the devastating reality of the mafia, in contrast to the literary and romantic stereotypes that fueled the myth of a 'good' mafia, which respected a code of honour, which defended and supported the weakest, in their guaranteeing services that the state denied them. We sought to remove the mafia consensus of the new generations."[38] Zecchin believed that

> the real effective strength of pictures is built through the coherence of an ensemble of photographs organized in a visual narrative (as an exhibition or a publication) much more than with a single and isolated photograph. Our photographs could be used more effectively to construct a memory and to develop a social conscience as opposed to the practice of forgetting (that is essential to the power of the mafia) because they constitute a coherent ensemble.[39]

Zecchin felt that photography could be used to restore a public realm that might, in Arendt's terms, create a common world in which collective and public recognition of the brutality of mafia criminality could be experienced as a force of affect that, although felt immediately, is not always easy to understand or to articulate. It is in the force of affect felt as a sensory intensity – a wince, a gasp, a tightness in the throat – that difficult knowledge begins to register. Perhaps this is what the congregation in Corleone felt as they viewed Zecchin's photographs before quickly returning to their homes, but we cannot know. This force of affect holds the potential, argues Roger Simon, who follows Deleuze and Guttari, "to place a disruptive claim on viewers and provide the possibilities of new thought without guarantees as to its substance and movement."[40] This force of emotion might work on a pedagogical level that exceeds contemplation and moves the viewers to encounter the physical conditions of fellow human beings and the forms of existence they share. This force of emotion is necessary, argues Azoulay, for the photograph to inspire the forms of action that Arendt attributed to bringing something new to the public as well as something that might be unforeseen by its own creator. This type of encounter provokes one, not out of force but voluntarily, to take on new perspectives, pose new questions, or take a course of action not previously planned. The question of affect posed by Simon inspires educators to pursue affect's relation to the possibility of thought.[41] Posted in the open-air exhibit in Palermo and Corleone and housed in Zecchin's archive is a photograph of the murder of Mario Francese, an accomplished antimafia crime reporter for the moderate *Giornale di Sicilia*. Francese's murder was recorded by Zecchin on 26 January 1979. Shot five times in front of his home in Palermo by Leoluca Bagarella, the brother-in-law of Totò Riina, Francese's death was recorded by the state as a crime of passion. The investigation into his death was immediately closed and his murder soon forgotten. In Zecchin's photograph is a line-up of six men standing at Francese's feet. The men are police officers and journalists and colleagues of the victim. Some look directly at his body – spread out like a Christ figure outlined in chalk – some look away, others at one another, one directly at the camera. The second man from the right with a moustache and facing the camera was Boris Giuliano, the head of the mobile police unit. He was murdered six months later by Corleonesi boss Leoluca Bagarella. A tableau of men clustered together can be seen in the background. Alongside Francese's body is another chalk outline stained with blood. The outline takes the shape of Francese's body. What is not captured in this photograph is Francese's 21-year-old son Giulio, a young reporter, arriving to report on the crime, not knowing that the victim was his father. Just a few blocks from this dead journalist, hundreds of thousands of people are terrified to leave their homes, to speak of what they know or see. They are, in Azoulay's words, "the present absentees in this photograph."[42] Confined to their homes, silent, behind shuttered windows, they are restricted from access to the spaces of plurality Arendt believes to be the necessary condition for action.

Azoulay's concept of "the practical gaze" helps to further understand Zecchin's pedagogy of action and remembrance.[43] Seeking to foster "the practical gaze," which extends beyond the photographic frame, is, argues Azoulay, the central condition for the accumulation of civil knowledge that cannot be controlled by sovereign powers or authoritative political domains. Here Azoulay shares the concerns expressed by Zecchin early in his career at *L'Ora* when he recognized the level of control authoritative channels of communication exert on photographic images and the necessity of creating an alternative, publicly accessible archive apart from state control. The practical gaze aims to generate a photographic civil discourse within the realm of the civil imagination that restores life stories neglected by the state and forgotten by history. This work of memory entails recognizing what Italian philosopher Giorgio Agamben calls "*homo sacer*" and "bare life." Radically excluded by the polis but at the same time sufficiently included to be the subject of murder, sacred or bare life cannot, in Agamben's words "be sacrificed and yet may be killed."[44] As if in conversation with Agamben, Arendt expresses her concern for "totalitarian man's" – both past and latent – intent on destroying human life after having destroyed the meaning of all lives, including his own. She writes:

> The tragedy began ... when it turned out that there was no mind to inherit and to question, to think about and to remember. The point of the matter is that the "completion," which indeed every enacted event must have in the minds of those who then are to tell the story and to convey its meaning, eluded them; and without this thinking completion after the act, without the articulation accomplished by remembrance, there simply was no story left that could be told.[45]

Implicit in Arendt's account of the failure of remembrance is the loss of "the who" or the "agent" of the story. Francese, one of the very first "excellent cadavers,"[46] was well known for exposing the corruption and bidding wars among the mafia; consequently, he was feared by the Cosa Nostra. The Cosa Nostra, an integral part of the state, operated from the very institutions where people like Francese worked. It would be 24 years before his killers would be imprisoned and the full story of Mario Francese's death told. Similar to Impastato's family's pursuit of justice, Giulio Francese worked tirelessly to contest the state and establish the truth about the murder of his father.

Zecchin's photograph of Francese's murder circulated and re-circulated during the time of the state's disavowal. It continues to circulate today, not only in his archive but also on antimafia websites, commemorative gatherings honouring journalists killed by the mafia, blogs, and Facebook pages. The life of this photograph continues to hold the potential to carry difficult knowledge and to work towards cultivating a "practical gaze" among spectators, asking them to take part in evoking and keeping memories and histories alive that were abandoned and silenced by a global network that houses and too often sanctions mafia violence. If photography is to work as an ethical pedagogy of remembrance, the photographic image must work as an activating strategy, not a truth to be displayed and always and already "there," independent of the photojournalist and passively viewed. The event of photography, argues Azoulay, includes not the information regarding where the photograph was taken (although this too is important), but the specific details and relevant data pertaining to the photograph. As well, the "event of photography" involves disrupting the existing unjust social order and redistributing the range of social places shut down by totalitarian authorities.

Franco Zecchin continues to raise concerns about the risks involved when a photograph escapes the photojournalist's control. When photographs become icons, they do so, argues Zecchin, because the image adheres to an existing collective imaginary of the mafia, and this indeed escapes the author's control.[47] Zecchin's concern pertains specifically to the ways in which his images can be used to promote stereotyped images of mafia violence and romanticize and sensationalize life under mafia rule. Moreover, argues Zecchin, when photographs escape the author's control and are shown out of their social and cultural contexts for uses that fail to correspond to effective antimafia practices, or worse, legitimate stereotypic images of the mafia as an invincible, immortal organization, they contribute to cultivating lives of precarity rather than civility and justice.

In *Frames of War: When Is Life Grievable?* Butler argues that the capacity to apprehend a life as valuable is in part dependent on the extent to which that life is produced "according to norms that qualify it as a life, or indeed as part of a life ... We have decided that some particular notion of 'personhood' will determine the scope and meaning of recognizability."[48] The "frames of war" delineated by the mafia exert a particular kind of war effort. They produce an operation of power and rationale that distinguishes between valuable and grievable lives on the one hand, and devalued and ungrievable lives on the other.[49] Is the photograph Zecchin offers of Francese an answer to Butler's question when she asks: "What allows a life to become visible in its precariousness and its need for shelter, and what is it that keeps us from seeing or understanding certain lives in this way?"[50] To what extent does Zecchin's public pedagogy inspire an action-oriented solidarity that opens the viewers of this photograph up to seeing and responding to the precarious lives not only of journalists and antimafia activists but also of men, women, and children most vulnerable to mafia terrorism and other acts of state-sponsored violence? What stories are called forth by this photograph? In what ways are we, as viewers of this photograph, complicit in failing to recognize the lives of men, women, and children vulnerable to poverty, violence, and war as grievable?

In his discussion of photography and ethical pedagogies of remembrance, Roger Simon argues that "encountering photographs creates a political space and it remains an open question as to the terms on which the politics of this space will be enacted."[51] Simon's claim resonates with the way in which Azoulay puts Arendt's concept of action to work when she conceptualizes the citizenry of photography. This citizenry, explains Azoulay, is open, borderless, and distinguished by civil characteristics.[52] "Much like action, which always occurs within a political sphere of plurality, the ... civil gaze, also exists – always and only – within a plurality. The spectator activating this gaze views the photograph and recognizes instantly that what is inscribed in it and discernible in it are products of plurality."[53] The murders of Antonio Scardina, Claudio Domino, and Mario Francese offer examples of one tragic potential product of plurality too often overlooked by education. Their deaths stand as a tragic outcome of difference, inequality, aggression, poverty, and what Arendt describes as "the calamities of action."[54] Action can be treacherous. "The chief hazard of action," observes Elisabeth Young-Bruehl in her reading of Arendt, "is that it has effects that are uncontrollable, unstoppable and unpredictable."[55] The conditions marking the deaths of Francese, Scardina, and Domino, while different, are each tied to acts of dissent and witnessing. The meaning of these actions can only be understood after they have ended – only when action has become a story susceptible to narration.

To recognize the singular death of any one victim of mafia violence as grievable requires more than simply identifying what is shown in the photograph of their murder and marking it as part of an evidentiary record. It requires attention of a particular sort, what Azoulay describes as "watching" the photograph as one would a moving picture. This resonates with Zecchin's concept of arranging photographs alongside one another to create an ensemble of actions. The capacity to watch involves inscribing dimensions of time and movement into the interpretation of the still photograph. This "practical gaze" asks when and where the subject of the photograph suffered the injury, reconstructing the photographic situation and distinguishing the reading of the injury from an exercise in aesthetic appreciation.[56] The "practical gaze" is activated the moment that one understands that citizenship, in Azoulay's words, "is a tool of a struggle or an obligation to others to struggle against injuries inflicted on those others, citizen and noncitizen alike ... the civil spectator has a duty to employ that skill the day she encounters photographs of those injuries – to employ it in order to negotiate the manner in which she and the photographed are ruled."[57] Education's challenge is to create the conditions necessary for the "civil spectator" of the photograph to reconstruct the photographic situation and to feel the obligation to take action against the injuries represented.

The challenges posed to the spectator watching a photograph in the midst of state-sanctioned terror are evident in an RAI video clip made during Zecchin's open-air exhibit on 7 October 1979 in Corleone. There, the exhibit featured the impact of mafia criminality: photographs of car bombings initiated by Corleonesi mafia bosses, meetings among bosses, murders, and agricultural devastation. The narrative voice-over introduces the exhibit by detailing the economic domination sustained by the mafia in the region and led by Totò Riina, Leoluca Bagarella, and Luciano Leggio. When asked by an interviewer what they thought of the photographs of car bombings and street murders, most of the older men walked away or stated that they preferred not to respond, that "it is better not to speak." When pressed about the photographs of the murders ordered by Leggio, another young man walked away stating that he didn't understand politics. Another man (only one woman was interviewed in the entire sequence) insisted that he did not see Leggio in the photographs ("*non lo visto*"). At the end of this clip, when asked to comment on spectators' claims that the exhibit was difficult to see, Letizia Battaglia makes a distinction between difficulty and fear. She argues that as journalists, she and her colleagues reported on the ordinary activity in Palermo and the surrounding regions. In her estimation people were afraid to look at the photographs in the midst of relentless violence. "Here," she states in the video, "we experience a paralyzing fear." Yet despite their fear, the people of Corleone did look at the photographs. They moved in close and studied them carefully before walking away from the interviewer, before retreating to their homes.

In her essay "On the Nature of Totalitarianism," Arendt raises concerns about forms of government defined by lawfulness: "The greatness, but also the perplexity of laws in free societies, is that they only tell what one should not, but never what one should, do."[58] She offers three principles of action guiding both the governed and the government: *virtue* in a republic, *honour* in monarchy, and *fear* in tyrannical forms of government.[59] For Arendt, fear in tyranny destroys the potential for action and eradicates the public realm of politics. This is clearly made evident in many of the responses spectators had to Zecchin's public exhibit. The state of isolation and impotence combines to destroy any use for a principle of action. What Zecchin and his colleagues offer education, however, is an example of just how imperfect and porous totalitarianism is. Totalitarianism does not eliminate all forms of spontaneous human action, freedom, or the inherent human capacity to make a new beginning. This is made evident by the photography of Zecchin and Battaglia, as well as the activism of Addiopizzo and Addiopizzo Travel, Corleone Dialogos, and activists and educators, such as Umberto Santino, Anna Puglisi, Don Luigi Ciotti, and so many others who have struggled against the mafia for generations.

Zecchin's duty to report offers a paradigmatic case of using photography to document crises in citizenship, civic status, and state-sanctioned violence. The duty to report evokes the stories of lives that might be forgotten or rendered ungrievable, and in turn endows these stories with an indeterminate historical force in present and future social life. Taken as a form of public pedagogy, Zecchin's open-air exhibits represent abject images of difficult knowledge that exceed any discourse that might establish their final significance or legacy. While Arendt does not write of photography and art as generative forms for cultivating non-violent spaces where the uniqueness of plurality can thrive, she no doubt would recognize Zecchin's photography as generating a form of socially committed persuasive action that inspires remembrance and narrative exchange.

Conclusion

I want to end this chapter by returning to a discussion of how Zecchin's belief in a duty to report informs a public pedagogy of remembrance. Zecchin's photography serves as a public record of commitment to use photojournalism to offer representations of mafia violence that stood apart from narratives that were saturated with private, economic, and political interests. After Impastato's death, Zecchin recalls the urgency he felt to find avenues to share public information apart from state control. Together with his colleagues, and inspired by the political activism of Giuseppe Impastato, Zecchin transformed public spaces of silence and fear into public gallery spaces for ordinary citizens to experience social engagement and exercise the duty to confront mafia criminality and political corruption. In the main square in Cinisi, on 9 May 1979, the anniversary of Impastato's death, the first national demonstration against the mafia – composed of two thousand people from across the country – took place. The mounted photographic exhibits, accompanied by detailed explanatory text, included images of murders, arrests, trials, and funerals, as well as poverty and social injustice in order to, writes Zecchin,

> highlight the collusion between the corrupt politicians and local leaders with the mafia. People stopped to look at each photo, read the captions, giving their opinions and offering their remarks. This was the first time that the mafia was debated openly in a public space ... slowly but surely we had begun to ... shatter its dissemination of a widespread culture of passive acceptance, subjection and silence.[60]

I suggest that the pop-up exhibits set up by Zecchin and his colleagues enact a spatialization of the duty to report that invites collective ethical engagements with the geographies of individual and collective life. The pop-up exhibits provoked participants to act as collective eyewitnesses to poverty, environmental ruin, and state complicities in violence. Moreover, these exhibits challenged the isolation that the force of tyranny can bring about. Arendt reminds us that tyranny relies on isolation – the isolation of the tyrant from his or her subjects and the isolation of subjects from one another through mutual fear and suspicion.[61] Arendt underscores that tyranny not only eradicates diversity but also destroys spaces where human action, plurality, and conversation are possible.

Zecchin's call to not abandon the pursuit of justice is also, in my estimation, a pedagogical commitment to assuage the pain of what Jill Stauffer describes as "ethical loneliness."[62] Stauffer uses this term to describe the experience of a double abandonment that comes with being condemned to a life of precarity, as happens in cases of societal trauma, compounded by the experiences of not being heard when one testifies to what happened. This sense of ethical loneliness is portrayed in the stories of Impastato and Francese, as well as those of Francesca Morvillo, Giovanni Falcone, and Libero Grassi. In each instance, the state refused to listen well. Consequently, the memories of their complex and singular lives were depoliticized. By not listening well, the state worked to promote forgetfulness and foreclose on collective mourning. Stauffer's insights into the importance of hearing testimony and its impact on communities in transition resonates with Winnicott's and Khan's concept of the necessity for the state to sustain social protective shields that can filter danger in the external world. The capacity to hear well as a witness to suffering is crucial to releasing people from the loneliness felt when they are dehumanized and confined to conditions of injustice. The condition of ethical loneliness can emerge, as made evident by the scholarship of Bronwen Leebaw, when we have a strong urge to hear stories of victimization rather than resistance, thereby relegating stories of resistance to the margins of collective memory. As well, argues Stauffer, in wanting to hear stories of resilience, one might fail to hear stories of a self's destruction. When asked how ethical loneliness might be produced, Stauffer offers the following examples:

> When academic discourse analysis takes testimony aiming to demonstrate strength *and* loss and transforms it into a story only about pain; when the legalized goal of isolating victims from perpetrators fails to see how porous the lines between the two can be in protracted complex conflict; or when those empowered to judge do not adequately understand the context in which histories and stories are conveyed, or the forms they might take, for indigenous or other minority communities.[63]

Ethical loneliness haunts societies in transition. Beyond the political impact of this loneliness, the failure to hear marginalized, half-spoken stories affects the present and how the past is remembered, and destroys the potential legacies of persons marginalized and abandoned by their communities. Zecchin's commitment to use photography as a means through which to see and to listen closely offers education insights into the power of aesthetics to re-appropriate city spaces, town centres, and countrysides as sites for collective life and civil responsibility within the interstices of economic and political injustices and social, geographical, and cultural transition. Zecchin's spontaneous exhibits can be understood as a practice of story-taking and storytelling that is devoted to a quality of human interaction where people act and speak together, and respect difference and all that is strange, while sustaining the conditions under which action is possible and freedom can appear. In this sense Zecchin's public pedagogy of remembrance contributes to an understanding of how the citizenry of photography might open spaces for deliberation and judgment about the common good, and promote plurality and freedom by recasting non-violent civil dissent against the mafia as an aesthetic encounter. This pedagogical encounter is committed to restoring the loneliness instiled by the silence, fear, and isolation inherent in the mafia's imposition of *omertà*. As well, it represents a form of collective action that understands social pain as a fundamental injury to participants' well-being and sense of belonging on intimate, local, and transnational scales.

Epilogue

On 10 July 2015 *The New York Times* reported a new development in Casal di Principe, hometown to Roberto Saviano and the Casalesi clan, one of the most powerful groups within the Camorra. As a result of the Rognoni-La Torre Law and a collaboration between the Uffizi Museum in Florence and the Capodimonte Museum in Naples, a concrete villa once owned by local mafia boss Edigio Coppola was transformed into a temporary museum. Antonio Natali, director of the state-run Uffizi Museum, explained that the exhibit stood as a symbolic gesture to show that the state was present. Renato Natale, the antimafia mayor of Casal di Principe, reported to *The Guardian* that it was only through the promotion of civil society that communities could protect themselves from mafia infiltration.

The exhibition, entitled "Light Defeats the Shadows," included paintings by Caravaggio and his followers, among whom was artist Pacecco De Rosa. Dedicated to the memory of Peppe Diana, a local priest who was shot by Camorra members as he prepared for mass in 1994, the title of the exhibit explicitly cites the chiaroscuro technique used by painters like Caravaggio to make their figures emerge from dimly lit backgrounds. In an interview with *New York Times* writer Elisabetta Povoledo, Saviano expressed hope for what he called "a miracle – a sign of the will to start something radically different in a territory that is a historic center of the Camorra."[1] As the paintings, rather than mafiosi, arrived under the protection of armed guards, art historian Antonella Diana also remarked on what a joy it was to see the people in Casale witness art of value presented to their community. Youth in the area have been recruited as guides for the exhibition and to talk with visitors about what many public officials are describing as the rebirth of the town of Casal.

To what extent does this exhibit offer the forms of story-taking and story-telling that Saviano inspires and that speak to the theme of natality structuring the activism of Addiopizzo and Addiopizzo Travel, Corleone Dialogos, and the photojournalism of Franco Zecchin and Letizia Battaglia? Are the stories the recruited museum guides tell about the claimed rebirth of Casal attuned to the challenges that trauma poses to language and to narrative? Do these narratives resist the narrative fetishism Eric Santner cautions against? Does this exhibit take and tell stories in ways that present difficult knowledge, marginalized histories, and political complexities? Perhaps it is too soon to tell.

I started this book by arguing that at the very heart of transitional justice is a pedagogical impulse made evident in the antimafia struggle against the Cosa Nostra in Sicily. The communities in transition represented in this book work to challenge denial, to learn from the past, and to engage in a set of ethical questions: Which memories are worthy of our collective attention? Which legacies are restored and sustained amid social breakdown? How should past violence be judged? Following Leebaw, I argued that the use of legalistic and restorative frameworks are often inclined to pursue new forms of forgetting and mythmaking by relying on criminal justice models that depoliticize the terms of investigation and, most relevant to this book, limit official remembrance of past suffering to victims or passive bystanders rather than recognizing the role of those who took action, engaged in dissent, and resisted state-sanctioned violence. Throughout this book I too have used a type of chiaroscuro technique to portray figures who, while relegated to the shadows of memory, engaged in non-violent dissent against the Cosa Nostra. The activists and public pedagogues I have portrayed offer educators lessons in the complexities of working towards justice, particularly given that mafias continue to extend their grip on local and global markets, political and cultural fields. Drawing on Arendt's concept of natality, I pursued a pedagogical ethic of remembrance that persisted, as I discussed in the Introduction, in marshalling the life drive, placing value on new beginnings, and resisting narratives of disavowal, naive hope, or consolation.

Yet although the public pedagogy of organizations such as Corleone Dialogos and Addiopizzo create a political sphere of communication that has emancipatory potential for cultural and social renewal, particularly within the context of a society in transition, the imperfect erasures of mafia influences continue to haunt antimafia efforts. I illustrate this influence in my discussion of Corleone Dialogos and the stories the members tell of Bernardino Verro and the agricultural cooperatives in Sicily. Many of these cooperatives sustain class divisions and hierarchies and jeopardize, as argued by Rakopoulos, internal democratic work relations. The case of Corleone Dialogos raises important questions about recalling multiple memories of violence and speaks to the cross-cutting nature of public memories. I showed how the messy historical contingencies associated with the stories told of Verro, Impastato, Falcone, and Borsellino are too often relegated to the shadows in an effort to create a selective genealogy of martyrs who serve the antimafia project. To my mind this simplification of, for example, Verro's complicated history of mafia involvement becomes assimilated into an archive of triumphant narratives, reminding us of Simon's claim that remembrance alone is not the secret of redemption. One of the most important questions I leave you with is, What would it mean for antimafia public pedagogies to revisit and rewrite hegemonic sites of memory that collapse into what Puccio-Den astutely described as the antimafia religion?

The Story-Takers illustrates how transitional justice marks a specific and most complicated moment in a nation's development, particularly with respect to mourning a traumatic past. While I accept Renga's claim that Italy continues to inhabit a state of national melancholia because it has yet to experience the period of latency so necessary for a trauma to be spoken about and worked through, I question the idea that societies must exist in a post-traumatic state to take up the work of mourning. Following Freud and the work of R.M. Kennedy, Deborah Britzman, Roger Simon, Michael Rothberg, Mario Di Paolantonio, and Eric Santner, I argued that the experience of trauma can never be put behind us. In fact, traumatic histories persist in exerting their influence on the present. In the chapters on Addiopizzo, Corleone Dialogos, Letizia Battaglia, and Franco Zecchin, I found that within the dynamics of political transition, the work of mourning is possible within the interstices of trauma when storytaking and storytelling provide alternatives to the neo-liberal narrative of denial and consolation that depoliticize transitional justice and efface the singularities of human subjects. I hope to have shown that the pedagogical impulse of transitional justice is most educative when stories of resistance, refusal, and non-violent dissent are part of the public memorial landscape. Italian activists, teachers, and artists offer educators examples of how the work of mourning can take hold and sustain itself amid social breakdown. We learn from public pedagogues, such as Edo Zaffuto, Francesca Vannini Parenti, and Dario Riccobono, that a pedagogy inspired by the life drive, by a hope for new beginnings, need not slide into denial or rely on consoling narratives that forget past atrocities in the name of a happy ending. We learn from photojournalist Letizia Battaglia of the importance of persistently and ritualistically transforming narratives of the difficult legacies people have inherited, and to sustain in these narratives the traces of the trauma's impact. Each of these activists offers lessons in the challenges that accompany the work of mourning. As well, the narratives appended to the Falcone Tree and registered on Francesca Morvillo's Facebook page present clear cases of how societies in transition can take up, refuse, fail, and defer the work of collective mourning amid social breakdown. Both these cases raise questions about the impact the institutionalization of memory has on mourning in transitional times.

The Story-Takers stands as a timely study, as I hope to have made clear. Despite the innovative non-violent dissent against the mafia, the mafia continues to thrive. It is the most globalized multinational corporation in the world, with drug trafficking working as its largest revenue source. Not only do mafia organizations modify democracies from within the state by tethering their illegal revenue streams to the legal economy, but they also garner, in the words of Saviano, social consensus: "In cases where the state is absent, the mafia "offers services" to citizens. Their winning formula is simple: an extreme tendency towards economic evolution combined with a minimal tendency towards cultural evolution."[2] Although the story-takers I introduce in this book work at the level of the law, they also recognize that law and policies must work in partnership with an education committed to taking and telling stories that remember dissent, sustain rather than neutralize political discourse, and recognize the traumatizing impact that the mafia has on individual and collective identities. In evoking the necessity of retaining rather than expunging the traces of trauma from stories of non-violent dissent against the mafia, a public pedagogy of remembrance that has the capacity to more fully politicize the partial and lost memories of complicities through memory work that values and sustains a critical dialogue with normative frameworks for civility and justice will be needed. This will require taking and telling stories that interrupt the violent and triumphant genealogy of mafia and antimafia heroism that celebrates the death drive and short-circuits the power of ingenuity fused throughout storytelling practices committed to Arendt's ideals for renewing a common world free from coercion, totalitarianism, and fear.

To conclude I will briefly outline the signatures of a public pedagogy that sustains an abiding concern with the pedagogical impulse of transitional justice – to prevent a violent past from being repeated and heal the wounds of the past. As I have argued throughout this book, societies in transition yearn for narratives to mediate traumatic experience. Directed both at people who lived through trauma and at future generations, a public pedagogy of remembrance directs its attention to renewing a public sphere where shared subjectivity and public civic life can flourish without the threat of violence. Each case study in this book portrays the complex ways in which a public pedagogy of remembrance combines rhetorics of repetition, erasure, and re-elaborations to accomplish, and at other times undermine, collective mourning and practices of remembrance. As Freud came to understand later in his life, mourning is an interminable process and cannot easily be disentangled from the symptoms associated with melancholia – an enduring attachment to the love object and a refusal to turn to the world and risk love again. The idea of working through traumatic loss implies a transformation in which traumatic memories are given representational and narrative form and a person, culture, or society experiences a new state of being in which the trauma is managed. Yet where is the line to be drawn between consoling, repetitive, or triumphant narratives that undermine a working through and multidirectional narratives that draw on the creativity of memory to acknowledge loss and make a working through possible?

In writing about her experience of rape and assault, philosopher Susan Brison challenges easy binaries between repetition or repeating the trauma and having worked it through. In fact, Brison argues that acts of repetition, such as the stories told about Bernardino Verro by Corleone Dialogos or those appended to the Falcone Tree, can be read as an important part of the process of working through trauma. The work of repetition itself can, according to Brison, lead to greater control of the trauma narrative and create the potential for more integrated narratives in the future.[3] Drawing on the work of Brison in her analysis of cultural trauma, Marita Sturken argues that repetition can serve as a means through which cultures make sense of trauma and work to make grief and loss manifest in daily life, specifically in times of suffering.[4]

A public pedagogy of remembrance recognizes that expressions of trauma can be represented on a continuum. As stories are told, repeated, listened to, and repeated once again in the company of others, the interminable work of mourning is made possible within the interstices of societal trauma. This possibility emerges, in part, because storytelling and story-taking disclose what Arendt and Cavarero described as our subjective uniqueness and our intersubjective connection to others. Narratives of the self in the presence of others represent singular histories, experiences, longings, and injuries. As relational practices that respect unique subjectivities, story-taking and storytelling have the capacity to re-signify normative ideals about who and what are remembered and thus re-signify the political frames that organize responses to trauma. Simply put, the practice of story-taking and storytelling inspired by the antimafia activism represented in this book speaks to the vital necessity for transitional justice to take up a pedagogical impulse grounded in a commitment to, in the words of Cavarero, the singularity of speakers who, in the act of speaking with one another, create the "taking-place of politics."[5] This pedagogical commitment recognizes the specificity of social injury and the dangers inherent in depoliticizing the actions and experiences of victims and perpetrators. This approach to public pedagogy works to understand trauma within its larger historical and political contexts, rather than relying on competitive memories or notions of a clear victim-perpetrator divide that ignores, as portrayed, for example, in the cases of Corleone Dialogos and the Falcone Tree, the complex areas of complicity and non-violent dissent.

To what extent can these public pedagogical principles operate in a context of ongoing mafia conflict, gross economic inequality, poor health care, unemployment, clientelism, and lingering mistrust of government? Transitional justice relies as much on legislation and formal principles as it does on informal principles – material and imagined – to address the needs of victims and localities. Such informal principles create, in the words of Umberto Santino, micro-entrepreneurial subjectivities and antimafia practices of daily living that generate a renewed sense of social citizenship. These micro-subjectivities, portrayed throughout the case studies in this book, challenge stereotypic images of southern Italy as lacking any capacity for civic engagement and ingenuity. Santino challenges this idea, described as amoral familism – set forth first in research by E.C. Banfield and later taken up by Robert Putnam in his 1993 publication *Making Democracy Work: Civic Traditions in Modern Italy*. Santino argues that the pursuit of transitional justice takes place within the interstices of daily mafia violence. As well, within the interstices of daily life, the work of mourning takes shape not as a linear, normative sequential process, but rather as an iterative, collective, imaginative pursuit of narratives that shatter the binary split between mourning and melancholia, trauma and post-trauma. In the context of antimafia non-violent dissent, the interminable work of mourning involves a process of making meaning through storytelling and story-taking practices that are provoked from sites of difficulty and may often result in people turning away from, disavowing, or avoiding the difficult knowledge they cannot bear to know. Inherent in any space of learning that interferes with or challenges a person's valued understandings is loss: the loss of assumptions, ideals, and imaginings. Among the most challenging pedagogical projects is the work of creating possibilities to work through the internal loss so that participants do not flee the site of difficulty. The anti-extortion campaigns of Addiopizzo, and the work of re-elaboration taken up by Letizia Battaglia in her contemporary photography, offer educators lessons in forging new meanings and imagined socialities from sites of difficulty, and they do so amid rather than after social breakdown and injustice. Taken together, the public pedagogies explored in this book have implications that reach far beyond antimafia public pedagogies. The work of story-taking and storytelling, so poignantly taken up by antimafia activists, recognizes the nonlinear, recursive process of making sense of disruptive, violent histories that continue to sustain a presence in contemporary times. As well, they recognize that, and here I paraphrase Pulitzer Prize–winning author Ta-Nehisi Coates: you have to find peace within the chaos, you have to find some sort of mission in the chaos ... you have to devote yourself to the struggle within the chaos with no assurance that you will see any victory within your lifetime.[6]

Notes

Introduction: Story-Taking, Public Pedagogy, and the Challenges of Transitional Justice

1 All translations from Italian have been made by the author unless otherwise noted.
2 Nina E. Rothe, "The Face of Courage: An Exclusive Interview with Roberto Saviano," *Huffington Post*, January 8, 2012, http://www.huffingtonpost.com/e-nina-rothe/roberto-saviano_b_1184140.html.
3 Rothe, "The Face of Courage."
4 Roberto Saviano, "My Life under Armed Guard," *The Guardian*, January 14, 2015, https://www.theguardian.com/world/2015/jan/14/-sp-roberto-saviano-my-life-under-armed-guard-gomorrah.
5 Rothe, "The Face of Courage."
6 Ibid.
7 Sebastian Rotello, "He Fights the Italian Mob with Words," *Los Angeles Times*, October 19, 2008, http://articles.latimes.com/2008/oct/19/world/fg-mafia19.
8 Leopoldo Franchetti, *Condizioni politiche e amministrative della Sicilia*, vol. I of L. Franchetti and S. Sonnino, *Inchiesta in Sicilia*, 2 vols, Florence, 1974, quoted in Nelson Moe, *The View from Vesuvius: Italian Culture and the Southern Question* (Los Angeles: University of California Press, 2002), 224.
9 Rothe, "The Face of Courage."
10 Ossigeno per L'Informazione Italian Observatory, *2010 Report: Protecting Threatened Journalists in Italy: Challenges and Suggestions*, trans. Silvia Cuomo (Rome: Ossigeno per L'Informazione, 2011), 14, http://www.odg.it/files/O2_Full_English_2010_Report_0.pdf.
11 Ibid.
12 See Michael Scarlett, "Imagining a World Beyond Genocide: Teaching about Transitional Justice," *The Social Studies* 100, no. 4 (2009).

13 "What Is Transitional Justice?" International Center for Transitional Justice, accessed May 2015, https://www.ictj.org/about/transitional-justice.

14 Pablo de Greiff, "Trial and Punishment, Pardon and Oblivion: On Two Inadequate Policies for the Treatment of Former Human Rights Abusers," *Philosophy and Social Criticism*, 22 (1996): 93–111 (quotation from p. 94).

15 de Greiff, "Trial and Punishment, Pardon and Oblivion," 29.

16 See Kerry Clamp and Jonathan Doak, "More Than Words: Restorative Justice Concepts in Transitional Justice Settings," *International Criminal Law Review* 12 (2012): 339–60.

17 Bronwyn Leebaw, *Judging State-Sponsored Violence: Imagining Political Change* (New York: Cambridge University Press, 2011), 14–15.

18 Ibid., 15.

19 Ibid., 15.

20 Ibid., 15–16.

21 I first underscored the relationship between corruption and human rights violations in my essay "'A Taste of Justice': Digitial Media and Libera Terra's Antimafia Public Pedagogy of Agrarian Dissent," in *The Italian Antimafia, New Media, and the Culture of Legality*, ed. Robin Pickering-Iazzi (Toronto: University of Toronto Press, 2017), chap. 3.

22 Chris Cuneen, "Exploring the Relationship between Reparations, the Gross Violation of Human Rights, and Restorative Justice," in *Handbook of Restorative Justice: A Global Perspective*, ed. Dennis Sullivan and Larry Tifft (New York: Routledge, 2005), 355–67.

23 See Leebaw, *Judging State-Sponsored Violence*, 187.

24 See Michael Rothberg, "Progress, Progression, Procession: William Kentridge and the Narratology of Transitional Justice," *Narrative* 20, no. 1 (2012): 1–24; Ruti Teitel, *Transitional Justice* (New York: Oxford University Press, 2001).

25 Ruti Teitel, "Transitional Justice as Liberal Narrative," in *Globalizing Transitional Justice: Contemporary Essays*, chap. 6 (New York: Oxford University Press, 2014), 249.

26 Rothberg, "Progress, Progression, Procession," 5.

27 Teitel, "Transitional Justice as Liberal Narrative," 241–55.

28 Rothberg, "Progress, Progression, Procession," 6.

29 Ibid., 7.

30 See Judith Butler, *Precarious Life: The Powers of Mourning and Violence* (New York: Verso Press, 2004); Paula M. Salvio, *Anne Sexton: Teacher of Weird Abundance* (New York: State University of New York Press, 2007).

31 Butler, *Precarious Life*, 41.

32 Butler, *Precarious Life*, 140.

33 Natasha Levinson, "Teaching in the Midst of Belatedness: The Paradox of Natality in Hannah Arendt's Educational Thought," *Educational Theory* 47, no. 4 (1997): 435–51.

34 Dana Renga, *Unfinished Business: Screening the Italian Mafia in the New Millennium* (Toronto: University of Toronto Press, 2013), 11.

35 Ibid., 10.

36 Jill Stauffer, *Ethical Lonelines: The Injustice of Not Being Heard* (New York: Columbia University Press, 2015).

37 E. Ann Kaplan, *Trauma Culture: The Politics of Terror and Loss in Media and Literature* (New Jersey: Rutgers University Press, 2005), 137.

38 Ulrich Baer, *110 Stories: New York Writes after September 11* (New York: New York University Press, 2002), quoted in E. Ann Kaplan, *Trauma Culture: The Politics of Terror and Loss in Media and Literature* (New Jersey: Rutgers University Press, 2005), 137.

39 Jeffrey C. Alexander, *Trauma: A Social Theory* (Malden, MA: Polity Press, 2013), 11; Max Weber, *The Sociology of Religion* (Boston: Beacon Press, 1978), 468–517.

40 Alexander, *Trauma: A Social Theory*, 11.

41 Ibid., 1.

42 Ibid., 8.

43 See Alexander, *Trauma*, 11.

44 See Rothberg, "Progress, Progression, Procession," 12.

45 Jennifer A. Sandlin, Brian D. Schultz, and Jake Burdick, ed., *Handbook of Public Pedagogy: Education and Learning Beyond Schooling* (New York: Routledge, 2010); Alice Pitt and Deborah Britzman, "Speculations on Qualities of Difficult Knowledge in Teaching and Learning: An Experiment in Psychoanalytic Research," *Qualitative Studies in Education* 16, no. 6 (2003): 755–76.

46 Roger I. Simon, *A Pedagogy of Witnessing: Curatorial Practice and the Pursuit of Social Justice* (Albany: State University of New York Press, 2013), 194.

47 Ibid., 195.

48 Ibid., 195.

49 Ibid., 194.

50 Peter Robb, *Midnight in Sicily: On Art, Food, History, Travel and La Cosa Nostra* (New York: Picador, 1996), xii.

51 Alexander Stille, *Excellent Cadavers: The Mafia and the Death of the First Italian Republic* (New York: Vintage, 1996).

52 Ibid., 5.

53 Corleone Dialogos website, Giuseppe Crapisi, last modified April 3, 2017, http://www.corleonedialogos.it/.

54   Adriana Cavarero, *Relating Narratives: Storytelling and Selfhood*, trans. Paul A. Kottman (New York: Routledge, 2000). First published in Italian as *Tu che mi guardi, tu che mi racconti*, ed. Giagiacomo Feltrinelle (Milan, Andegari: 1997).

55   Anna Freud and Dorothy T. Burlingham, *War and Children* (Greenwood Press: Westport, CT, 1943).

56   Simon, *A Pedagogy of Witnessing*, 2013.

57   Roger I. Simon, *The Touch of the Past: Remembrance, Learning, and Ethics* (New York: Palgrave Macmillan, 2005), 35.

58   Ibid., 15.

59   Simon, *The Touch of the Past*, 16.

60   See Eric L. Santner, "History beyond the Pleasure Principle: Some Thoughts on the Representation of Trauma," in *Probing the Limits of Representation: Nazism and the"Final Solution,"* ed. Saul Friedlander (Cambridge: Harvard University Press, 1992); Rothberg, "Progress, Progression, Procession," 7.

61   Adriana Cavarero, *Relating Narratives: Storytelling and Selfhood* (London: Routledge Press, 1997), 64. First published in Italian as *Tu che mi guardi, tu che mi racconti*, ed. Giagiacomo Feltrinelle (Milan, Andegari: 1997).

62   Ibid., 64.

63   John Dickie, *Cosa Nostra: A History of the Sicilian Mafia* (London: Hodder and Stoughton, 2004), 231.

64   "Giuseppe Impastato," Centro Siciliano di Documentazione; Umberto Santino, "Fighting the Mafia and Organized Crime: Italy and Europe," in *Crime and Law Enforcement in the Global Village*, ed. W.F. McDonald (Cincinnati: Anderson Publishing, 1997), 151–66, http://www.centroimpastato.com/ fighting-the-mafia-and-organized-crime-italy-and-europe/.

65   See Peter T. Schneider and Jane Schneider, *Reversible Destiny: Mafia, Antimafia, and the Struggle for Palermo* (Los Angeles: University of California Press, 2002); Paul Ginsborg, *Italy and Its Discontents: Family, Civil Society, State: 1980–200* (New York: Palgrave Macmillan, 2003), 100–1, 146–52.

66   Schneider and Schneider, *Reversible Destiny*, 78.

67   Ibid., 77.

68   Ibid., 79.

69   For a historical analysis of the status of state support for antimafia movements in Italy, see Ginsborg, *Italy and Its Discontents*, 324.

70   Teresa de Lauretis, "Eccentric Subjects: Feminist Theory and Historical Consciousness," *Feminist Studies* 16, no. 1 (Spring, 1990), 115–50.

71   Eric L. Santner, *Stranded Objects: Mourning, Memory and Film in Postwar Germany* (Ithaca, NY: Cornell University Press, 1990).

72   Vito Lo Monaco, personal interview with the author, July 2013.

73 Hannah Arendt, "The Crisis in Education," in *Between Past and Future*, 173–96 (New York: Penguin Books, 1977), 189.

74 See Baris Cayli, "Creating Counterpublics against the Italian Mafia: Cultural Conquerors of Web-Based Media," *Javnost–The Public* 20, no. 3 (2013): 59–76.

75 See Leebaw, *Judging State-Sponsored Violence*, 28.

76 Leebaw, *Judging State-Sponsored Violence*, 118 and 168.

77 See R.M. Kennedy, "Toward a Cosmopolitan Curriculum of Forgiveness," *Curriculum Inquiry* 41, no. 1 (2011): 373–93, for an astute discussion about the role narrative can play in replacing Western universal identity categories with an embodied epistemology that recognizes the significance of social difference. As well, Kennedy persuasively argues that the work of reimagining and renewing our social world can indeed take place amid social breakdown if narrative practices are sensitive to the specificity of experience (390).

1 "To Tarry with Grief": Spontaneous Shrines, Public Pedagogy, and the Work of Mourning

1 Alison Jamieson, *Antimafia: Italy's Fight against Organized Crime* (London: Palgrave Macmillan, 1999), 304.

2 John Dickie, *Cosa Nostra: A History of the Sicilian Mafia* (New York: St. Martin's Press, 2004), xx.

3 Deborah Puccio-Den, "The Anti-Mafia Movement as Religion?: The Pilgrimage to the Falcone Tree," in *Shrines and Pilgrimage in the Modern World. New Itineraries into the Sacred*, ed. Peter Jan Margry (Amsterdam: Amsterdam University Press, 2008), 380; Dickie also discussed this phenomenon: John Dickie, "Falcone and Borsellino: Truth and Memory" (lecture, Casa Italiana Zerilli-Marimo, New York City, NY, May 1, 2012).

4 Cyrille Fijnaut and Letizia Paoli, "Organized Crime and Its Control Policies," *European Journal of Crime, Criminal Law and Criminal Justice* 14, no. 3 (2006): 307–27.

5 Falcone had wanted a united European approach to combating the mafia precisely because he believed the mafia affected all of Europe and specifically the European Union. At an international symposium in Germany in November 1990, he argued that the Sicilian and Calabrian migrants brought the mafia with them when they immigrated to Belgium, France, Germany, and elsewhere. He believed that by eliminating internal border controls, the EU helped to facilitate the spread of mafia activity; see Cyrille Fijnaut, "Transnational Organized Crime and Institutional Reform in the European Union: The Case of Judicial Cooperation," in *Combating Transnational Crime: Concepts, Activities and Responses*, ed. P. Williams and D. Vlassis (London: Frank Cass, 2001), 278.

6   Letizia Paoli, ed. *The Oxford Handbooks of Organized Crime* (NewYork: Oxford University Press, 2014); Puccio-Den, "The Anti-Mafia Movement as Religion?"

7   The letters from the Falcone Tree I draw from cover 1992 to 2014.

8   Jack Santino, ed., *Spontaneous Shrines and the Public Memorialization of Death* (New York: Palgrave, 2006), 12.

9   Peter Jan Margry and Cristina Sánchez-Carretero, "Memorializing Traumatic Death," *Anthropology Today* 23, no. 3 (2007): 1–2.

10   Santino, *Spontaneous Shrines*, 369.

11   Sandra Amurri, ed., *L'Albero Falcone* (Palermo: Fondazione Giovanni e Francesca Falcone, 1992), 13.

12   Deborah Puccio-Den, "A Máfia siciliana: a transformação num mal global" [The Sicilian Mafia: Transformation to a Global Evil], *Etnografica (Lisboa)* 12, no. 2 (2008): 55.

13   Amurri, *L'Albero Falcone*, 120.

14   Ibid., 24; Puccio-Den, "The Sicilian Mafia," 60.

15   Santino, *Spontaneous Shrines*, 202.

16   See Cheryl R. Jorgensen-Earp and Lori A. Lanzilotti, "Public Memory and Private Grief: The Construction of Shrines at the Sites of Public Tragedy," *Quarterly Journal of Speech* 84, no. 2 (1998): 150–70.

17   Santino, *Spontaneous Shrines*.

18   See Michael Rothberg, "Progress, Progression, Procession: William Kentridge and the Narratology of Transitional Justice," *Narrative* 20, no. 1 (2012): 1–24.

19   Judith Butler, *Precarious Life: The Powers of Mourning and Violence* (New York: Verso Press, 2004), 27.

20   Ibid., 28.

21   Ibid., xvii and 30.

22   Ibid., 21.

23   Ibid., 30.

24   Curriculum scholars such as R.M. Kennedy, Mario Di Paolantonio, Chloe Brushwood Rose, Bronwen Low, Warren Crichlow, and Sarah Matthews have made and continue to make significant contributions to the ways in which the curriculum – both inside and outside conventional classroom settings – might "tarry with grief." Among the signature features of their work are storytelling and story-taking practices grounded in relational theories that respect the singularity of subjectivities and re-signify normative ideals about who and what are remembered, and thus re-signify the political frames that structure responses to trauma.

25   Public materials developed by the Foundation describe its work as follows: "The Giovanni and Francesca Falcone Foundation was established in Palermo on 10 December 1992 by the family of Falcone and Morvillo. Since 1996, the Foundation has been recognized as a Non Governmental Organization. The main

aim of the Foundation is to promote cultural activities, study and research that encourage the development of anti mafia culture in society and specifically among youth particularly. The Foundation is also dedicated to fostering cooperation among the European legal systems for more effective coordination of all the states and the agencies appointed to the prevention of organized crime. Its overarching goal is to eradicate mafia culture from society.

26 See Peter T. Schneider and Jane Schneider, *Reversible Destiny: Mafia, Antimafia, and the Struggle for Palermo* (Los Angeles: University of California Press, 2002), 445.

27 For an extensive analysis of the evolution of Freud's theories of melancholia, see Tammy Clewell, "Mourning beyond Melancholia: Freud's Psychoanalysis of Loss," *Journal of the American Psychoanalytic Association* 52, no. 1 (2004): 43–67.

28 Ibid.

29 Ibid., 44.

30 Ibid., 47.

31 I use the term *absent referent* to refer to the half-formed discourse or signifiers in search of expression and to represent the loss of Falcone, as well as the meanings embodied in this loss.

32 I write extensively on using poetry to challenge normative prohibitions on grieving in *Anne Sexton: Teacher of Weird Abundance* (Albany: State University of New York Press, 2007); Clewell, "Mourning beyond Melancholia," 52.

33 Clewell, "Mourning beyond Melancholia."

34 Ibid., 57.

35 Ibid., 60.

36 Ernst L. Freud, ed., and Tania Stern and James Stern, trans., *Letters of Sigmund Freud* (New York: Dover Publications, 1992), 386.

37 For a collection of critical essays on Freud's theories of loss, see Jon Mills, ed., *Rereading Freud: Psychoanalysis through Philosophy* (Albany: State University of New York Press, 2004). In this collection, the essay by Emily Zakin, "The 'Alchemy of Identification': Narcissism, Melancholia, Femininity," offers a particularly close reading of Freud's writings on loss and challenges the idea that melancholia is solely a sadistic expression of revenge.

38 Zakin's reading of Sprengnether posits the ego as an "elegiac formation" that memorializes loss and is deeply tied to the work of identity (84–85).

39 Amurri, *L'Albero Falcone*, 13; Puccio-Den, "The Sicilian Mafia," 53.

40 Amurri, *L'Albero Falcone*, 46.

41 Puccio-Den, "The Sicilian Mafia," 55.

42 One example of a "register of action" called "Waves of Legality, Waves of Citizenship" was tied to the public school curricula. This project, sponsored by the Giovanni and Francesca Falcone Foundation and the European Forum for Urban

Security, promoted human right and "legality and the role of civil society in countering organized crime." The international seminar brought together students ages 18 to 30 and international human rights activists throughout Europe until it was discontinued in 2015. The seminar concluded with another event on May 23 called "Boats of Legality," in which approximately 10,000 students from all over Italy would arrive in Palermo in "Boats of Legality" and gather in front of the Falcone Tree to celebrate the memory of Falcone, Morvillo, and their escorts.

43 Amurri, *L'Albero Falcone*, 51; Puccio-Den, "The Sicilian Mafia," 55.

44 Clewell, "Mourning beyond Melancholia."

45 Puccio-Den, "The Sicilian Mafia," 58.

46 Amurri, *L'Albero Falcone*, 199.

47 Puccio-Den, "The Sicilian Mafia," 58.

48 In *Aftermath: Violence and the Remaking of a Self* (Princeton: Princeton University Press, 2003), Susan J. Brison offers insights into the dangers inherent in establishing simple binaries between "repetition" and "working through" trauma. She argues that repetition can be understood as an important part of the process of working through loss and trauma. This theme emerges in the work of contemporary antimafia activists.

49 Roger I. Simon, *The Touch of the Past: Remembrance, Learning and Ethics* (New York: Palgrave Macmillan, 2005).

50 Vikki Bell and Mario Di Paolantonio, "The Haunted *Nomos*: Activist-Artists and the (Im)possible Politics of Memory in Transitional Argentina," *Cultural Politics* 5, no. 2 (2009), 149–78.

51 Simon, *The Touch of the Past*.

52 Ibid.

53 Ibid., 35.

54 Simon, *The Touch of the Past*, 35; Bell and Di Paolantonio, "The Haunted *Nomos*," 149.

55 Simon, *A Pedagogy of Witnessing*, 34.

56 Ibid., 34.

57 Ibid., 36

58 Ibid., 39.

59 Eric L. Santner, "History beyond the Pleasure Principle: Some Thoughts on the Representation of Trauma," in *Probing the Limits of Representation: Nazism and the "Final Solution,"* ed. Saul Friedlander (Cambridge: Harvard University Press, 1992), 144.

60 Ibid., 144.

61 E. Ann Kaplan, *Trauma Culture: The Politics of Terror and Loss in Media and Literature* (New Brunswick, NJ: Rutgers University Press, 2005); Dana Renga,

Unfinished Business: Screening the Italian Mafia in the New Millennium (Toronto: University of Toronto Press, 2013), 163.

62 Jorgensen-Earp and Lanzilotti, "Public Memory and Private Grief."

63 Hannah Arendt, *The Human Condition* (Chicago: University of Chicago Press, 1958), 188.

2 "Eccentric Subjects": Female Martyrs and the Antimafia Public Imaginary

1 Alexander Stille, *Excellent Cadavers: The Mafia and the Death of the First Italian Republic* (New York: Pantheon Books, 1995), 354.

2 According to Stille, the most thorough reconstruction of this assassination is presented in the documents filed by the *Procura distrettuale anti-mafia* of Caltanisetta (Stille, *Excellent Cadavers*, 440, n. 36).

3 The "Women of the Sheets" and "Women of the Fast" were groups formed by Sicilian women who fasted soon after the deaths of Morvillo, Falcone, and Borsellino to generate critical public discussion about the mafia. For an analysis of how women and other marginalized groups in Sicily established public space to articulate half-spoken traumas that were censored by sovereign powers, see Valeria Fabj, "Private Symbols as Vehicles for a Public Voice: 'Women of the Fast' Reject the Mafia," *Global Media Journal* 8, no. 15 (2009), 1–22.

4 For an extensive analysis of the role of women in the mafia and antimafia movements, see the work of Robin Pickering-Iazzi. Many of the points I make are developed based on Pickering-Iazzi's scholarship, most especially, "(En)gendering Testimonial Bodies of Evidence and Italian Antimafia Culture: Rita Atria," *Italian Culture* 28, no. 1 (2010): 21–37; and *Politics of the Visible: Writing Women, Culture and Fascism* (Minneapolis and London: University of Minnesota Press, 1997).

5 Deborah Puccio-Den, "A Máfia siciliana: a transformação num mal global" [The Sicilian Mafia: Transformation to a Global Evil], *Etnográfica (Lisboa)* 12, no. 2 (2008): 377–86. Peter Schneider and Jane Schneider offer an extensive historical and anthropological analysis of the antimafia movements at work in Sicily since the nineteenth century in *Reversible Destinies: Mafia, Antimafia and the Struggle for Palermo* (Berkley: University of California Press, 2003).

6 I want to thank my colleague Amy Boylan for directing me to the Francesca Morvillo Facebook page and for her insights into social media and the work of mourning.

7 Stefania Gargioni, personal correspondence with the author, 13 March 2012.

8 Henry Giroux, "Public Pedagogy and the Politics of Neo-Liberalism: Making the Political More Pedagogical," *Policy Futures in Education* 2 (2004): 494–503 (494).

9 Jacques Rancière, *The Ignorant Schoolmaster: Five Lessons in Intellectual Emancipation*, trans. Kristin Ross (Stanford, CA: Stanford University Press, 1991).

10 Solange Guenoun, James H. Kavanagh, and Roxanne Lapidis, "Jacques Rancière: Literature, Politics, Aesthetics: Approaches to Democratic Disagreement," *SubStance* 29 (2000): 3–24.

11 Marie-Laure Ryan, *Avatars of Story* (Minneapolis: University of Minnesota Press, 2006).

12 Listed among the most widely read antimafia blogs and Facebook sites are Ammazzateci Tutti (http://www.ammazzatecitutti.org), Addiopizzo (http://www .addiopizzo.org), and Corleone Dialogos (http://it-it.facebook.com/corleonedialogos).

13 For a discussion of feminist public pedagogies and their impact on public spheres, see Carmen Luke, *Feminisms and Pedagogies of Everyday Life* (Albany: State University of New York Press, 1996).

14 See Jacques Rancière, *The Future of the Image*, trans. Gregory Elliott (London: Verso, 2007), 514.

15 Giorgio Agamben, *State of Exception*, trans. Kevin Attell (Chicago: University of Chicago Press, 2005).

16 Ewa Plonowska Ziarek offers an incisive analysis of the neologism *dissensus* and the ways in which racial and sexual differences play out in the public sphere when persons engage in what she describes, following Levinas, as a "transformative praxis motivated by an obligation for the Other": *An Ethics of Dissensus: Postmodernity, Feminism, and the Politics of Radical Democracy* (Stanford California: Stanford University Press, 2001), 90.

17 Ziarek discusses whether the wounded, expendable, and endangered body (Agamben's "bare life") can, after being stripped of political significance, develop the capacity to effectively take part in emancipatory movements: Ewa Plonowska Ziarek, "Bare Life on Strike: Notes on the Biopolitics of Race and Gender," *South Atlantic Quarterly* 107 (2008): 89–105.

18 Ann Cvetkovich, *An Archive of Feelings: Trauma, Sexuality, and Lesbian Public Cultures* (Durham, NC: Duke University Press, 2003), 268.

19 Ibid., 268

20 For an extensive analysis of women and the antimafia public imaginary, see Pickering-Iazzi's, "(En)gendering Testimonial Bodies of Evidence."

21 In the context of this project, the concept of "civil society" extends beyond the borders of Western politics to include global landscapes and political practices that derive from non-Western traditions. My interest is in exploring the ways in which the antimafia movement works to enhance public participation, consultation, transparency, and accountability within Italy, as well as the influence this project has on international movements working to fight transnational organized crime.

22 Teresa de Lauretis, "Eccentric Subjects: Feminist Theory and Historical Consciousness," *Feminist Studies* 16, no.1 (1990): 115–50 (p. 115).

23 See Pickering-Iazzi, "(En)Gendering Testimonial Bodies," 102.

24 *Francesca Laura Morvillo Facebook Page*, administered by Stefania Gargioni, http://www.facebook.com/pages/Francesca-Laura-Morvillo/132846650955.

25 *Francesca Laura Morvillo Facebook Page*, page description by Stefania Gargioni, 9 September 2009 (10:28 a.m.), https://www.facebook.com/permalink.php?story_fbid=150143161634&id=132846650955. Translated from Italian by author.

26 Stefania Gargioni, personal correspondence with the author, 13 March 2012.

27 *Francesca Laura Morvillo Facebook Page*, comment by Stefania Gargioni, 10 September 2009 (https://www.facebook.com/permalink.php?story_fbid=146400779154&id=132846650955).

28 "Felice Cavallaro sul 'Corriere della Sera' 25 maggio 1992," *Francesca Laura Morvillo Facebook Page*, https://www.facebook.com/permalink.php?story_fbid=147016118022&id=132846650955, 9 September 2009.

29 This procession is named after a red diary that belonged to Borsellino and disappeared after his murder, believed stolen because it held information about negotiations between the Italian state and the mafia.

30 Robin Pickering-Iazzi, "The Politics of Gender and Genre in Italian Women's Autobiography of the Interwar Years," *Italica* 71 (1994): 176–97.

31 Michel De Certeau, *The Practice of Everyday Life*, trans. Stephen Rendall (San Diego: University of California Press, 2001), 125.

32 Leoluca Orlando, *Fighting the Mafia and Renewing Sicilian Culture* (San Francisco: Encounter Books, 2001), 32.

33 Jan Masschelein and Maarten Simons, "The Hatred of Public Schooling: The School as the Mark of Democracy," *Educational Philosophy and Theory* 42 (2010): 666–82 (512).

34 See Rancière, *The Ignorant Schoolmaster*; Masschelein and Simons, "The Hatred of Public Schooling."

35 Renate Siebert, *Secrets of Life and Death: Women and the Mafia* (New York: Verso Press, 1996).

36 de Lauretis, "Eccentric Subjects," 115.

37 Ibid., 116.

38 Ibid., 127.

39 Ibid., 138.

40 Puccio-Den, "The Sicilian Mafia," 377.

41 Don Luigi Ciotti, preface to *L'altra storia*, ed. Laura Anello (Milan: Sperling & Kupfer, 2012), xi–xxiii, quoted in Robin Pickering-Iazzi, *The Mafia in Italian Lives and Literature* (Toronto: University of Toronto Press, 2015), 148.

42 See, for example, Hannah Arendt, *The Life of the Mind: The Groundbreaking Investigation on How We Think* (New York: Harcourt. 1971).

3 "Children of the Massacre": Public Pedagogy and Italy's Non-violent Protest against Mafia Extortion

1 Grassi's letter reads: "I want to warn our unknown extortionist that he can save himself the trouble of the threatening phone calls and expenses for buying bombs and bullets. Since we are not inclined to give contribution and are now under police protection. I set up this factory with my own hands and I have no intention of closing it down."

2 Renate Siebert, *Secrets of Life and Death: Women and the Mafia* (New York: Verso Books, 1996), 100.

3 Ibid., 66.

4 Ibid., 26.

5 Ibid., 26.

6 Ibid., 26.

7 See Dana Renga, *Unfinished Business: Screening the Italian Mafia in the New Millennium* (Toronto: University of Toronto Press, 2013), 44.

8 Carola Mamberto, producer, *Italy: Taking on the Mafia* (Boston: WGBH Educational Foundation, 2009), 21 min., http://www.pbs.org/frontlineworld/stories/italy801/video/video_index.html.

9 While Addiopizzo focuses on extortion, Libera Terra focuses on repurposing land confiscated from the mafia for the public. Their efforts are directed at improving the land and strengthening the La Torre Law (Edo Zaffuto in discussion with the author, 26 July 2013).

10 Other antimafia organizations working in partnership with Addiopizzo include the national anti-pizzo association FAI (the Italian Federation for Anti-Racket Associations), Libera, the anti-corruption network FLARE, and Addiopizzo Catania and Messina.

11 Philip Jacobson, "Addiopizzo: The Grassroots Campaign Making Life Hell for the Sicilian Mafia," *Newsweek*, September 17, 2014, http://www.newsweek.com/2014/09/26/addiopizzo-grassroots-campaign-making-life-hell-sicilian-mafia-271064.html.

12 Foundazione BNE, conducted in 2003.

13 Edo Zaffuto in discussion with the author, 26 July 2013.

14 Ibid.

15 Ibid.

16 See Jacobson, "Addiopizzo."

17 Chiara Superti, "Addiopizzo: Can a Label Defeat the Mafia?" (paper prepared for Professor Peter Gourevitch, University of California, San Diego, 2008), 5.

18 Ibid., 5.

19 See the policy brief by Elena Sciandra and Antonio Iafano, *Countering Extortion Racketeering: The Italian Experience* (Madrid, Spain: Center for the Study of Democracy, Universita Cattolica del Cacro Cuore, 2014), http://www.csd.bg/fileSrc.php?id=22973.

20 Jacobson, "Addiopizzo."

21 See Vittorio Daniele, "Organized Crime and Regional Development: A Review of the Italian Case," *Trends in Organized Crime* 12, no. 3 (2009): 211–34.

22 "Italian Mafia Has 'Larger Annual Budget Than European Union,'" *The Week*, March 27, 2014, http://www.addiopizzo.org/public/theweek.co.uk_27-03-2014.pdf.

23 Richard Barley, "Italy: At the Heart of Europe's Growing Pains," *Wall Street Journal*, August 12, 2016, https://mpra.ub.uni-muenchen.de/16547/1/MPRA_paper_16547.pdf.

24 Falcone and Padovani, *Men of Honour*, 12.

25 Renga, *Unfinished Business*, 5.

26 Ibid., 11.

27 Ibid., 11.

28 Ibid., 11.

29 Roger I. Simon, *A Public Pedagogy of Witnessing: Curatorial Practice and the Pursuit of Social Justice* (Albany: State University of New York Press, 2014), 4.

30 Ibid., 4.

31 Jeffrey Champlin, "Born Again: Arendt's Natality as Figure and Concept," *The Germanic Review* 88, no. 2 (2013): 151.

32 See R.M. Kennedy, "Toward a Cosmopolitan Curriculum of Forgiveness," *Curriculum Inquiry* 41, no. 1 (2011): 376.

33 Hannah Arendt, *The Human Condition* (Chicago: University of Chicago Press, 1958), 247.

34 Hannah Arendt, *Between Past and Future: Eight Exercises in Political Thought* (London: Penguin Books, 1977), 174.

35 Arendt, *The Human Condition*, 8–9.

36 Natasha Levinson, "The Paradox of Natality," *Educational Theory* 47, no. 4 (1997): 439.

37 Arendt, *Between Past and Future*, 174.

38 Levinson, "The Paradox of Natality," 437.

39 Ibid., 437.

40 Ibid., 437.

41 Arendt, *The Human Condition*, 233–4.

42 See Levinson, "The Paradox of Natality," 442.

43 Hannah Arendt, *Essays in Understanding, 1930–1954* (New York: Schocken Books, 1954), 178.

44 Kennedy, "Towards a Comopolitan Curriculum," 379.
45 See Addiopizzo Travel home page, http://www.addiopizzotravel.it/default.asp.
46 Addiopizzo Travel, http://www.addiopizzotravel.it/eng/gitescolastiche.asp?frame_puls=2, accessed July 5, 2015.
47 See Chris Gibson, "Geographies of Tourism: (Un) Ethical Encounters," *Progress in Human Geography* 34, no. 4 (2010): 521–7.
48 see Rothberg, "Progress, Progression, Procession," 4.
49 See Ruti Teitel, *Liberal Narrative*, 241 and 255
50 Eric Santner, *Stranded Objects*, 144.
51 Ibid., 150.
52 Controversy continues today about the extent to which the state was involved in the deaths of Falcone and his colleague Paolo Borsellino, who was killed a few months later. Because Falcone and Borsellino had developed an innovative method to investigate the connections between organized crime, politicians, and corporate businesses, they were particularly vulnerable.
53 "On Our Legs," Addiopizzo Travel, http://www.addiopizzotravel.it/default.asp?hl=en&tour=71.
54 See Roger I. Simon with Sharon Rosenberg, "Beyond the Logic of Emblemization: Remembering and Learning from the Montreal Massacre," in *The Touch of the Past*, ed. Roger I. Simon (New York: Palgrave Macmillan, 2005), 65–86. Roger I. Simon, *The Touch of the Past: Remembrance, Learning, and Ethics* (New York: Palgrave Macmillan, 2005), 35.
55 Sigmund Freud, "Mourning and Melancholia," in *The Standard Edition of the Complete Psychological Works of Sigmund Freud*, vol. 14, ed. James Strachey (London: Hogarth Press, 1940), 243–58. 1917.
56 Ibid., 243.
57 Ibid., 245.
58 Ibid., 246.
59 Ibid., 246.
60 Hannah Arendt, "The Crisis in Education," *Between Past and Future* (New York: Viking Press, 1961), 196.
61 Zygmunt Bauman, "Has the Future a Left?," *Soundings* 35 (2007), https://www.lwbooks.co.uk/sites/default/files/s35_02bauman.pdf.
62 Bauman, "Has the Future a Left?"
63 "Sicilian Mafia and Anitmafia Strategies," Addiopizzo Travel, http://www.addiopizzotravel.it/default.asp?hl=en&tour=30.
64 Kevin Strand, "Danilo Dolci Leads Fast and Reverse Strike for Employment, 1956," Global Nonviolent Action Database, March 23, 2012, http://nvdatabase.swarthmore.edu/content/danilo-dolci-leads-fast-and-reverse-strike-employment-1956.

65 Walter Benjamin, "Thesis on the Philosophy of History," ed. Hannah Arendt, trans., Harry Zohn, *Illuminations: Essays and Reflections* (New York: Schocken, 1969), 257–58.
66 Also see Clarence W. Joldersma, "Benjamin's Angel of History and the Work of Mourning in Ethical Remembrance: Understanding the Effect of W.G. Sebald's Novels in the Classroom," *Studies in Philosophy of Education* 33, no. 2 (2014), 138.
67 Jan Assmann, *Moses the Egyptian: The Memory of Egypt in Western Monotheism* (Cambridge, MA: Harvard University Press, 1997), quoted in Amy Boylan, "Memory, History and a Mother's Resistant Mourning in Giuseppe Dessi's Il Disertore," *Quaderni d'italianistica* 33, no. 2 (2012): 133–49.
68 Arendt, *The Human Condition.*
69 Edo Zaffuto, interview with the author, July 2014.

4 On the Road to a New Corleone: Digital Screen Cultures and Citizen Writers

1 Roberto Rossellini, dir. *Stromboli* (Italy: Berit Films, 1950), 107 min. The film (also known as *Stromboli, Land of God*) was produced and distributed by Berit Films, a joint company set up by Rossellini and Ingrid Bergman (who starred in the movie). Bergman secured funding from RKO Pictures owner Howard Hughes and other international investors.
2 See John Dickie, *Cosa Nostra: A History of the Sicilian Mafia* (New York: St. Martin's Press, 2004), 284.
3 David Williams, "Performing Palermo: Protests against Forgetting," in *Performing Cities*, ed. Nicolas Whybrow (New York: Palgrave, 2014), 21–38.
4 Francis Ford Coppola, dir., *The Godfather* (Los Angeles: Alfran Productions, 1972), 177 min.; Francis Ford Coppola, dir., *The Godfather Part II* (Los Angeles: The Coppola Company, 1974), 200 min.; Francis Ford Coppola, dir., *The Godfather Part III* (San Francisco: Zoetrope Studios 1990), 162 min.
5 Known as "smart tourism in Sicily," the project of ethical tourism in Corleone is part of a project called INTUS: Environmental Intelligence, Narratives, Tagging of Urban Resources and Spreading Sensors and is supported by the Ministry of Education and Research (MIUR) under the National Operational Programme Research and Competitiveness 2007–2013, Smart Cities and Communities and Social Intervention (see http://meltingpro.org/en/progetti-en/intus/).
6 Michael Hardt and Antonio Negri, *Commonwealth* (Cambridge: Belknap Press of Harvard University Press, 2009), viii. For an extensive discussion of the concept of multidirectional memory, see Michael Rothberg, *Multidirectional Memory: Remembering the Holocaust in the Age of Decolonization* (Stanford: Stanford University Press, 2009).

7 Roger I. Simon, *A Public Pedagogy of Witnessing: Curatorial Practice and the Pursuit of Social Justice* (Albany: State University of New York Press, 2014).

8 See Chris Atton, "Alternative and Citizen Journalism," *The Handbook of Journalism Studies: International Communication Association Handbook Series* (Abingdon: Routledge, 2009), 265–78.

9 Walter Benjamin, "The Work of Art in the Age of Mechanical Reproduction (a 1935 essay)," in *Illuminations: Essays and Reflections*, ed. Hannah Arendt, trans. Harry Zohn (New York: Schocken Books, 1969).

10 Atton, "Alternative and Citizen Journalism."

11 For an overview of the rationale for creating *Libera Informazione*, see "Italia: nasce Libera Informazione, osservatorio contro le mafie," Unimondo.org, September 24, 2007, http://www.unimondo.org/Guide/Salute/Droghe/Italia-nasce-Libera-Informazione-osservatorio-contro-le-mafie-77383.

12 With a circulation of about 1500, it is distributed in Corleone, Bisacquino, Bolognetta, Campofiorito, Chiusa Sciafani, Giuliana, Marineo, and Palermo.

13 *Corleone Dialogos Facebook Page*, https://www.facebook.com/corleonedialogos.

14 Many of the ideas on communicative capitalism expressed in this chapter have also been explored in my essay "'A Taste of Justice': Digitial Media and Libera Terra's Antimafia Public Pedagogy of Agrarian Dissent," included in *The Italian Antimafia, New Media, and the Culture of Legality*, ed. Robin Pickering-Iazzi (Toronto: University of Toronto Press, 2017), chap. 3.

15 Dan Gillmor, *We the Media: Grassroots Journalism by the People, for the People* (North Sebastopol, CA: O'Reilly Media, 2006).

16 In his critique of direct forms of citizen journalism, Matt Sienkiewicz traces the evolution of citizen journalism from 2008 to 2014. In 2011, writes Sienkiewicz, "CNN initiated its iReports awards, recognizing stories that were reported first and sometimes exclusively through the re-transmission of materials obtained from non-professional journalists. Months later, a retired Chinese bureaucrat, Liu Futang, won the first Chinese Environmental Press award for citizen journalism for an expose on pollution in the oil industry" (693). See Matt Sienkiewicz, "Start Making Sense: A Three-Tier Approach to Citizen Journalism," *Media, Culture and Society* 36, no. 5 (2014), 691–701.

17 Jodi Dean, *Blog Theory: Feedback and Capture in the Circuits of Drive* (Cambridge: Polity Press), 2010.

18 Ibid., 51–74.

19 Ibid., 70.

20 Malcolm Gladwell, "Small Change: Why the Revolution Will Not Be Tweeted," *The New Yorker*, October 4, 2010, http://www.newyorker.com/magazine/2010/10/04/small-change-malcolm-gladwell; Evgeny Morozov, "The Brave New World of Slacktivism," *Foreign Policy*, May 19, 2009, http://www.npr.org/templates/story/

story.php?storyId=104302141; Evgeny Morozov, *The Net Delusion: How Not to Liberate The World* (London: Allen Lane, 2001).

21 Morozov, "The Brave New World."
22 Michael Rothberg, *Multidirectional Memory: Remembering the Holocaust in the Age of Decolonization* (Stanford: Stanford University Press, 2009), 2.
23 Ibid.
24 Ibid., 11.
25 Ibid., 11–12.
26 Leonardo Sciascia, *The Day of the Owl* (New York: NYRB Classics, 2003), first published in 1968.
27 Michael Hardt and Antonio Negri, *Commonwealth* (Cambridge: Belknap Press of Harvard University Press, 2009).
28 Ibid.
29 Corleone Dialogos blog, http://corleonedialogos.blogspot.com.
30 Addiopizzo Travel, "No Mafia One-Day Tour," http://www.addiopizzotravel.it/default.asp?hl=en&p=309.
31 Cosimo Lo Sciuto, interview with the author, July 2014.
32 The intention to overcome shame emerges in discussions with activists at Addiopizzo and Addiopizzo Travel as well. Implicit in their slogan, "A whole people who pay the pizzo is a people without dignity," is a desire to overcome indignity and establish respect.
33 Roger I. Simon, *A Pedagogy of Witnessing: Curatorial Practice and the Pursuit of Social Justice* (Albany: State University of New York Press, 2013), 211–12.
34 Hardt and Negri, *Commonwealth*, 6.
35 Pablo Alonso Gonzalez, "From a Given to a Construct," *Cultural Studies* 23, no. 3 (2014): 359–90.
36 See Hardt and Negri, *Commonwealth*, 151.
37 Rothberg, *Multidirectional Memory*, 21.
38 In Italian, *fascio* means "bundle," or solidarity. The Fasci were brotherhoods that united the peasants against the landowners and the intermediaries, *gabelloti*, who were employed to safeguard the land of landowners and keep the peasants in check. The Fasci were unrelated to Benito Mussolini's fascist movement founded a generation later (see Dickie, *Cosa Nostra*, 157).
39 See Theodoros Rakopoulos, "Cooperative Modulations: The Antimafia Movement and Struggles over Land and Cooperativism in Eight Sicilian Municipalities," *Journal of Modern Italian Studies* 19, no. 1 (2014): 15–33.
40 Ibid., 17.
41 Ibid.
42 Ibid.
43 Ibid., 16.

44 Carlo Cattaneo, *The Kingdom of the Two Sicilys* (1845), quoted in L. Franchetti, *Condizioni politiche e amministrative della Sicilia*, vol. I of L. Franchetti and S. Sonnino, *Inchiesta in Sicilia*, 2 vols, Florence, 1974, quoted in Nelson Moe, *The View from Vesuvius: Italian Culture and the Southern Question* (Los Angeles: University of California Press, 2002), 106–8.

45 *Corleone Trofeo Podistico Città della Legalità*, 31 August 2015. Corleone Marathon, http://www.corleonemarathon.it.

46 Bronwen Leebaw, *Judging State-Sponsored Violence: Imagining Political Change* (Cambridge: Cambridge University Press, 2011), 264.

47 Rakopoulos, "Cooperative Modulations," 19.

48 See Dickie, *Cosa Nostra*, 158.

49 See Moe, *The View from Vesuvius*, 17.

50 Dickie, *Cosa Nostra*, 158.

51 Ibid., 158.

52 Ibid., 161.

53 Lucy Riall, *The Italian Risorgimento: State, Society and National Unification* (London: Routledge Press, 1994), 224.

54 Rakopoulos, "Cooperative Modulations," 57.

55 Ibid., 60.

56 Ibid., 66.

57 Rothberg, *Multidirectional Memory*, 35.

58 Ibid., 36.

59 Ibid., 131.

60 Ibid., 26.

61 Simon, *A Pedagogy of Witnessing*, 204.

62 Ibid., 204.

63 Ibid., 205.

64 Ibid., 210.

65 Ibid., 210.

66 Ibid., 211.

67 Deborah Puccio-Den, "A Máfia siciliana: a transformação num mal global" [The Sicilian Mafia: Transformation to a Global Evil], *Etnografica (Lisboa)* 12, no. 2 (2008).

68 Rotheberg, *Multidirectional Memory*, 313.

69 Baris Cayli, "Creating Counterpublics against the Mafia," *Cultural and Ethical Turns: Interdisciplinary Reflections on Culture, Politics and Ethics*, ed. Ben Garner, Sonia Pavlenko, Salma Shaheen, and Alison Wlanski (Oxford: Interdisciplinary Press, 2011).

70 Robin Pickering-Iazzi, *The Mafia in Italian Lives and Literature* (Toronto: University of Toronto Press, 2015), 193–4.

71 Ibid., 193–4.
72 Rotherberg, *Multidirectional Memory*.
73 Pickering-Iazzi, *The Mafia in Italian Lives and Literature*, 152.
74 Ibid., 191.
75 Ibid., 191.
76 Rotherberg, *Multidirectional Memory*.

5 Reconstructing Memory through the Archives: Public Pedagogy, Citizenship, and Letizia Battaglia's Photographic Record of Mafia Violence

1 For an incisive analysis of the ways in which public pedagogy provides a basis for establishing an understanding of political agency, see Henry Giroux, "Public Pedagogy as Cultural Politics: Stuart Hall and the Crisis of Culture," *Cultural Studies* 14, no. 2 (2000): 341–60.

2 See Hannah Arendt, *The Human Condition* (Chicago: University of Chicago Press, 1958).

3 See Gert Biesta, "Making Pedagogy Public: For the Public, of the Public, or in the Interest of Publicness?," in *Problematizing Public Pedagogy*, ed. Jake Burdick , Jennifer A. Sandlin, and Michael P. O'Malley (New York: Routledge, 2014), 23–4.

4 John Dickie, *Cosa Nostra: A History of the Sicilian Mafia* (London: Hodder and Stoughton, 2004), 91.

5 Dickie, *Cosa Nostra*, 101.

6 Ibid., 91.

7 Sigmund Freud, "Outline of Psychoanalysis," in *The Standard Edition of the Complete Psychological Works of Sigmund Freud*, vol. 23, ed. James Strachey (London: Hogarth Press, 1940), 195–207.

8 Ibid., 204.

9 Christopher Bollas, "The Structure of Evil," in *The Christopher Bollas Reader* (East Sussex: Routledge, 2011), 173.

10 For documentation of human rights violations not addressed by the state because of legal obstacles, see, for example, the Amnesty International reports on Uruguay, the United States, and Argentina at http://www.amnesty.org/en.

11 Jacques Derrida, *Archive Fever: A Freudian Impression* (Chicago: University of Chicago Press, 1996), 84.

12 Ibid., 11.

13 Ibid., 19.

14 One way to define a trauma is as an experience or a series of experiences that are absolutely unthinkable. The unthinkable, at once persistently haunting, resists an integrated narrative or even an integrated neuronal memory. Often, traumatic memory is made manifest in compulsive thinking or, conversely, is denied,

dissociated, or disavowed. See Elisabeth Young-Bruehl, *The Clinic and the Context: Historical Essays* (New York: Karnac, 2013), 40–1.

15 Young-Bruehl, *The Clinic and the Context*, 45.

16 Ibid., 45.

17 Ibid., 45.

18 The UN Convention on the Rights of the Child has secured signatures from all UN members except the United States.

19 Elizabeth Povinelli, "The Woman on the Other Side of the Wall: Archiving the Otherwise in Postcolonial Digital Archives," *Differences: A Journal of Feminist Cultural Studies* 22, no. 1 (2011): 149.

20 Adriana Cavarero, *Relating Narratives: Storytelling and Selfhood*, trans. Paul A. Kottman (London: Routledge, 1997), 142. First published in Italian as *Tu che mi guardi, tu che mi racconti*, ed. Giagiacomo Feltrinelle (Milan, Andegari: 1997).

21 Ibid., 87.

22 Alexander Stille et al., *Passion, Justice, Freedom: Photographs of Sicily by Letizia Battaglia* (New York: Aperture Foundation, 1999), 12.

23 Carlo Ruta, "*L'Ora*, the Mafia and Palermo," *Libera Informazione*, June 5, 2013, http://www.liberainformazione.ort/2013/06/05/lora-la-mafia-e-palermo/.

24 Stille et al., *Passion, Justice Freedom*, 15.

25 Ibid., 18.

26 Ibid., 82.

27 A selection of Battaglia's work can be seen online at "Shooting the Mafia – in Pictures," *The Guardian*, March 4, 2012, https://www.theguardian.com/artanddesign/gallery/2012/mar/04/shooting-mafia-photography-in-pictures; the Maxxi Museum in Rome has had several exhibits of her work (see, for example, http://www.fondazionemaxxi.it/en/events/letizia-battaglia-per-pura-passione/).

28 Stille et al., *Passion, Justice, Freedom*, 84.

29 Ibid., 16.

30 Jerzy Growtowski, *Towards a Poor Theatre* (Denmark: Odin Teatret Forlag, 1968), 22.

31 Giorgio Agamben, *State of Exception*, trans. Kevin Attell (Chicago: University of Chicago Press, 2005).

32 Dora Apel, *War Culture and the Contest of Images* (New Brunswich: Rutgers University Press, 2012), 9.

33 Ariella Azoulay, *The Civil Contract of Photography* (New York: Zone Books, 2008), 9.

34 Stille et al., *Passion, Justice, Freedom*, 15.

35 "Shooting the Mafia," image 8, https://www.theguardian.com/artanddesign/gallery/2012/mar/04/shooting-mafia-photography-in-pictures#img-8

36 Azoulay, *The Civil Contract of Photography*, 201.

37 Ibid., 302.

38 See Bruehl, *The Clinic and the Context*, 46.

39 Stille et al., *Passion, Justice, Freedom*, 91.

40 Bruehl, *The Clinic and the Context*, 41.

41 Ibid., 41.

42 Ibid., 41.

43 Stille et al., *Passion, Justice, Freedom*, 13.

44 Ibid.,12.

45 Cavarero, *Relating Narratives*, 58.

46 Apel, *War, Culture and the Contest of Images*, 8.

47 Renate Siebert, *Secrets of Life and Death: Women and the Mafia* (New York: Verso Books, 1996), 178.

48 Siebert, *Secrets of Life and Death*, 26.

49 Schifani's position challenges that of the female martyr who trades political engagement for her life, as we see, for example, in the public memories of Rita Atria. As well, Schifani represents a departure from the discourse of martyrdom so prevalent in the antimafia imaginary. For an astute analysis of this discourse, see the scholarship of Deborah Puccio-Den and Robin Pickering-Iazzi.

50 Siebert, *Secrets of Life and Death*, 24.

51 Ibid., 22.

52 Ibid., 121.

53 Ibid., 181.

54 Ibid., 179.

55 Ibid., 180.

56 Felice Cavallaro and Fabio Vannini, *Ho Vinto Io*, dir. Fabio Vannini, prod. Cerioni. (Rome, Italy: Rai Tre Radiotelevisione Italiana, 2012), 63 min.

57 Lucio Ganci, interview with the author, 2013.

58 Stille et al., *Passion, Justice, Freedom*, 91.

59 Nicoletta Di Ciolla, "Perfecting Females/Pursuing Truths: Texts, Subtexts and Postmodern Genre-Crossing in Salvatori's Noir, *Sublime Anima Di Donna*," in *Trends in Contemporary Italian Narrative: 1980–2007*, ed. Gillian Ania and Ann Hallamore Caesar (Newcastle: Cambridge Scholars Publishing, 2007), 40; Paula M. Salvio, "Uncanny Exposures: A Study of the Wartime Photojournalism of Lee Miller," *Curriculum Inquiry* 39, no. 4 (2009): 521–36.

60 For studies of the dangers inherent in the discourse of martyrdom in antimafia activism, see the scholarship of Puccio-Den, Pickering-Iazzi, and Salvio: Deborah Puccio-Den, "A Máfia siciliana: a transformação num mal global" [The Sicilian Mafia: Transformation to a Global Evil], *Etnografica (Lisboa)* 12, no. 2 (2008): 55; Deborah Puccio-Den, "The Anti-Mafia Movement as Religion?: The Pilgrimage to the Falcone Tree," in *Shrines and Pilgrimage in the Modern World. New Itineraries*

into the Sacred, ed. Peter Jan Margry (Amsterdam: Amsterdam University Press, 2008); Robin Pickering-Iazzi, "(En)gendering Testimonial Bodies of Evidence and Italian Antimafia Culture: Rita Atria," *Italian Culture* 28, no. 1 (2010): 21–37; and Paula Salvio, "'Eccentric Subjects': Female Martyrs and the Antimafia Public Imaginary." *Italian Cultural Studies* 67, no. 3 (2012): 397–410.

61 Apel, *War, Culture and the Contest of Images*, 5.

62 Robin Pickering-Iazzi, *Mafia and Outlaw Stories from Italian Life and Literature* (Toronto: University of Toronto Press, 2007), 65.

63 Ibid., 69.

6 "The Duty to Report": Political Judgment, Public Pedagogy, and the Photographic Archive of Franco Zecchin

1 Franco Zecchin, "The Duty to Report," http://picturetank.com/___/series/e72bc619228758d17bd3f94ffbaac42f/en/o/ZEF_The_Duty_to_Report.html.

2 Ibid.

3 Quote from *L'Ora.* The story ran in Milan in 1978.

4 Franco Zecchin, "The Duty to Report." http://picturetank.com/___/series/e72bc619228758d17bd3f94ffbaac42f/en/a/ZEF_The_Duty_to_Report.html.

5 Ibid.

6 Deborah Puccio-Den, "The Ethnologist and the Magistrate: Giovanni Falcone's Investigation into the Sicilian Mafia," *Ethnologie Francaise* l, no. 31 (2001): 15–27.

7 Francesco Renda, *Storia della mafia* (Palerme, Sigma Edizioni, 1997), 168 and 184.

8 Puccio-Den, "The Ethnologist and the Magistrate."

9 Renda, *Storia della mafia*, 26.

10 Deborah Puccio-Den, "Photographing the Mafia or How to Photograph Something That Doesn't Exist" (paper presented at the 13th European Association of Social Anthropologists Biennial Conference, Tallinn University, Estonia, July 31–August 3, 2014).

11 See Hannah Arendt, *The Human Condition* (Chicago: University of Chicago Press, 1958); and Adriana Cavarero, *Relating Narratives: Storytelling and Selfhood*, trans. Paul A. Kottman (London: Routledge, 1997). First published in Italian as *Tu che mi guardi, tu che mi racconti*, ed. Giagiacomo Feltrinelle (Milan, Andegari: 1997).

12 Adriana Cavarero, *Horrorism: Naming Contemporary Violence* (New York: Columbia University Press, 2009), 11.

13 Ibid.

14 Cavarero, *Relating Narratives*, 20–9.

15 Cavarero, *Relating Narratives*, 57.

16 Ibid.

17 Renate Siebert, *Secrets of Life and Death: Women and the Mafia* (New York: Verso Press, 1996), 138.

18 Ibid.

19 Also see Judith Butler, *Precarious Life: The Powers of Mourning and Violence* (New York: Verso Press, 2004), 42.

20 See Alison Jaimson, *The Antimafia: Italy's Fight against Organized Crime* (London: Palgrave, 1992), 28.

21 Umberto Santino, "The Mafia and the Antimafia Fight: An Analisys beyond the Stereotypes," Centro Siciliano di Documentazione "Giuseppe Impastato," http://www.centroimpastato.com/the-mafia-and-the-antimafia-fight-an-analisys-beyond-the-stereotypes/.

22 See Umberto Santino, *Mafia and Antimafia: A Brief History* (London: Tauris, 2015).

23 Jaimson, *The Antimafia*, 24.

24 Ibid., 24–25.

25 Arendt, *The Human Condition*, 26.

26 Ibid., 26.

27 Ibid.

28 Cavarero, *Relating Narratives*, 51.

29 Sharon Todd, *Toward an Imperfect Education: Facing Humanity, Rethinking Cosmopolitanism* (Boulder: Paradigm, 2009), 12.

30 Tom Behan, *Defiance: The Story of One Man Who Stood Up to the Sicilian Mafia* (London: I.B. Tauris, 2008), 82–3.

31 Ibid.

32 Ibid., 135.

33 Arendt, *The Human Condition*, 27.

34 Cavarero, *Relating Narratives*, 3–4.

35 Ibid., 5.

36 See Bronwyn Leebaw, *Judging State Sponsored Violence: Imagining Political Change* (New York: Cambridge University Press, 2011), 188 and 168–88.

37 Franco Zecchin, interview with the author, 2015.

38 "L'Arsenal de Metz expose *Antimafia* de Franco Zecchin et Letizia Battaglia" (photograph), http://fr.actuphoto.com/23972-l-arsenal-de-metz-expose-antimafia-de-franco-zecchin-et-letizia-battaglia.html.

39 Franco Zecchin, personal correspondence with the author, 2015.

40 Roger I. Simon, *A Pedagogy of Witnessing: Curatorial Practice and the Pursuit of Social Justice* (Albany: State University of New York Press, 2013), 179.

41 Roger I. Simon, "A Shock to Thought: Curatorial Judgment and the Public Exhibition of "Difficult Knowledge," *Memory Studies* 4 (2011): 432–49.

42 Ariella Azoulay, *The Civil Contract of Photography* (New York: Zone Books, 2008), 141.

43 Ibid.

44 Giorgio Agamben, *Homo Sacer: Sovereign Power and Bare Life*, trans. Daniel Heller-Roazen (Stanford: Stanford University Press, 1998), 82.

45 Hannah Arendt, *Between Past and Future* (New York: Viking Press, 1961), 6.

46 Alexander Stille, *Excellent Cadavers: The Mafia and the Death of the First Italian Republic* (New York: Vintage, 1996).

47 Franco Zecchin, interview with the author, 2015.

48 Butler, Judith. *Frames of War: When Is Life Grievable?* (New York: Verso, 2009), 3 and 6.

49 Ibid., 22.

50 Ibid., 51.

51 Simon, *A Pedagogy of Witnessing*, 37.

52 Azoulay, *The Civil Contract of Photography*, 97.

53 Ibid., 97.

54 Arendt, *The Human Condition*, 220.

55 Elisabeth Young-Bruehl, *Why Arendt Matters* (New Haven: Yale University Press, 2007), 99.

56 Azoulay, *The Civil Contract of Photography*, 14.

57 Ibid., 14.

58 Hannah Arendt, *The Origins of Totalitarianism* (Berlin: Schocken Books, 1951), 238.

59 Ibid.

60 Franco Zecchin, interview with the author, 2015.

61 Arendt, *The Human Condition*, 202.

62 Jill Stauffer, *Ethical Lonliness: The Injustice of Not Being Heard* (New York: Columbia University Press), 2015.

63 "Interview with Jill Stauffer, author of *Ethical Loneliness*," Columbia University Press Blog, October 1, 2015, http://www.cupblog.org/?p=17545.

Epilogue

1 Elisabetta Povoledo, "With a Nod to Italian Mafia, a Notorious Crime Hub Gets a Museum," July 9, 2015, https://www.nytimes.com/2015/07/10/world/europe/with-a-nod-to-italian-mafia-a-notorious-crime-hub-gets-a-museum.html?_r=0

2 Roberto Saviano, "Mafia Organizations Are More Dangerous Than Terrorist Groups," *New York Times*, April 28, 2014, http://www.nytimes.com/roomfordebate/2014/04/28/is-the-mafia-europes-new-security-threat/mafia-organizations-are-more-dangerous-than-terrorist-groups.

3 Susan J. Brison, *Aftermath: Violence and the Remaking of a Self* (Princeton: Princeton University Press), 2003.
4 Marita Sturken, *Tourists of History: Memory, Kitsch, and Consumerism from Oklahoma City to Ground Zero* (Durham: Duke University Press), 30.
5 Adriana Cavarero, *For More Than One Voice: Toward a Philosophy of Vocal Expression*, trans. Paul A. Kottman (Stanford: Stanford University Press, 2005), 204.
6 Ta-Nehisi Coates, *Between the World and Me* (New York: Spiegel and Grau, 2015).

Works Cited

Agamben, Giorgio. *Homo Sacer: Sovereign Power and Bare Life*. Translated by Daniel Heller-Roazen. Stanford: Stanford University Press, 1988.

– *State of Exception*. Translated by Kevin Attell. Chicago: University of Chicago Press, 2005. http://dx.doi.org/10.1215/9780822386735-013.

Alexander, Jeffrey C. "Toward a Theory of Cultural Trauma." In *Cultural Trauma and Collective Identity*, edited by Jeffrey C. Alexander, Ron Eyerman, Bernard Giesen, Neil J. Smelser, and Piotr Sztompka, 1–30. Berkeley: University of California Press, 2004. http://dx.doi.org/10.1525/california/9780520235946.003.0001.

Amurri, S., ed. *L'Albero Falcone*. Palermo: Fondazione Giovanni e Francesca Falcone, 1992.

Ania, G., and A. Hallamore Caesar. *Trends, Contemporary Italian Narrative: 1980–2007*. Newcastle: Cambridge Scholars Publishing, 2007.

Apel, Dora. *War Culture and the Contest of Images*. New Brunswick: Rutgers University Press, 2012.

Arendt, Hannah. "The Crisis in Education." In *Between Past and Future*, 173–96 New York: Penguin Books, 1977.

– *Eichmann in Jerusalem: A Report on the Banality of Evil*. New York: Penguin, 1963.

– *Essays in Understanding, 1930–1954: Formation, Exile, and Totalitarianism*. New York: Harcourt Brace & Company, 1994.

– *The Human Condition*. Chicago: University of Chicago Press, 1958.

– *On Revolution*. London: Penguin Books, 1963.

– *The Origins of Totalitarianism*. 3rd ed. New York: Harcourt Brace, 1973.

Azoulay, Ariella. *The Civil Contract of Photography*. New York: Zone Books, 2008.

Baer, Ulrich, ed. *110 Stories: New York Writes after September 11*. New York: New York University Press, 2002.

Bauman, Zygmunt. "Has the Future a Left?" *Soundings* 35 (2007). http://www.iceta.org/zb150507.pdf.

Bell, Vikki, and Mario Di Paolantonio. "The Haunted *Nomos*: Activist-Artists and the (Im)possible Politics of Memory in Transitional Argentina." *Cultural Politics* 5, no. 2 (2009): 148–78. http://dx.doi.org/10.2752/175174309X428199.

Benjamin, Walter. "Theses on the Philosophy of History." In *Illuminations: Essays and Reflections*, edited by Hannah Arendt. New York: Schocken Books, 1968.

Bollas, Christopher. *The Christopher Bollas Reader*. New York, NY: Routledge, 2011.

Boylan, Amy. "Pasquale Scimeca's Placido Rizzotto: A Different View of Corleone." In *Mafia Movies: A Reader*, edited by Dana Renga. Toronto: University of Toronto Press, 2011.

Brison, Susan J. *Aftermath: Violence and the Remaking of a Self*. Princeton: Princeton University Press, 2003.

Britzman, Deborah. "Between Psychoanalysis and Pedagogy: Scenes of Rapprochement and Alienation." *Curriculum Inquiry* 43, no. 1 (2013): 95–117. http://dx.doi.org/10.1111/curi.12007.

– "If the Story Cannot End: Deferred Action, Ambivalence, and Difficult Knowledge." In *Between Hope and Despair: Pedagogy and the Remembrance of Historical Trauma*, edited by Roger I. Simon, Sharon Rosenberg, and Claudia Eppert, 27–58. New York: Rowman and Littlefield, 2000.

– *Novel Education*. New York: Peter Lang, 2006.

Brushwood Rose, Chloe. "The (Im)possibilities of Self Representation: Exploring the Limits of Storytelling in the Digital Stories of Women and Girls." *Changing English* 16, no. 2 (2009): 211–20. http://dx.doi.org/10.1080/13586840902863194.

Brushwood Rose, Chloe, and Colette Granger. "Unexpected Self-Expression and the Limits of Narrative Inquiry: Exploring Unconscious Dynamics in a Community-Based Digital Storytelling Workshop." *International Journal of Qualitative Studies in Education* 26, no. 2 (2012): 1–22.

Butler, Judith. *Frames of War: When Is Life Grievable?* New York: Verso, 2009.

– *Precarious Life: The Powers of Mourning and Violence*. New York: Verso, 2006.

Cavarero, Adriana. *For More Than One Voice: Toward a Philosophy of Vocal Expression*. Translated by Paul A. Kottman. Stanford: Stanford University Press, 2005.

– *Horrorism: Naming Contemporary Violence*. Translated by William McCuaig. New York, Chichester: Columbia University Press, 2009.

– *Relating Narratives: Storytelling and Selfhood*. Translated by P.A. Kottman. London: Routledge, 1997.

Cavarero, Adriana, and Elisabetta Bertolino. "Beyond Ontology and Sexual Difference: An Interview with the Italian Feminist Philosopher Adriana Cavarero." *Differences: A Journal of Feminist Cultural Studies* 19, no. 1 (2008): 128–67. http://dx.doi.org/10.1215/10407391-2007-019.

Cayli, Baris. "Italian Mafia in the Spectrum of Culture and Politics." In *Cultural and Ethical Turns: Interdisciplinary Reflections on Culture, Politics and Ethics*, edited by

Ben Garner, Sonia Pavlenko, Salma Shaheen, and Alison Wlanski, 51–7. Oxford: Interdisciplinary Press, 2011.

Anello, Laura, ed. *Ciotti, don Luigi. Preface to L'altra storia*, xi–xxiii. Milan: Sperling & Kupfer, 2012.

– "Creating Counterpublics against the Italian Mafia." *Public* 20, no. 3 (2013): 59–76.

Clamp, Kerry Leigh, and Jonathan Doak. "More than Words: Restorative Justice Concepts in Transitional Justice Settings." *International Criminal Law Review* 12, no. 3 (2012): 339–60. http://dx.doi.org/10.1163/157181212X648824.

Clewell, Tammy. "Mourning beyond Melancholia: Freud's Psychoanalysis of Loss." *Journal of the American Psychoanalytic Association* 52, no. 1 (2004): 43–67. http://dx.doi.org/10.1177/00030651040520010601.

Coates, Ta-Nehisi. *Between the World and Me*. New York: Spiegel and Grau, 2015.

Comay, Rebecca. *Lost in the Archives*. Toronto: Alphabet City Media, 2002.

Cuneen, Chris. "Exploring the Relationship between Reparations, the Gross Violation of Human Rights, and Restorative Justice." In *Handbook of Restorative Justice: A Global Perspective*, edited by Dennis Sullivan and Larry Tifft, 355–67. New York: Routledge, 2005.

Cvetkovich, Ann. *An Archive of Feelings: Trauma, Sexuality, and Lesbian Public Cultures*. Raleigh: Duke University Press, 2003. http://dx.doi.org/10.1215/9780822384434.

Dean, Jodi. *Blog Theory: Feedback and Capture in the Circuits of the Drive*. Malden: Polity Press, 2010.

– "Communicative Capitalism: Circulation and the Foreclosure of Politics." *Cultural Politics* 1, no. 1 (2005): 51–74. http://dx.doi.org/10.2752/174321905778054845.

De Certeau, Michel. *The Practice of Everyday Life*. Translated by Stephen Rendall. San Diego: University of California Press, 2001.

De Ciolla, Nicoletta. "Perfecting Females/ Pursuing Truths: Texts, Subtexts and Postmodern Genre-Crossing in Salvatori's, Noir, Sublime Anima Di Donna." In *Trends in Contemporary Italian Narrative 1980–2007*, edited by Gillian Ania and Ann Hallamore Caesar, 29–49. Newcastle: Cambridge Scholars Publishing, 2007.

de Lauretis, Teresa. "Eccentric Subjects: Feminist Theory and Historical Consciousness." *Feminist Studies* 16, no. 1 (Spring 1990): 115–50. http://dx.doi.org/10.2307/3177959.

de Greiff, Pablo. *Transitional Justice and Development*. New York: Social Science Research Council, 2009.

Derrida, J. *Archive Fever: A Freudian Impression*. Translated by E. Prenowitz. Chicago: University of Chicago Press, 1996.

Dickie, John. *Cosa nostra: A History of the Sicilian Mafia*. London: Hodder and Stoughton, 2004.

Di Paolantonio, M. "A Site of Struggle, a Site of Conflicting Pedagogical Proposals: The Debates over Suitable Commemorative Form for ESMA." *Journal of the Canadian Association for Curriculum Studies* 6, no. 2 (2008): 25–42.

Fabj, Valeria. "Private Symbols as Vehicles for a Public Voice: Women of the Fast Reject the Mafia." *Global Media Journal* 8, no. 15 (2009): 1–22.

Falcone, Giovanni. *Men of Honour: The Truth about the Mafia.* London: Warner, 1992.

Farley, Lisa. "Operation Pied Piper: A Psychoanalytic Narrative of Authority in a Time of War." *Psychoanalysis and History* 14, no. 1 (2012): 29–52. http://dx.doi.org/10.3366/pah.2012.0098.

– "Radical Hope: Or, the Problem of Uncertainty in History Education." *Curriculum Inquiry* 39, no. 4 (2009): 537–54. http://dx.doi.org/10.1111/j.1467-873X.2009.00456.x.

Featherstone, Mike. "Archive." *Theory, Culture & Society* 23, no. 2–3 (2006): 591–6. http://dx.doi.org/10.1177/0263276406023002106.

Freud, Sigmund. "Outline of Psychoanalysis." In *The Standard Edition of the Complete Psychological Works of Sigmund Freud*, vol. 23, edited by James Strachey, 141–216. London: Hogarth Press, 1940.

– "Thoughts for the Times on War and Death." In *The Standard Edition of the Complete Psychological Works of Sigmund Freud*, vol. 14, edited by James Strachey, 273–302. London: Hogarth Press, 1915.

– "The Ego and the Id." In *The Standard Edition of the Complete Psychological Works of Sigmund Freud*, vol. 19, edited by James Strachey, 19–27. London: Hogarth Press, 1923.

Freud, Anna, and Dorothy T. Burlingham. *War and Children.* California: Greenwood Publishing Group, 1973.

Frigerio, L. "La Confisca dei Benni alle mafia: Luci e Ombre di un Percorso Civile," *Aggiornamenti sociali* 01 (2009): 38–48.

Ganci, Lucio. 2013. "Letizia Battaglia," accessed December 9, 2013, http://www.demotix.com/news/1857617/letizia-battaglia-photo-exibition#media-1857261.

Georgis, Dina. *The Better Story: Queer Affects from the Middle East.* Albany: State University of New York Press, 2013.

Ginsborg, Paul. *A History of Contemporary Italy: Society and Politics, 1943–1988.* New York: Palgrave, 2003.

Giroux, Henry A. "Cultural Studies in Dark Times: Public Pedagogy and the Challenge of Neoliberalism." *Fast Capitalism* 1, no. 2 (2005). http://www.henryagiroux.com/online_articles/DarkTimes.htm.

– "Cultural Studies, Public Pedagogy, and the Responsibility of Intellectuals." *Communication and Critical/Cultural Studies* 1, no. 1 (2004): 59–79. http://dx.doi.org/10.1080/1479142042000180926.

– "Public Pedagogy and the Politics of Neo-liberalism: Making the Political More Pedagogical." *Policy Futures in Education* 2, no. 3 (2004): 494–503. http://dx.doi.org/10.2304/pfie.2004.2.3.5.

Gladwell, Malcolm. "Small Change: Why the Revolution Will Not Be Tweeted." *New Yorker*, October 4, 2010, http://www.newyorker.com/magazine/2010/10/04/small-change-malcolm-gladwell.

Gordon, Mordechai. *Hannah Arendt and Education: Renewing Our Common World.* Boulder: Westview Press, 2001.

Guenoun, Solange, James H. Kavanagh, and Roxanne Lapidus. "Jacques Rancière: Literature, Politics, Aesthetics: Approaches to Democratic Disagreement." *SubStance* 29, no. 2 (2000): 3–24. http://dx.doi.org/10.2307/3685772.

Growtowski, Jerzy. *Towards a Poor Theatre.* Denmark: Odin Teatret Forlag, 1968.

Hardt, Michael, and Antonio Negri. *Empire.* Cambridge: Harvard University Press, 2001.

Harris, Melissa. *Passion, Justice, Freedom: Photographs of Sicily by Letizia Battaglia.* New York: Aperature, 1999.

Harvey, David. "The Future of the Commons." *Radical History Review* 214 (2011): 101–7.

Hill, Dan. "Journal: Roberto Saviano at Fabrica." Cityofsound, May 21, 2013, http://www.cityofsound.com/blog/2013/05/roberto-saviano-fabrica.html.

International Center for Transitional Justice. "What Is Transitional Justice?" Accessed February 12, 2014. https://www.ictj.org/about/transitional-justice.

Ihanus, Juhani. "The Archive and Psychoanalysis: Memories and Histories Towards Futures." *International Forum of Psychoanalysis* 16, no. 2 (2007): 119–31. http://dx.doi.org/10.1080/08037060701299970.

Jamieson, Alison. *The Antimafia: Italy's Fight against Organized Crime.* London: Macmillan Press Ltd, 2000.

Jan Margry, Peter, and Cristina Sánchez-Carretero. "Memorializing Traumatic Death." *Anthropology Today* 23, no. 3 (2007): 1–2. http://dx.doi.org/10.1111/j.1467-8322.2007.00508.x.

Jorgensen-Earp, Cheryl R., and Lori A. Lanzilotti. "Public Memory and Private Grief: The Construction of Shrines at the Sites of Public Tragedy." *Quarterly Journal of Speech* 84, no. 2 (1998): 150–70. http://dx.doi.org/10.1080/00335639809384211.

Kaplan, E. Ann. "Global Trauma and Public Feelings: Viewing Images of Catastrophe." *Consumption Markets & Culture* 11, no. 1 (2008): 3–24. http://dx.doi.org/10.1080/10253860701799918.

Kennedy, R.M. "Toward a Cosmopolitan Curriculum of Forgiveness." *Curriculum Inquiry* 41, no. 3 (2011): 373–93. http://dx.doi.org/10.1111/j.1467-873X.2011.00551.x.

Khan, M.M. "The Concept of Cumulative Trauma." In *The Privacy of the Self*, 42–58. New York: International Universities Press, 1963.

La Spina, Antonio. *Mafia Legalita Debole e Sviluppo del Mezzogiorno.* Bologna: Ricerca, 2005.

Leebaw, Bronwyn. *Judging State-Sponsored Violence: Imagining Political Change.* Cambridge: Cambridge University Press, 2011. http://dx.doi.org/10.1017/CBO9780511976490.

Lehrer, Erica, Cynthia E. Milton, and Monica Eileen Patterson, eds. *Curating Difficult Knowledge: Violent Pasts in Public Places.* New York: Palgrave, 2011. http://dx.doi.org/10.1057/9780230319554.

Levinson, Natasha. "Teaching in the Midst of Belatedness: The Paradox of Natality in Hannah Arendt's Educational Thought." *Educational Theory* 47, no. 4 (Fall 1997): 435–51. http://dx.doi.org/10.1111/j.1741-5446.1997.00435.x.

Low, Bronwen. "At the Edge of Writing and Speech: New Oralities and Curriculum." *Journal of the Canadian Association for Curriculum Studies* 8, no. 2 (2012): 50–75.

Luke, Carmen. *Feminisms and Pedagogies of Everyday Life.* Albany: State University of New York Press, 1996.

Marcus, Millicent. "In Memoriam: The Neorealist Legacy in the Contemporary Anti Mafia Film." In *Italian Neorealism and Global Cinema*, edited by Laura E. Rorato and Kristi M. Wilson, 290–306. Detroit: Wayne State University Press, 2007.

Masschelein, Jan, and Maarten Simons. "The Hatred of Public Schooling: The School as the Mark of Democracy." *Educational Philosophy and Theory* 42, no. 5–6 (2010): 666–82. http://dx.doi.org/10.1111/j.1469-5812.2010.00692.x.

Miller, Janet. *The Sounds of Silence Breaking: Women, Autobiography, Curriculum.* New York: Peter Lang, 2005.

Moe, Nelson. *The View from Vesuvius: Italian Culture and the Southern Question.* Berkeley: University of California Press, 2002.

Mohanty, G.S. *Modern Sociology: Globalization and Urban Sociology.* New York: Isha Books, 2005.

Morozov, Evyeny. "The Brave New World of Slacktivism." *Foreign Policy*, May 19, 2009. http://foreignpolicy.com/2009/05/19/the-brave-new-world-of-slacktivism/.

– *The Net Delusion: How Not to Liberate the World.* London: Allen Lane, 2001.

Orlando, Leoluca. *Fighting the Mafia and Renewing Sicilian Culture.* San Francisco: Encounter Books, 2001.

Picciotto, Loredana. "Social Entrepreneurship and Confiscated Mafia Properties in Italy" 4th EMES-SOCENT Conference Selected Papers, no. LG13-73, Liege, Belgium, 2013. http://www.iap-socent.be/sites/default/files/Picciotto%20ECSP-LG13-73.pdf.

Pickering-Iazzi, Robin. *Mafia and Outlaw Stories from Italian Life and Literature.* Toronto: University of Toronto Press, 2013.

– *The Mafia in Italian Lives and Literature: Life Sentences and Their Geographies.* Toronto: University of Toronto Press, 2015.

– "(En)gendering Testimonial Bodies of Evidence and Italian Antimafia Culture: Rita Atria." *Italian Culture* 28, no. 1 (2010): 21–37. http://dx.doi.org/10.1179/016146210X12626054653135.

Paoli, Letizia, ed. *The Oxford Handbooks of Organized Crime*. New York: Oxford University Press, 2014. http://dx.doi.org/10.1093/oxfordhb/9780199730445.001.0001.

Pinar, William. *The Worldliness of a Cosmopolitan Education: Passionate Lives in Public Service*. New York: Routledge, 2009.

Pitt, Alice, and Deborah Britzman. "Speculations on Qualities of Difficult Knowledge in Teaching and Learning: An Experiment in Psychoanalytic Research." *International Journal of Qualitative Studies in Education: QSE* 16, no. 6 (2003): 755–76. http://dx.doi.org/10.1080/09518390310001632135.

Povinelli, Elizabeth. "The Woman on the Other Side of the Wall: Archiving the Otherwise in Postcolonial Digital Archives." *Differences: A Journal of Feminist Cultural Studies* 22, no. 1 (2011): 146–71. http://dx.doi.org/10.1215/10407391-1218274.

Puccio-Den, Deborah. "A Máfia siciliana: a transformação num mal global" [The Sicilian Mafia: Transformation to a Global Evil]. *Etnográfica (Lisboa)* 12, no. 2 (2008): 377–86. http://dx.doi.org/10.4000/etnografica.1763.

Puglisi, Anna. *Donne, Mafia e Antimafia*. Trapani, Italy: Di Girolamo Editore, 2005.

Putnam, Robert. *Making Democracy Work: Civic Traditions in Modern Italy*. Princeton: Princeton University Press, 1993.

Rakopoulos, Theodoros. "Cooperative Modulations: The Antimafia Movemement and Struggles over Land and Cooperativism in Eight Sicilian Municipalities." *Journal of Modern Italian Studies* 19, no. 1 (2014): 15–33. http://dx.doi.org/10.1080/1354571X.2014.851964.

– "Which Community for Cooperatives?: Peasant Mobilizations, the Mafia, and the Problem of Community Participation in Sician Co-Ops." *Focaal* 71, no. 71 (Spring 2015): 57–70.

Rancière, Jacques. *The Ignorant Schoolmaster: Five Lessons in Intellectual Emancipation*. Translated by Kristin Ross. Stanford: Stanford University Press, 1991.

Rancière, Jacques. *The Future of the Image*. Translated by Gregory Elliot. London: Verso, 2007.

Renga, Dana. *Unfinished Business: Screening the Italian Mafia in the New Millennium*. Toronto: University of Toronto Press, 2013.

Reski, Petra. *The Honored Society: The Secret History of Italy's Most Powerful Mafia*. New York: Basic, 2013.

Robb, Peter. *Midnight in Sicily: On Art, Food, History, Travel, and La Cosa Nostra*. New York: Harvill, 1999.

Rotella, Sebastian. "He Fights the Italian Mob with Words." *Los Angeles Times*, October 19, 2008, http://articles.latimes.com/2008/oct/19/world/fg-mafia19.

Rothberg, Michael. "Progress, Progression, Procession: William Kentridge and the Narratology of Transitional Justice." *Narrative* 20, no. 1 (2012): 1–24. http://dx.doi.org/10.1353/nar.2012.0005.

Rothberg, Michael. *Multidirectional Memory: Remembering the Holocaust in the Age of Decolonization*. Stanford: Stanford University Press, 2009.

Rothe, Nina E. "The Face of Courage: An Exclusive Interview with Roberto Saviano." *Huffington Post: The Blog*, August 1, 2012, http://www.huffingtonpost.com/e-nina-rothe/roberto-saviano_b_1184140.html.

Ruta, Carlo. 2013. "'L'Ora,' the Mafia and Palermo." *Libera Informazione*, June 5, 2013, http://www.liberainformazione.org/2013/06/05/lora-la-mafia-e-palermo/.

Ryan, Marie-Laure. *Avatars of Story*. Minneapolis: University of Minnesota Press, 2006.

Scarlett, Michael. "Imagining a World Beyond Genocide: Teaching about Transitional Justice." *Social Studies* 100, no. 4 (2009): 169–76. http://dx.doi.org/10.3200/TSSS.100.4.169-176.

Salvio, Paula M. *Anne Sexton: Teacher of Weird Abundance*. Albany: State University of New York Press, 2007.

– "'Eccentric Subjects': Female Martyrs and the Antimafia Public Imaginary." *Italian Cultural Studies* 67, no. 3 (2012): 397–410. http://dx.doi.org/10.1179/0075163412Z.00000000026.

– "Uncanny Exposures: A Study of the Wartime Photojournalism of Lee Miller." *Curriculum Inquiry* 39, no. 4 (2009): 521–36. http://dx.doi.org/10.1111/j.1467-873X.2009.00455.x.

Sandlin, Jennifer A., Brian D. Schultz, and Jake Burdick, eds. *Handbook of Public Pedagogy: Education and Learning Beyond Schooling*. New York: Routledge, 2010.

Santino, Umberto. Centro Siciliano di documentazione "Giuseppe Impastato." July 2015, http://www.centroimpastato.it

– "Fighting the Mafia and Organized Crime: Italy and Europe." In *Crime and Law Enforcement in the Global Village*, edited by W.F. McDonald, 151–66. Cincinnati: Anderson Publishing, 1997. http://www.centroimpastato.com/fighting-the-mafia-and-organized-crime-italy-and-europe/

– *Mafia and Antimafia: A Brief History*. London: Tauris, 2015.

Santner, Eric. "History beyond the Pleasure Principle: Some Thoughts on the Representation of Trauma." In *Probing the Limits of Representation: Nazism and the Final Solution*, edited by Saul Friedlander, 143–54. Cambridge, London: Harvard University Press, 1992.

– *Stranded Objects: Mourning, Memory and Film in Postwar Germany*. New York: Cornell University Press, 1993.

Savage, Glenn C. "Problematizing Public Pedagogy in Educational Research." In *Handbook of Public Pedagogy: Education and Learning Beyond Schooling*, edited by Jennifer A. Sandlin, Brian D. Schultz, and Jake Burdick, 103–15. New York: Routledge, 2010.

Saviano, Roberto. *Gomorrah: A Personal Journey into the Violent International Empire of Naples' Organized Crime System*. New York: Picador, 2008.

Scarlett, Michael. "Imagining a World Beyond Genocide: Teaching about Transitional Justice." *Social Studies* 100, no. 4 (2009): 169–76. http://dx.doi.org/10.3200/TSSS .100.4.169-176.

Schneider, Jane, and Peter Schneider. *Reversible Destiny: Mafia, Anti-Mafia, and the Struggle for Palermo.* Berkeley: University of California Press, 2003.

– "Suggestions from the Antimafia Struggle in Sicily." *Anthropological Quarterly* 75, no. 1 (Winter 2002): 155–8. http://dx.doi.org/10.1353/anq.2002.0020.

Sciascia, Leonardo. *The Day of the Owl.* Translated by Archibald Colquhoun and Arthur Oliver. New York: New York Review Books, 2003.

Siebert, Renate. *Secrets of Life and Death: Women and the Mafia.* New York: Verso Books, 1996.

Simon, Roger I. *A Pedagogy of Witnessing: Curatorial Practice and the Pursuit of Social Justice.* Albany: State University of New York Press, 2014.

– *The Touch of the Past: Remembrance, Learning, and Ethics.* New York: Palgrave Macmillan, 2005. http://dx.doi.org/10.1007/978-1-137-11524-9.

Simon, Roger I., and Claudia Eppert. "Remembering Obligation: Pedagogy and the Witnessing of Testimony of Historical Trauma." *Canadian Journal of Education* 22, no. 2 (1997): 175. http://dx.doi.org/10.2307/1585906.

Steedman, Carolyn. *Dust: The Archive and Cultural History.* New Brunswick: Rutgers University Press, 2001.

Stille, Alexander. *Excellent Cadavers: The Mafia and the Death of the First Italian Republic.* New York: Vintage, 1995.

Stille, Alexander, Renate Siebert, Roberto Scarpinato, Leoluca Orlando, Simona Mafai, Milissa Harris, and Angela Casiglia Battaglia. *Passion, Justice, Freedom: Photographs of Sicily by Letizia Battaglia.* New York: Aperture Foundation, 1999.

Sturken, Marita. *Tourists of History: Memory, Kitsch, and Consumerism from Oklahoma City to Ground Zero.* Durham: Duke University Press, 2007. http://dx.doi. org/10.1215/ 9780822390510.

Taubman, Peter M. "I Love Them to Death." In *Love's Return: Psychoanalytic Essays on Childhood, Teaching and Learning,* edited by G. Boldt and P. Salvio, 19–32. New York: Routledge, 2006.

Teitel, Ruti. *Transitional Justice as Liberal Narrative.* Durham: Duke University Press, 2003.

Todd, Sharon. *Toward an Imperfect Education: Facing Humanity, Rethinking Cosmopolitanism.* Boulder: Paradigm, 2009.

Valenzuela, Sebastián, Namsu Park, and Kerk F. Kee. "Is There Social Capital in a Social Network Site?: Facebook Use and College Students' Life Satisfaction, Trust, and Participation." *Journal of Computer-Mediated Communication* 14, no. 4 (2009): 875–901. http://dx.doi.org/10.1111/j.1083-6101.2009.01474.x.

Cavallaro, Felice, and Fabio Vannini. *Ho Vinto Io*. Directed by Fabio Vannini. Produced by Cerioni. Music by Fabrizio Mancinelli. Rome, Italy: Rai Tre Radiotelevisione Italiana, 2012, 63 min.

Winnicott, Donald W. *Collected Papers: Through Pediatrics to Psychoanalysis*. New York: Basic Books, 1958.

Young-Bruehl, Elisabeth. *The Clinic and the Context: Historical Essays*. London: Karnac, 2013.

Ziarek, Ewa Plonowska. "Bare Life on Strike: Notes on the Biopolitics of Race and Gender." *South Atlantic Quarterly* 107, no. 1 (2008): 89–105. http://dx.doi.org/10.1215/00382876-2007-057.

Index

Abbate, Ciccio, 76

absent referent, 33, 149n31

activism and activists. *See* antimafia movements; narrative practices of activists; non-violent acts of public dissent; photojournalism and antimafia activism; public pedagogy of remembrance; story-taking and story-takers

Addiopizzo: action in face of totalitarianism, 132; anti-extortion stickers, 61, 79–80; overview, 15, 22, 154n10; *pizzo* explanation, 62; strategies of, 6, 11, 22, 61–5, 66–7, 69, 79–80, 141

Addiopizzo Travel (tourism website), 63, 69–73; analysis of ethics of, 74–5, 77, 79–80, 89–90, 159n32

Agamben, Giorgio, 45, 56, 106–7, 128–9

Alexander, Jeffrey C., 12

Alton Belice, Sicily, 91

Anderson, Benedict, 91

"angelic historian" persona (Benjamin), 77

anti-extortion organizations, 154n10; ethics of self-preservation, 11; *pizzo* explanation, 62. *See also* Addiopizzo; Addiopizzo Travel; public pedagogy of remembrance

antimafia cooperatives, 93–5

antimafia imaginary: art exhibit, 136; civil society, 46, 152n21; female role in, 43, 53–5, 163n49; hope juxtaposed with martyrdom, 113; photography of, 129–30; social networking projects, 50; terminology, 18

antimafia movements: action in face of totalitarianism, 132; agrarian dissent history, 16, 82, 87, 88, 90–6; antimafia and mafia entanglements, 95–6, 137–8; continuing threat of mafia, 50–1, 65–7, 71–3 (*see also* trauma and post-traumatic state); history in ethical tours, 75–6, 89–90; iconic images of, 105–6, 109–11; impact on mafia's activities, 77–8; photography and exhibits, 117, 124–5, 126–32; social cooperatives, 91–6; social networking projects, 45–7, 49–50; success and vulnerabilities, 19–20. *See also* Addiopizzo; Addiopizzo Travel; Battaglia, Letizia; public pedagogy of remembrance; Zecchin, Franco

antimafia museum, 70

antimafia religion, 34, 43, 51–2, 55, 138

antimafia vocabulary, 34

Anzaldua, Gloria, 54

Apel, Dora, 107, 109, 113

archives: literal and figurative, 99–104; as social protective shields, 102–4, 108. *See also* Battaglia, Letizia; Zecchin, Franco